On the Drafting of Tribal Constitutions

American Indian Law and Policy Series
Lindsay G. Robertson, General Editor

Felix S. Cohen, from a portrait by Joseph Margulies.
Courtesy Beinecke Rare Book and Manuscript Library, Yale University.

On the Drafting of Tribal Constitutions

By Felix S. Cohen

Edited by David E. Wilkins

Foreword by Lindsay G. Robertson

University of Oklahoma Press : Norman

Also by Felix S. Cohen

Ethical Systems and Legal Ideas: An Essay on the Foundations of Legal Criticism (New York, 1933)

Handbook of Federal Indian Law (Washington, D.C., 1942)

Combating Totalitarian Propaganda: A Legal Appraisal (Washington, D.C., 1944)

(with Morris Raphael Cohen) *Readings in Jurisprudence and Legal Philosophy* (New York, 1951)

Legal Conscience: Selected Papers, edited by Lucy Cramer Cohen (New Haven, 1960)

Also by David E. Wilkins

Diné Bibeehaz'áanii: A Handbook of Navajo Government (Tsaile, Ariz., 1987)

American Indian Sovereignty and the U.S. Supreme Court: The Masking of Justice (Austin, 1997)

(with Vine Deloria, Jr.) *Tribes, Treaties, and Constitutional Tribulations* (Austin, 1999)

(with K. Tsianina Lomawaima) *Uneven Ground: American Indian Sovereignty and Federal Law* (Norman, 2001)

(ed. with Richard A. Grounds and George E. Tinker) *Native Voices: American Indian Identity and Resistance* (Lawrence, Kans., 2003)

American Indian Politics and the American Political System, 2nd ed. (Lanham, Md., 2007)

Library of Congress Cataloging-in-Publication Data

Cohen, Felix S., 1907–1953.
    On the drafting of tribal constitutions / by Felix S. Cohen ; edited by David E. Wilkins ; foreword by Lindsay G. Robertson.
      p. cm. — (American Indian law and policy series ; 1)
    Includes bibliographical references and index.
    ISBN 978-0-8061-3806-0 (hard cover)
    ISBN 978-0-8061-6606-3 (paper)
      1. Indians of North America—Legal status, laws, etc.—United States. 2. Indians of North America—Politics and government. 3. Tribal government—United States. 4. Constitutional law—United States. I. Wilkins, David E. (David Eugene), 1954– II. Robertson, Lindsay Gordon. III. Title.

KF8221.C64 2007
342.7308'7—dc22   2006050468

On the Drafting of Tribal Constitutions is Volume 1 in the American Indian Law and Policy Series.

The paper in this book meets the guidelines for permanence and durability of the Committee on Production Guidelines for Book Longevity of the Council on Library Resources, Inc. ∞

Copyright © 2006 by the University of Oklahoma Press, Norman, Publishing Division of the University. Paperback published 2020. Manufactured in the U.S.A.

All rights reserved. No part of this publication may be reproduced, stored in a retrieval system, or transmitted, in any form or by any means, electronic, mechanical, photocopying, recording, or otherwise—except as permitted under Section 107 or 108 of the United States Copyright Act—without the prior written permission of the University of Oklahoma Press.

CONTENTS

SERIES EDITOR'S FOREWORD

Lindsay G. Robertson

Native American tribal governments are in a widespread state of resurgence. Tribal legislatures, judiciaries, constitutions, and legal codes have become fixed in the political framework of North America. Given these developments, it is propitious that David Wilkins should now have rediscovered and offered to the public the manuscript of Felix Cohen's "Basic Memorandum on Drafting of Tribal Constitutions."

Cohen prepared his "Basic Memorandum" in 1934 while serving as assistant solicitor in the U.S. Department of the Interior and chair of the Tribal Organization Committee established to assist participating tribes in organizing their political systems under the Indian Reorganization Act. While not uncontroversial, the memorandum contains materials of continuing use to tribal governments. Moreover, its reappearance coincides with the publication of the fourth version of Felix Cohen's Handbook of Federal Indian Law, still the most cited reference in the field. In furthering the understanding and development of tribal political institutions, On the Drafting of Tribal Constitutions is a fine complement to Cohen's Handbook. Adding to the value of the book is Wilkins's insightful introduction, which provides a biographical portrait of Cohen and places Cohen's "Basic Memorandum" in historical context.

This book also marks an important volume in the history of the University of Oklahoma Press. In 1932, two years before the passage of the Indian Reorganization Act and the drafting of the "Basic Memorandum," the Press published Alfred B. Thomas' Forgotten Frontiers: A Study of the Spanish Indian Policy of Don Juan Bautista de Anza, Governor of New Mexico 1777–1787, the first volume in The Civilization of the American Indian Series. That series very quickly came to set the standard in scholarship on Native American issues. As of today, The Civilization of the American Indian Series includes more than 250 titles, among them such classics as Grant Foreman's The Five Civilized Tribes, Karl Llewellyn and E. Adamson Hoebel's

vii

The Cheyenne Way, Angie Debo's The Road to Disappearance, and Black Elk's The Sacred Pipe. With its publication of On the Drafting of Tribal Constitutions, the Press inaugurates a new series devoted to Native American issues: The American Indian Law and Policy Series. This series, which is hemispheric in scope, will include titles encompassing the modern political and legal experiences of the Native peoples of the Americas. The University of Oklahoma Press and I are proud to offer David Wilkins's masterful edition of Felix Cohen's On the Drafting of Tribal Constitutions as our inaugural volume.

ACKNOWLEDGMENTS

As always, I thank my family for their love and support—Evelyn, Sion, Niłtooli, and Nazhone. They endure much during my writing moments yet never complain. I am also deeply indebted to Elmer Rusco, who first made me aware of Cohen's "Basic Memorandum." Special thanks to Lucy Kramer Cohen for sanctioning this project and for all the important work that she has engaged in for many years and that has proven so beneficial to First Nations sovereignty and self-determination.

I thank George Miles and Jill Haines of the Beinecke Rare Book and Manuscript Library for their help during my brief stint at their fine institution. Cohen's papers are a treasure, and it is with great pleasure that I acknowledge the Yale Collection of Western Americana, Beinecke Rare Book and Manuscript Library, as the location holding this "Basic Memorandum" and Cohen's other enlightening works.

Two other institutional programs deserve mention: the American Indian Studies Department at the University of Minnesota and Dartmouth College's Native American Program. First, special thanks to Pat Albers, chair of Minnesota's department, for her friendship, and to Steven Rosenstone, dean of the College of Liberal Arts, for his unwavering support throughout my tenure at Minnesota. I am also appreciative of Colin Calloway, director of Dartmouth's Native American Program, for the invitation to be a visiting professor during the fall quarter of 2005. Not only did I enjoy my tenure at Dartmouth, but it was a short drive down to the Yale collection from Hanover, New Hampshire.

Finally, a special thanks to Alex Johnson, dean of the University of Minnesota Law School from 2002 to 2006, for his support of my work. His office provided the financial support that brought in Katy Kimble, who did an outstanding job typing the hard-to-read original manuscript.

It is with great joy and profound sadness that I acknowledge and dedicate this study to Vine Deloria, Jr., incomparable scholar, outstanding teacher, dear friend, and the most significant figure in contemporary indigenous activism. I first learned of Cohen's importance in an early conversation with Vine years ago as I geared up to begin graduate study with him at the University of Arizona. Vine walked on in the fall of 2005 while I was pursuing completion of this project. I wish I could put this book in his hands now.

David E. Wilkins

INTRODUCTION

Felix Solomon Cohen, a vaunted legal realist considered by many the leading architect of the Indian New Deal in the 1930s, is once again receiving the attention he deserves. The current spate of attention is reflected in the recent literature (see selected bibliography) analyzing his philosophy of law, including his work in American Indian law. A major academic conference, held at the University of Connecticut School of Law in the fall of 2005 and titled "Indian Law at a Crossroad," had a two-pronged purpose—to assess the current state of federal Indian law and to hail the latest incarnation of Cohen's most widely known accomplishment, the *Handbook of Federal Indian Law*, first produced in 1941. After a lengthy and tortured process, Cohen's *Handbook* was published in December 2005 by LexisNexis. It was the product of a large board of authors and editors led by editor in chief Nell Jessup Newton.

Cohen's return to the attention of those who plow the fields of federal Indian law, tribal sovereignty and self-governance, and American jurisprudence in general coincides with a number of contemporary political, legal, and human rights developments, developments that might give Cohen pause. He would likely express deep dismay over the current drift in ideological and institutional interpretations of democracy and the rule of law. As Theodore Haas, a close friend of Cohen's and his chief collaborator on the *Handbook*, noted in 1956, Cohen simultaneously occupied two roles in the course of his short but memorable public and private careers: He was both a man of ideas and a man of action. Cohen, said Haas, "was no cloistered philosopher, no impractical idealist, but an effective defender of disadvantaged people against powerful opponents."[1]

In his last major article, "The Erosion of Indian Rights, 1950–1953: A Case Study in Bureaucracy," published in 1953, the year of his death at age forty-six from lung cancer, Cohen systematically showed how the Department of the Interior, especially the Bureau of Indian Affairs (BIA), had concocted a number of highly questionable rules and regulations that were decisively restricting the human, civil, proprietary, and treaty rights of nearly half a million American Indians and Alaskan Natives. Indigenous peoples were experiencing constraints upon their personal and property freedoms in areas as diverse as tribal elections; use of federal funds; the right to counsel; freedom of speech and religion; and freedom from arrest, search, and seizure without a warrant.[2]

It was in "Erosion of Indian Rights" that Cohen wrote one of his more noteworthy lines: "Like the miner's canary, the Indian marks the shift from fresh air to poison gas in our political atmosphere; and our treatment of Indians, even more than our treatment of other minorities, reflects the rise and fall in our democratic faith."[3] While I have never been as smitten as some others with this metaphor, since it situates indigenous nations in an extremely vulnerable and abused role, there is no dispute that Native peoples have often been used in federal social experiments. Sometimes these experiments have then been extrapolated to other groups.

Cohen ended his article by more aptly observing that those abusing others' rights—one thinks here of the BIA, as Cohen was, or the National Security Agency (NSA) today—often justify their actions by arguing that their behavior is necessary to bring about a society that will eventually have no need for such intrusive and coercive acts. But as Cohen said, "what they forget, and what we need another John Maynard Keynes to remind us of, is that in the long run we are all dead, and that while the means we use may be molded by the ends we seek, it is the means we use that mold the ends we achieve."[4]

COHEN'S PHILOSOPHY OF LAW

Cohen described his own legal philosophy as "functional jurisprudence," by which he meant that he believed that law must not be studied in isolation but must incorporate the fields of anthropology, economics, psychology, sociology, the social and hard sciences, and, most importantly, history. Only by embracing the interconnections with these other fields can law reach its potential as a true instrument of justice. Although practicing, in his own words, a functional jurisprudence, Cohen and others of his ideological bent were more often viewed as practitioners of what was termed "legal realism." Legal realists, according to Thomas Clarkin, "maintained that the legal process was not merely the rational application of understood laws; rather, emotions and value judgments played important roles in the interpretation of law."[5]

Stephen M. Feldman, who has also written about Cohen's jurisprudence, echoes Clarkin but adds that for legal realists "law is not autonomous from society and that abstract preexisting principles do not objectively dictate judicial decisions. Consequently, the heart of realism was the belief that the study of law should be focused on concrete disputes and on what officials at all levels do about those disputes. Realists focused on factual realities, and, correspondingly, distrusted abstract legal rules, principles, and systems."[6]

Cohen has also been called an "academic humanist," one who believed in the equality of all peoples and their unique cultural manifestations and in their right to freely choose their own forms of government.[7] He has also been deemed a "legal pluralist," specifically, a man whose ideals evolved through three types of pluralism—socialist, systematic, and comparative.[8]

One of the ideological distinctions of Cohen's philosophy of law was that he believed "that ethical and policy dimensions provide an external standard against which to measure legal behavior and also provide a set of policy objects toward which the law should strive."[9] In other words, his approach to the study of law had a pragmatic, instrumentalist, and consequential thrust as well. "Law," said Cohen, "is the most powerful and flexible instrument of social control and has the power to enhance the 'good life.'"[10]

COHEN'S DEMOCRACY AT WORK

Cohen and John Collier, the commissioner of Indian affairs from 1933 to 1945, are often treated as ideological twins regarding the dynamics of Indian policy during the Indian Reorganization period—an era in which the morally bankrupt, culturally discriminatory, and economically repressive tide of allotment* and assimilation of Native peoples was finally stemmed and the reemergence of Indian self-rule and cultural regeneration was encouraged. It is certainly true that both men showed a passion for human rights, social justice, and a degree of tribal self-governance. But as Stephen Haycox has argued, "for Collier, Indians were *the* minority [emphasis in original]. But for Cohen, Indians were one of many minorities, to all of which he accorded the same legitimacy and the same rights."[11] In fact, Cohen's close friend, Theodore Haas, noted that while Cohen was a gifted lawyer and activist, it was in his intercultural work that he stood out. Haas observed that "one of the dominant notes of his thinking in intergroup relations was that the soil of cultural pluralism, when watered with competing

---

*Congress initiated the General Allotment policy (also known as the Dawes Act) in 1887. It was designed to break up tribal governments and abolish Indian reservations by the "allotment" of communally held reservation lands to individual Indians for private ownership. This was considered a critical step in the assimilation of Indians into Euro-American cultural society. The policy was ended in 1934 with the enactment of the Indian Reorganization Act.

ideas and customs, nurtures the finest fruits of democracy; and that a key challenge faced by our government and philosophy is the problem facing the world—the achieving of intercultural understanding."[12]

As an American Jew, Cohen was actively involved in cases contesting anti-Semitism. He also supported the rights of immigrants, African Americans, and Puerto Ricans. During his lengthy stint in the Department of the Interior—1933 to 1948—his position changed from assistant solicitor to associate solicitor and finally to chairman of Interior's Board of Appeals. For many, Cohen is most often associated with his vigorous Indian political and legal work. But his interests and involvement ranged widely beyond Indian and minority work. During his Interior phase, he helped draft economic development plans for Alaska and the Virgin Islands; helped address the currency problems in the Philippines; worked on natural resource issues involving water power, public lands, helium, coal, and minerals; dealt with atomic energy legislation; and worked on fair-employment practices.[13]

COHEN'S PERSONAL LIFE

Felix Cohen was born in New York City on July 3, 1907. He was the son of Morris R. Cohen, a prominent professor and philosopher, and Mary Ryshpan, who had also taught. He attended Townsend Harris High School in New York, which was then part of an educational system institutionally linked with City College. At age eighteen he graduated magna cum laude. He proceeded to Harvard College, where he earned an M.A. in philosophy in 1927. During his M.A. work, he read broadly in law, anthropology, and political science as well as philosophy. He also audited classes outside his primary field from such luminaries as Roscoe Pound and Felix Frankfurter.[14]

In 1928, while continuing work on his Ph.D. at Harvard, Cohen enrolled at Columbia's law school. He secured his doctorate in 1929 and his L.L. B. from Columbia in 1931.[15] His dissertation was published by Falcon in 1933 under the title *Ethical Systems and Legal Ideals: An Essay on the Foundations of Legal Criticism.*

Upon graduation in 1931, he became a legal apprentice to Bernard L. Shientag, a New York supreme court justice. He also married Lucy M. Kramer that year. Ms. Kramer, who was studying at Barnard College at the time, already had a keen interest in American Indian issues. She had worked closely with Franz Boas, a leading anthropologist, on several projects and had taken graduate-level courses in both anthropology and linguistics.[16] The marriage produced two children and a personal and professional relationship that proved quite fertile. Kramer worked for a number of years at the Department of the Interior and played a significant role in the development of the first edition of Cohen's *Handbook*. After her husband's death in 1953, she gathered, edited, and published, in 1960 with Yale University Press, his collected works under the title *The Legal Conscience: Selected Papers of Felix Cohen.* In 1932, a year after his marriage to Kramer, Cohen entered the private practice of law in New York, but within months, he received a one-year appointment from Nathan Margold, solicitor for the Department of the Interior, as an assistant solicitor, expressly to help draft the basic legislation that came to be known as the Wheeler-Howard bill, or the Indian Reorganization Act (IRA).[17] Margold had been involved with the 1928 Meriam Report that had critiqued federal Indian policy. He was well aware of Cohen's talents, and he assigned him the task of focusing on the Indian reforms that were just getting underway.[18]

Cohen, always a quick study, soon immersed himself in the unique challenge of his Indian-focused work and proved so adept that he and Margold agreed that he should remain on board after the passage of the IRA in June 1934. Thus, Cohen's temporary one-year assignment became a fifteen-year career in public service that transformed the face and substance of federal Indian law, policy, and tribal self-governance.[19]

By 1948, Cohen had grown increasingly unhappy with Interior's drift into conservatism, and he resigned on January 2 to reenter private practice. The issue that finally prompted his resignation was Interior's opening of Alaska's Tongass National Forest to massive logging over strenuous indigenous objections in 1947. Despite his frustration with the department, Cohen was awarded Interior's highest honor, the Distinguished Service Award, by the secretary in 1949.[20]

Freed from federal bureaucratic constraints, Cohen now became deeply involved in many activities. He served as lead attorney in a number of lawsuits in support of Indian rights regarding voting, land claims, social security, and the consumption of liquor.* He began teaching law at Yale and philosophy at New York City College. He worked with a number of organizations, including the Association on American Indian Affairs, the American Jewish Committee, the Institute of Ethnic Affairs, and the New York Association for New Americans. He did a significant amount of writing. And he continued an active outdoor life of mountain climbing, camping, and canoeing.

---

*Until 1953 it was illegal for American Indians to drink alcoholic beverages. Cohen's advocacy led to congressional action that decriminalized consumption of alcohol by Natives and granted tribal governments the right to decide whether liquor could be sold within reservation boundaries.

In June 1953, four months before he died, Cohen pulled together his major written works into three unbound volumes as a graduation gift to his older daughter, Gene Maura.[21] The volumes, titled "Law and Ethics," "The Indian's Quest for Justice," and "Studies in the Philosophy of American Democracy," indicate the true breadth of his intellectual passion.

COHEN AND FEDERAL INDIAN LAW: POSITIVES AND NEGATIVES

Although Felix Cohen led a diverse and richly rewarding vocational and intellectual life, many consider his work in Indian affairs to be his most impressive set of achievements. A number of recent articles (see selected bibliography) have analyzed his major contributions in this important area. These articles, for the most part, focus on Cohen's work on the Indian Reorganization Act; his efforts behind the 1934 "Solicitor's Opinion,which identified the inherent governing powers vested in indigenous nations; his leadership of the Indian Law Survey in the Department of Justice, where he, Theodore Haas, and a well-trained team of officials compiled a forty-six-volume collection of federal laws and treaties that would later be distilled in the *Handbook*; his role in drafting the Indian Claims Commission Act of 1946 that authorized Native nations to file lawsuits against the federal government for compensation for lands and treaty violations; his work in leading Congress to repeal the discriminatory Indian liquor legislation in 1953; and the outstanding legal work he provided to a number of tribes—the Hualapai, San Carlos Apache, Blackfeet, Nez Perce, and Omaha, among others—before and especially after he had left public service as their lead attorney.

Generally, most commentators agree that Cohen deserves great credit for his Indian-related work, asserting that his not-inconsiderable efforts during the Indian New Deal paved the way for the revitalization of tribal sovereignty and cultural and economic self-determination, the reaffirmation of treaty rights, and the extension of civil liberties to tribal citizens. Of course, these very powers and rights were already coming under intense assault by federal and state officials even before Cohen's tenure at Interior ended in 1948. Termination[*] was brewing; plans were being made to relocate thousands of Indians

---

[*] The official federal policy from 1953 to the mid-1960s, "termination" entailed the legislative severing of federal benefits and support services to certain tribes, bands, and numerous California Native communities and forced the dissolution of their reservations and trust lands. The policy was embodied in House Concurrent Resolution 108 (August 1, 1953), the infamous "termination resolution," and Public Law 83–280 (August 15, 1953), which conferred upon several designated states full criminal and some civil jurisdiction over most Indian reservations within those states and allowed the assumption of such jurisdiction by any other state that chose to do so.

to urban areas; and states were clamoring for greater jurisdictional clout over tribal nations and their citizens. Several states received such power in 1953 with passage of Public Law 280. These devastating policy shifts would plague American Indians and Alaskan Natives for another generation.

Nevertheless, Cohen's work, in particular his individual and joint efforts in (1) overseeing the development of the *Handbook*, the first study to compile many of the federal statutes and court cases dealing with indigenous peoples, and (2) working with tribes as they struggled to create or, in some cases, revive systems of local governance, deserves special mention. These two critical contributions helped fuel the Native renaissance that burst forth in the 1960s. They provided the legal, political, and economic framework and the institutional mechanisms necessary to enable many tribal nations to challenge termination and other nefarious policies. They enabled many indigenous nations to develop the institutional machinery and wield the legal authority necessary to continue their march toward self-determination.

Cohen, without doubt, was a brilliant advocate for indigenous nations and their distinctive rights. Nevertheless, his scholarship has also drawn important criticisms from those active in federal Indian law and tribal governance. On the legal front, Vine Deloria, Jr., argued that, even though "the raw data of federal Indian law [was] the documentary record of how the United States government has treated Indians,"[22] Cohen's *Handbook*, by reducing the complicated and diverse set of legal and policy outputs to an oversimplified and largely mythical set of principles and doctrines, unwittingly did a profound disservice to tribal nations and their legal relationship to the federal and state governments.

By conflating tribal and issue diversity for the purpose of developing an organizational framework for the book, Deloria said, Cohen and Margold had shunted aside much of the actual historical record—despite their own warnings in the introduction to the *Handbook*. Moreover, while their study was explicitly identified as a "handbook," meaning it was not an authoritative treatise but a summary of the materials, too many commentators treat it as if it is the final word on the subject of federal Indian law. Deloria went on to say, "Paying homage to Cohen is proper, but elevating a handbook to the status of a treatise while doing so is highly suspect and means that principles and doctrines sketched out as a means of locating resources now achieve a status whereby it becomes unnecessary to use the *Handbook* as a resource. Scholars then start with the *Handbook* and not the data, erroneously believing that many questions have already been laid to rest."[23]

In a 1996 article in the *Arizona Law Review*, Deloria was even more critical of Cohen's *Handbook*. He pondered "whether Cohen's framework is at all useful in serving as the structure for arranging the materials that represent the relationship between the United States and American Indians." He went on to note that "Cohen was part of the educated elite, had no experience as an oppressed minority and could not understand what their experiences were at the grass-roots level where discrimination and injustice flourished."[24]

The *Handbook*, Deloria observed, had not been written from a pro-Indian, or even a neutral, perspective. In fact, many of the discussions and interpretations of Indian policy development and federal case law had a clear "federal bias in that no question is ever raised as to whether federal actions were proper or whether or not the federal government violated previously agreed upon principles of the federal-Indian relationship."[25]

Frank Pommersheim, while lauding Cohen's *Handbook*, has also assailed two dimensions of Cohen's understanding of Indian history and law. First, Pommersheim expressed some concern with Cohen's "miner's canary" metaphor. While noting that the metaphor remains quite powerful, he observed that "the present ratio of fresh air to poison gas is not necessarily encouraging." Moreover, because there is "no basic doctrinal stability or national moral commitment to ensure that the fresh air will not dissipate further," Pommersheim called for greater effort in strengthening federal Indian law.[26]

Pommersheim also clearly and convincingly criticized Cohen's articulation of tribal sovereignty, which Cohen had said included three principles: (1) tribes possess the powers of any sovereign entity; (2) having been conquered, tribes were thus subject to federal legislative power that effectively terminated their external sovereignty but generally sustained their internal, or self-governing, authority; and (3) tribal powers had been justifiably qualified by federal laws and treaty provisions, but any powers not expressly modified remained vested in the tribe and its governing bodies.[27]

While agreeing with Cohen's first principle, Pommersheim challenged the veracity of the other two. Many tribes had never, in fact, been militarily conquered, and federal plenary power, as defined by Cohen, vested far too much power in Congress, which, according to Pommersheim, might "also severely limit tribal sovereignty."[28]

Stephen Feldman has also criticized a dimension of Cohen's *Handbook*—the part that deals with state power in Indian Country. Feldman posits, and judicial history seems to bear him out, that Cohen's legal realism approach to federal Indian law provided states with an opportunity to intrude into tribal affairs. Cohen stated as a general principle in the opening of his chapter on state power over Indian affairs that state laws have no force inside Indian Country in matters affecting Indians. Yet he ended his introduction by asserting two exceptions to that principle. Courts, he maintained, will support state jurisdiction over Indians if either of two conditions applies: (1) Congress has expressly delegated to or recognized in a state the power to govern American Indians, or (2) a question that involves Indians also "involves non-Indians to a degree which calls into play the jurisdiction of a state government."[29]

According to Feldman, Cohen was essentially inviting "the court to focus on the concrete factual circumstances of each individual case." Such an invitation encourages a case-by-case analysis, which typically requires a balancing test. And since the courts are being asked to make particularized inquiries into the interests at stake in each case, "the continuance of legitimate tribal sovereignty is largely at the whimsical sway of political pressures: in any particular case, a court can reach the decision that is best for the majority of society at the time." Feldman concluded by noting that although Cohen was an advocate of Native peoples, "the Court's use of his functional approach has to some extent facilitated the weakening of Native American rights."[30]

Finally, Dalia Tsuk, who has written Cohen's biography as well as several lengthy articles on his role in the New Deal, has argued that Cohen, a Jew, naively assumed that federal law, "as a tool for remedying collective traumas, particularly the Indian trauma of colonization," was sufficient to rectify the problems that federal law itself had also instigated. According to Tsuk, Cohen, like John Collier, also failed, at least initially, to grasp that his plans for Indian land consolidation and tribal governance were rooted in Western ideologies and cultural paradigms that were products of his own socialist pluralism and were "not necessarily suitable for the customs and traditions of Indian tribes."[31]

Despite these criticisms, the vast majority of commentators, and Native nations themselves, express profound and continued admiration for the pathbreaking work that Cohen did in the area of federal Indian law. In fact, Supreme Court Justices Felix Frankfurter and William O. Douglas, and Collier himself, declared that Cohen was "the final authority on Indian law."[32]

Let us turn our attention now to the work that is the focus of this project: constitutional development in Indian Country.

COHEN ON TRIBAL CONSTITUTIONS

As noted above, Cohen had been hired expressly in 1933 to draft the legislation that would culminate in the Indian Reorganization Act the following year. Many scholarly analyses have been written about this important piece of legislation—touted by many as the most important Indian law of the twentieth century because it stemmed the tide of unilateral legislation aimed at forcibly assimilating Native peoples.[33] It effectively ended allotment, restored trust protections of remaining Indian lands, supported tribal political and economic organization, called for the establishment of new Indian reservations, and allowed Indian nations the right to choose whether they would even embrace the law's provisions.

Section 16 of the IRA, dealing with tribal political development, is the aspect we are most concerned with here. The section states, in pertinent part:

> Any Indian tribe, or tribes, residing on the same reservation, shall have the right to organize for its common welfare, and may adopt an appropriate constitution and bylaws, which shall become effective when ratified by a majority of the tribe, or of the adult Indians residing on such reservations, as the case may be, at a special election authorized and called by the Secretary of the Interior under such rules and regulations as he may prescribe. Such constitution and bylaws when ratified as aforesaid and approved by the Secretary of the Interior shall be revocable by an election open to the same voters and conducted in the same manner as herein above provided. Amendments to the constitution and bylaws may be ratified and approved by the Secretary in the same manner as the original constitution and bylaws.
>
> In addition to all powers vested in any Indian tribe or tribal council by existing law, the constitution adopted by said tribe shall also vest in such tribe or its tribal council the following rights and powers: To employ legal counsel, the choice of counsel and fixing of fees to be subject to the approval of the Secretary of the Interior; to prevent the sale, disposition, lease, or encumbrance of tribal lands, interests, in lands, or other tribal assets without the consent of the tribe; and to negotiate with the Federal, State, and local Governments.[34]

Unlike Collier, who had spent considerable time among Indians prior to his appointment as commissioner of the BIA, Cohen lacked substantial knowledge about Native peoples and their systems of governance at the time he drafted the bill. A quick learner, however, Cohen soon immersed himself in the examination of tribal peoples and their cultures, and his knowledge and respect for indigenous nations increased significantly during his remaining years. In fact, his interest in Native cultures intensified during the 1940s because he and his wife had a summer home near Onchiota, New York, in the Adirondack Mountains, where they spent time conversing with Ray Fadden, a respected Mohawk teacher. In these conversations, Cohen learned much about

Iroquois political philosophy and law and the significant impact that Iroquois statesmen and their political traditions, in particular, and indigenous cultures, in general, had on Anglo-American constitutional development.[35]

Cohen, of course, did not work alone in drafting the IRA, although it appears that he was its principal author. In the initial months after his hiring in October 1933, Cohen traveled to several reservations with another recently appointed attorney, Melvin Siegel.[36] Ward Shepard, the BIA's expert on land policy, was the third person providing the initial ideas for the IRA. John Collier, Nathan Margold, Allan G. Harper, Robert Marshall, and Walter V. Woehlke also had some involvement in developing the final draft of the lengthy bill.

Cohen and his colleagues were convinced, especially at the beginning of the process, that tribal organization via written constitutions, charters, and bylaws was the most appropriate means for Native nations to protect and exercise their basic right of political and economic self-determination. But why tribal constitutions? What were these documents to contain? How would tribes adopting constitutions relate to the BIA, state governments, and the federal government? If tribes had retained any traditional institutions of governance, how would the adoption of a constitution affect those traditions? And was there to be a "model" tribal constitution that aspiring tribes would be advised or required to adhere to?

Shortly after the IRA became law, but well before the major thrust of constitutional development had taken place, some sixty tribes had preexisting constitutions, or "documents in the nature of constitutions," that were already on file with the Department of the Interior.[37] It is not known precisely how many of these were early versions of IRA-type constitutions, but it seems fairly certain that at least forty of them well predate the New Deal period. Cohen, reflecting the informal education he had been receiving from Ray Fadden, wrote an article in 1939 titled "How Long Will Indian Constitutions Last?" in which he noted that "tribal constitutions, after all, are not an innovation of the New Deal. The history of Indian constitutions goes back at least to the Gayanashakgowah (Great Binding Law) of the Iroquois Confederacy, which probably dates from the 15th century. . . . So too, we have the written constitutions of the Creek, Cherokee, Choctaw, Chickasaw, and Osage nations, printed usually on tribal printing presses, constitutions which were in force during the decades from 1830 to 1900."[38]

Although Cohen would later learn a great deal about indigenous constitutional history that long predated non-Indian involvement, a close review of his archived papers reveals that in the early drafts of the IRA his understanding of, and vision for, tribal constitutional development was heavily influenced, not by preexisting tribal constitutions or other indigenous forms of governance, but by the regulations of the municipal governments that dot the American landscape.

In Cohen's view, tribal constitutional governments "were to be like town governments, except that they would have federal protection and their special rights."[39] Evidence supporting this town-structure arrangement is found in a nine-page "Bibliography for Use in Drafting Tribal Constitutions" in Cohen's papers. This bibliography contains over seventy-five references to books, articles, and government documents that deal with "administration," "city planning," "health and sanitation," "housing," "licenses," "nuisances," and other matters associated with establishing and running municipal governments.[40]

Even before the IRA became law on June 18, 1934, Cohen had already suggested to Collier that Indian tribes deserved an opportunity to meet with BIA personnel to discuss the ramifications of the bill. He said this would build support for what promised to be a controversial measure. He also believed that "contact with Indians would be very helpful when the time came to implement 'our plans concerning land development and self-government.'"[41] Collier wisely heeded Cohen's suggestion, and a series of "Indian congresses" was held throughout the country to provide federal officials valuable, if long-neglected, tribal input on Indian concerns of the day and on this major piece of legislation in particular[42] Cohen attended many of these meetings and was called upon to respond to questions from the Indian delegates about the claims process, the meaning of Indian self-government, the planned court of Indian offenses, and other issues.

After the IRA was adopted in the summer of 1934, 181 tribes adopted the act, with some 77 choosing to reject it. Although tribes that voted to accept the measure were not required to adopt constitutions, many tribes expressed interest in doing so, and Cohen intensified his efforts to learn more about tribal governance, to dig deeper into the prior constitutional history of Indian nations.

The process of modern tribal constitutional development has long been fraught with uncertainty and ambiguity. Many commentators have maintained that Western-styled constitutions were forced on reluctant tribes, thereby eclipsing extant traditional systems that, they argue, had survived the previous century of coercive assimilation. These authors also typically assert that the BIA developed a "model" constitution that it sent out to newly organizing tribes to structure the style and content of their organic documents, forcing a constitutional uniformity that denies the diverse nature of tribal nations.[43]

Contrarily, Elmer Rusco declared in his excellent 2000 study of the IRA, *A Fateful Time*, that the allegation that a coercive and uniform "model" tribal constitution had been sent out was in "error." While acknowledging that the idea had been "considered," Rusco says that this approach was ultimately rejected by the bureau. "Perhaps," said Rusco, "the confusion arose from the fact that the Bureau did develop an outline of topics that might be included in a constitution. However, listing a membership section imposed no uniform rule for determining membership, and the same thing is true in other areas."[44]

My analysis of Cohen's relevant papers and a review of his "Basic Memorandum" on tribal constitutions generally supports Rusco's interpretation of events, although there is incontrovertible evidence that some tribes did, in fact, receive a copy of a "model" constitution (see Appendix A) or in some cases an "outline" of what a constitution should contain (see Appendix B). These instruments were meant to guide them in their efforts to craft an organic document. (Appendix C contains a copy of a "model" corporate charter that was included in Cohen's papers.) Much more comprehensive and systematic research of all the BIA's records and the records of individual IRA tribes is required before we can definitively answer the question of precisely how many tribes received the "model" constitution, the "outline," or the corporate charter. Also open to further research is the question of whether the constitutional process in Indian Country effectively displaced extant traditional systems of governance—and, indeed, which tribes retained traditional forms of governance by the mid-1930s.

Cohen was soon appointed chairman of the Tribal Organization Committee (TOC) that was in charge of the constitutional development process. The committee early on consisted of the following individuals: Walter Woehlke, Fred H. Daiker, J. R. T. Reeves, Mrs. E. Smith, and Dr. Duncan Strong. Cohen and various members of the committee traveled into Indian Country to listen to Indians and to learn more about how they might structure tribal organization. It was during this period of study that Cohen learned of the status and utility of preexisting tribal constitutions and of the residual traditional governing systems that were still active in many places. Nevertheless, we still see evidence of the inherent ideological and policy tension that Cohen and his colleagues faced as federal employees. On the one hand, they wanted to facilitate and encourage a degree of Indian self-rule; on the other hand, they were operating under certain cultural and political presuppositions that elevated their own values and governing systems over those of indigenous nations. This produced a set of sometimes conflicting questions, policies, and views that led to contradictory constitutional results throughout Indian Country.

For example, on July 31, 1934, a little more than a month after the IRA's adoption, a memorandum was issued titled "Immediate Program for Organization of Indian Tribes." It called for about thirty tribes to be selected on the basis of (1) "the wishes of the Indians and their intelligent understanding of the problems of self-government"; (2) their responses to an earlier circular on self-governance; (3) "the sympathy and ability of the Superintendent, in whom must be placed chief responsibility for dealing with tribal representatives in reaching a satisfactory program of self-government"; (4) the economic status of the community; and (5) the relative ease of the organization process.[45]

From this list of tribes, which, unfortunately, were not identified, the number was to be reduced to about twelve, who would then receive the concentrated attention of Cohen and the TOC in an effort to develop constitutions, bylaws, and charters for each group by January 1, 1935. The seemingly hurried nature of the writing process for these "strategically located" tribes was considered important, "since the failure to do this will subject the Indian Office to considerable criticism, and since only through actual organization can the deficiencies of the Wheeler-Howard Act and the need for amendments of this Act and the permanent implications of this Act be clarified."[46] John Collier would later observe that the pace of tribal constitutional development was indeed remarkable. "These constitutions," he said, were "probably the greatest in number ever written in an equivalent length of time in the history of the world."[47]

Along with this major undertaking, the TOC was also charged with studying the nearly forty already approved—or awaiting approval—tribal constitutions. It was hoped that these documents might give committee members knowledge useful in helping other tribes gear up for the constitutional drafting process. The following specific questions were posed: (1) How was the constitution adopted? What part did Indians and/or the Indian Office play in its drafting? (2) To what extent does the constitution reflect Indian traditions and political experience? (3) Does the constitution provide for the exercise of any real powers by the tribal authorities, or does it provide for a merely advisory organization? (4) Are the provisions of the constitution clear and enforceable? (5) What incidents indicate the strength or weakness of the constitution? (6) What criticisms of particular constitutional provisions have been voiced?[48]

After this study was completed, the TOC was to draft a comprehensive memorandum correlating and integrating the data analyzed. The memorandum was to "contain an outline of the various topics to be dealt with in a constitution and, under each heading, any extant constitutional provision which may serve *as a model*, any extant constitutional provisions which may serve as horrible examples, and reference to any data showing actual experience with and criticism of relevant constitutional provisions" [emphasis added]. In effect, that memorandum—the "Basic Memorandum" reproduced in this text—was intended to show "what powers may be legally entrusted to an Indian tribal organization."[49]

Along with the study of the forty already approved or pending constitutions, and the memorandum that was to result from the study, the TOC was also to prepare reports for each of the thirty tribes that were included in the "immediate program" of organization. These were to be comprehensive and tribal-specific case studies that sought to ascertain (1) the persistence of social traditions, (2) the traditional legal or quasi-legal sanctions of conduct and whether these could be revived or perpetuated, (3) the political traditions of the tribe as reflected in a centralized or decentralized structure, (4) the kind of traditional symbols (that is, titles of office, insignia, and ceremonial inductions) used by the tribe's members—and whether such symbolism could be "used to lend authority to a government set up under the Wheeler-Howard Act," (5) the extent of factional differences within the tribe, and finally (6) the extent of the political experience of tribal members.[50]

On the basis of these case studies, the TOC was then "to prepare draft constitutions for approximately twenty of the thirty groups studied. These draft constitutions are to be submitted to the Indians concerned and to their superintendents for discussion and criticism. . . . Constitutional drafts should be submitted to the selected tribes between October 1 and November 1 [1934], allowing approximately two or three months for completing negotiations on the twelve reservations that respond most quickly to the program."[51]

According to this memorandum, we have evidence that the BIA officers did, in fact, plan not only to provide a "model" constitution for some tribes, but were going to draft the entire constitutions of a select number of tribes before submitting the preliminary document to these specific tribes for "discussion and criticism." But it is also seen, by the questions asked, that the committee, contrary to current opinion, was intent on learning and, if possible, incorporating "traditional" forms, symbols, and understandings of tribal governance into the modern written constitutions.

On October 29, 1934, an important document was produced that furthered the drive toward tribal self-government. Nathan Margold, the BIA solicitor, issued a detailed opinion titled "Powers of Indian Tribes." This document, which Cohen probably had a hand in developing, identified the essential powers of self-governance that were already "vested" in tribal nations and could be incorporated in their new IRA constitutions and bylaws.

Then, on November 19, 1934, Cohen, with an unspecified amount of assistance from his committee members, submitted to Commissioner Collier a draft of the "Basic Memorandum on Drafting of Tribal Constitutions." It was an effort, from Cohen's perspective, "to outline legal possibilities in the drafting of constitutions under the Wheeler-Howard Act." This draft did not, however, include the lengthy section on bylaws, which was submitted nine days later as a supplemental memorandum.[52]

The reason this lengthy, fascinating, and detailed memorandum on something as vital as tribal constitutions was not more widely distributed at the time it was written is spelled out in Cohen's cover letter to Collier: "I leave to your best judgment the question of whether this memorandum, or something closely or remotely similar to it, should be sent out to the field generally or to those reservations which have asked for advice on constitution drafting or for criticism of submitted constitutions, or whether such a memorandum should be used simply by those of us in Washington who are working on the job of organization (so far as I know, Messrs. Gordon, Woehlke, Daiker, Mrs. Welpley and myself)."

In a follow-up memorandum to Collier on November 27, Cohen asked a number of questions about various aspects of the constitutional material. He wondered, for instance, if the statements laid down in Section 12 on popular initiative and referendum [would] meet with the approval of the Indian Office." His final question is the most instructive: "Should this memorandum, or some other memorandum of a similar character, be sent to the ten or twenty tribes which are now preparing, or have already submitted for approval, Wheeler-Howard constitutions? Should some such memorandum be sent out to other tribes which have voted to accept the Wheeler-Howard Act? If not, what steps should be taken to satisfy the demand of many tribes for action?"

The reason this important and substantive document has received scant attention by contemporary commentators,[53] despite Cohen's obvious importance to the field of federal Indian law and governance, is partially explained by the fact that Lucy Kramer Cohen maintained vigilance over her husband's papers until 1989 and 1991 when she turned them over in two separate donations to the staff at Yale's Beinecke Library. Thus, they have been available for public review for only a relatively short period of time.

As tribal constitutions began arriving in Washington for consideration by BIA and Department of the Interior officials, it became clear that there was still a great deal of uncertainty about what form these documents should take and what powers tribes could legitimately wield. Cohen, in a memorandum to Collier on June 4, 1935, said, "I have, as you know, from the start, opposed the idea of sending out canned constitutions from Washington." He reminded Collier that his "Basic Memorandum" "makes it clear that constitutions must be worked out in the first place by the Indians in the field. . . . I think it would be very unfortunate to lay before the Sioux tribes, for instance, a model constitution prepared by a group of superintendents (with my help) in Washington."

Despite this statement, in an August 19, 1935, memorandum to Jane Jennings of the TOC office, Cohen attached a "model" constitution for office personnel to utilize as they worked with certain tribes. (See Appendix A.) Cohen did emphasize that he believed "it would be a mistake to furnish this outline to any Indian tribe, who would naturally be tempted to regard it as comprehensive rather than suggestive."[54] But he suggested it would be useful to BIA officials "to serve as an educational document" in working with tribes that met four qualifications: (1) the tribe was fairly small in population size; (2) the tribe had little experience in self-government and all their ordinances were subject to secretarial review; (3) the tribe was integrated with non-Indians to such a degree that they would not have the power to regulate their own domestic affairs; and (4) the tribe lacked effective social controls.

In October 1935 Margold issued a memorandum to Secretary of Interior Harold Ickes that explained Margold's response to and "approval" of the Blackfeet tribe's recently submitted constitution and bylaws. After examining the various issues and questions that had been raised by Commissioner Collier and the acting solicitor, Margold went on to say that it was "embarrassing" to have to question law and policy aspects of a tribe's constitution now, after the BIA had previously expressed support for the same document. But Margold insisted this was unavoidable until some "general understanding" was had as to what might or might not be involved in tribal constitutions that had to be approved by the Interior Department.

Margold then declared that "a comprehensive memorandum on Indian constitutional provisions, passed upon by the Indian Office, the Solicitor's Office, Assistant Secretary Chapman and yourself, would eliminate many sources of delay and disappointment in the drafting of these constitutions and would permit more mature consideration of certain difficult legal questions than is permissible under the present procedure." He then mentioned the "Basic Memorandum" that Cohen had drafted the previous year and "Powers of Indian Tribes," the 1934 "Solicitor's Opinion" that he and Cohen had worked on. Margold said these documents were "an attempt to delimit the provisions which law and sound policy permit in these Indian constitutions." Interestingly, Margold then noted that "unfortunately the memorandum first referred to is an informal document which has never been approved either by the Department, by the Commissioner of Indian Affairs, or by this Office. Many constitutions presented to this Office indicate that the repeated statement, 'Reference has been had to these documents,' is a polite fiction rather than a description of fact."[55]

Nothing in the rest of Margold's memo or in any of Cohen's papers indicates why the "Basic Memorandum" remained "informal" and was apparently "never approved" by the department. A meticulous search of Margold's, Ickes', and Collier's papers might help unravel this mystery, but for now we can only speculate. We do not know how many officials within the BIA or the Department of the Interior—or how many superintendents or Indian agents—knew of this document. We are also unable to say with any certainty how many Indians knew about it. Or even if it was ever viewed by any tribal persons. Was it not formally approved and distributed because the BIA and Interior officials simply wanted to keep it an in-house document that they could rely on for ideas on constitutional development? Or was it deemed a document too sensitive for Indian eyes because it contained valuable details about traditional governance that some in the bureau wanted displaced by modern constitutional law? We simply do not know. Much more research will have to be done before we can draw better conclusions about this important document's role, or nonrole, in Indian constitutional development.

When I wrote Lucy Kramer Cohen seeking her reaction to the publication of this memorandum, she gave her blessing to the project but also indicated that she, too, had been unaware of the document's existence. That is an interesting admission, since she was intimately involved in her husband's Indian policy affairs and was very familiar with most of his works.

Finally, to add further ambiguity to the question of whether tribes were presented with "model" constitutions, we have a Cohen memo dated December 14, 1935, titled "Criticisms of Wisconsin Oneida Constitution." In the opening paragraph he notes that "except for four provisions, discussed below, this constitution is identical with the 'Short Form Model Constitution' which *has been presented to and adopted by various other tribes"* [emphasis added]. In fact, it was apparent, said Cohen, that the Oneida had not given "any constructive thought on self-government in this constitution," meaning that it had probably been offered to them and that they had not had an opportunity to express their own views on the document, much less have had a role in its development.

The data reviewed confirms that while, indeed, some tribes were presented with prewritten "model" constitutions, this was not the case for all tribal nations. The "informal" "Basic Memorandum" presented in the following pages may have been relied on as an in-house document to guide

Cohen and the other staffers of the TOC in their review of tribal constitutions as they were submitted and to answer questions from tribal leaders, agents, and superintendents.

THE "BASIC MEMORANDUM"

The memorandum that follows contains a wealth of information on existing tribal constitutional provisions and a good deal of data as well on traditional aspects of indigenous governance still pertinent in 1934 in Indian Country. Thus it reveals that the concept of Indian "self-governance," which had not been generally respected by federal officials for the better part of six decades, was nevertheless not an alien concept to indigenous nations, but an idea still close to their hearts. This document also reveals that Felix Cohen acknowledged the difficulties and opportunities that accompanied the tremendous diversity evident in Indian Country and that he had respect for the importance of incorporating local tribal will into the constitutional process. As he noted in the memorandum's opening pages, "model constitutions" drawn up by the Indian Office would, "for the present," not be provided to tribes, since it would then "be only an adopted child and not the natural offspring of Indian hearts and minds."

Cohen's analysis of preexisting tribal constitutions and his continuing education in local tribal traditions led him to posit that IRA tribes had to carefully choose "between the older form of tribal government and the forms of government which are customary in white communities." He noted that each tribe "must consider for itself how far it wishes to preserve its own ancient traditions of self-government." Where those had been lost, tribes could rely on modern structures. But where they adhered, he observed that "they offer a very important source of knowledge and wisdom to those who are engaged in drafting a constitution."

This document also reveals that Cohen was aware that tribal court systems mattered. But he also doubted that many tribes would require three distinct branches since, in his opinion, "unified government" was the form "enjoyed by practically all Indian tribes before the coming of the white man, and it persists in the most successful self-governing Indian communities today." In his view, separation of powers was expensive and duplicative, caused friction and inefficiency, and led to uncertain responsibilities. This analysis might explain why, even today, few tribes have three distinct branches of government.

In the section titled "Relation of the Indian Service to Tribal Government," Cohen asserted that there were three "levels" of self-government, the third level constituting a tribal government that would have "complete independence of the Interior Department." But even in this case, Cohen declared that "it must be remembered that Congress would retain the power which it now has to nullify any tribal ordinances or resolutions. No constitution or charter could take that power away. Even Congress could not deprive itself of that power." In Cohen's mind, Congress's self-assumed superior authority—"self-assumed" since nothing in the Constitution or the many treaties authorizes such virtually absolute power over tribes—was an unquestionable reality of indigenous life.

Notwithstanding that ideological point of view, this "Basic Memorandum" is replete with examples of indigenous political, social, and cultural structure. It also contains Cohen's own ideas on how these structures might be, and, in fact, should be, incorporated in the newly forming tribal constitutions. As tribal nations and the federal government entered the self-determination phase of their relationship in the 1960s, and with the recent surge of tribes reengaging in much-needed constitutional reform, this long-neglected document should prove useful as tribes delve deeply into their own historic and constitutional pasts to mine ideas on how best to amend, modify, or in some cases completely restructure their organic documents.

The concepts of Indian self-government and self-determination did not start with Felix Cohen, John Collier, and Nathan Margold. Rather, these concepts were, and they remain, a vital force all Native nations exercised throughout history, as this document strikingly reveals.

EDITORIAL NOTE

The force and flow of Felix Cohen's original prose demanded that the editing of the document that follows be kept to a minimum. However, the formatting of headings and lists has been standardized throughout. Typographical errors, as few as there were, have been corrected, and minor stylistic changes have been made as necessary for clarity.

NOTES

1. Theodore Haas, ed., *Felix S. Cohen, a Fighter for Justice* (Washington, D.C.: Chapter of the Alumni of the City College of New York, 1956), 7.

2. Compare this with the recent developments in the Bush administration: (1) Scooter Libby's five-count indictment in the Valerie Plame scandal; (2) the recent revelations of the existence of a network of secret overseas prisons; (3) Vice President Dick Cheney's strenuous arguments regarding the "legality" of torturing individuals; (4) President Bush's illegal authorization of spying on American citizens by the National Security Agency (NSA); and (5) Repub-

lican lobbyist Jack Abramoff's criminal activities, including his defrauding several tribes of more than $82 million.

3. Felix S. Cohen, "The Erosion of Indian Rights, 1950–1953: A Case Study in Bureaucracy," *Yale Law Journal* 62 (1952–1953), 390.

4. Ibid.

5. Thomas Clarkin, "Felix Solomon Cohen," *American National Biography,* vol. 5, John A. Garraty and Mark C. Carnes, eds. (New York: Oxford University Press, 1999), 161.

6. Stephen M. Feldman, "Felix S. Cohen and His Jurisprudence: Reflections on Federal Indian Law," *Buffalo Law Review* 35 (Spring 1986), 483.

7. Stephen Haycox, "Felix Cohen and the Legacy of the Indian New Deal," *Yale University Library Gazette* 64 (April 1994), 138.

8. Dalia Tsuk, "The New Deal Origins of American Legal Realism," *Florida State University Law Review* 29, no. 1 (Fall 2001), 194.

9. Nell Jessup Newton et. al., *Cohen's Handbook of Federal Indian Law* (Newark, N.J.: LexisNexis, 2005), ix.

10. As quoted in Feldman, "Felix S. Cohen," 486.

11. Haycox, "Felix Cohen," 138.

12. Haas, *Felix S. Cohen*, 8.

13. "Biographical Sketch," *Rutgers Law Review* 9 (Winter 1954), 348.

14. Ibid., 346.

15. Clarkin, " Felix Solomon Cohen," 161.

16. Newton et al., *Cohen's Handbook,* xxix.

17. 48 Stat. 984 (1934).

18. Haycox, "Felix Cohen," 136.

19. Clarkin, "Felix Solomon Cohen," 161.

20. Haycox, "Felix Cohen," 147.

21. "Biographical Sketch," 349.

22. Vine Deloria, Jr., "Laws Founded in Justice and Humanity: Reflections on the Content and Character of Federal Indian Law," *Arizona Law Review* 31 (1989), 204.

23. Ibid., 212.

24. Vine Deloria, Jr., "Reserving to Themselves: Treaties and the Powers of Indian Tribes," *Arizona Law Review* 38 (Fall 1996), 966.

25. Ibid., 964.

26. Frank Pommersheim, *Braid of Feathers: American Indian Law and Contemporary Tribal Life* (Berkeley: University of California Press, 1995), 51.

27. Ibid., 51–52.

28. Ibid., 52–53.

29. Feldman, "Felix S. Cohen," 504.

30. Ibid., 505, 513, 525.

31. Dalia Tsuk, "Pluralisms: The Indian New Deal as a Model," *Margins Law Journal* (2001). Available on Lexis/Nexis, 3, 12.

32. John Collier, *From Every Zenith: John Collier, a Memoir* (Denver: Sage Books, 1963), 173.

33. See, for example, Graham Taylor, *The New Deal and American Indian Tribalism: The Administration of the Indian Reorganization Act, 1934–1945* (Lincoln: University of Nebraska Press, 1980); Kenneth R. Philp, *John Collier's Crusade for Indian Reform: 1920–1954* (Tucson: University of Arizona Press, 1977); Vine Deloria, Jr., and Clifford M. Lytle, *The Nations Within: The Past and Future of American Indian Sovereignty* (New York: Pantheon Books,

1984); and Elmer Rusco, *A Fateful Time: The Background and Legislative History of the Indian Reorganization Act* (Reno: University of Nevada Press, 2000).

34. 48 Stat. 984.

35. Donald A. Grinde, Jr., "A Symposium on *Native Pragmatism: Rethinking the Roots of American Philosophy*," *Transactions of the Charles S. Peirce Society* xxxix, no. 4 (Fall 2003), 559.

36. Rusco, *Fateful Time,* 193.

37. Felix S. Cohen, *Felix S. Cohen's Handbook of Federal Indian Law* (Albuquerque: University of New Mexico Press, reprint, 1972), 129. See note 59 of the *Handbook* for a list of the constitutions on file as of December 1934.

38. Felix S. Cohen, "How Long Will Indian Constitutions Last?" *Indians at Work* no. 10 (June 1939), 40.

39. Haycox, "Felix S. Cohen," 140.

40. Felix S. Cohen's Papers (hereafter FCP), Beinecke Rare Book and Manuscript Library, Yale University, Box 5, Folder 77, no date.

41. Rusco, *Fateful Time,* 211.

42. See Vine Deloria, Jr., ed., *The Indian Reorganization Act: Congresses and Bills* (Norman: University of Oklahoma Press, 2002). This volume provides a verbatim account of the fascinating discussions that took place at these congresses.

43. See, for example, Taylor, *New Deal,* xiii, 96; Theodore W. Taylor, *American Indian Policy* (Mount Airy, Md.: LeMond Publications, 1983), 10; Emma R. Gross, *Contemporary Federal Policy toward American Indians* (New York: Greenwood Press, 1989), 20; and Ward Churchill, *Struggle for the Land: Indigenous Resistance to Genocide, Ecocide, and Expropriation in Contemporary North America* (Monroe, Me.: Common Courage Press, 1993).

44. Rusco, *Fateful Time,* 307n7.

45. FCP, Box 8, Folder 117.

46. Ibid.

47. Collier, *From Every Zenith,* 177.

48. Ibid., 2.

49. Ibid.

50. Ibid., 3.

51. Ibid.

52. FCP, Box 7, Folder 100.

53. I have seen only two explicit references to this important document. The first person to mention it was Elmer Rusco, who discussed it briefly in his book on the IRA that was published in 2000. In fact, when I met Rusco in 2002 and asked him about this document, he was kind enough to share excerpts of it with me, and he was the person who encouraged me to pursue its publication. The only other work that mentions the memo is Robert Clinton, Carole Goldberg, and Rebecca Tsosie's federal Indian law casebook, *American Indian Law: Native Nations and the Federal System: Cases and Materials,* rev. 4th ed. (Charlottesville, Va.: Lexis/Nexis, 2003).

54. FCP, Box 8, Folder 106.

55. FCP, Box 7, Folder 100, p. 3.

BASIC MEMORANDUM
ON DRAFTING OF
TRIBAL CONSTITUTIONS

SECTION 1

INTRODUCTION

In the following pages an attempt is made to offer useful suggestions to Indians engaged in drawing up constitutions for adoption and approval under the Wheeler-Howard Act and to members of the Indian Service who may be called upon to assist in this task.

In particular, various constitutional provisions that Indians themselves have prepared, in places where they have enjoyed some measure of self-government, are offered for study. An attempt has been made to bring to bear upon the work of constitution-making the past experience of various Indian tribes with traditional and modern forms of legal government.

For the present, the Indian Office will not furnish Indian tribes with "model constitutions." In the first place, the situation of the various Indian tribes, with respect to experience in self-government, the nature of land ownership, the solidarity of the community, and the extent of contests with non-Indians, is so variable that no single constitution prepared by the Indian Office could possibly fit the varied needs of the different Indian tribes.

In the second place, a model furnished by the Indian Office might be "adopted" by an Indian tribe, but it would be only an adopted child and not the natural offspring of Indian hearts and minds. There is no assurance that an Indian community will be able to manage a form of government manufactured in Washington. On the other hand, what the Indians themselves create they will understand. In past years many Indian tribal councils have tried to operate under written constitutions prepared by the Indian Office. Frequently the Indians and even the officers of the tribe have not been familiar with the provisions of these constitutions, and the constitutions have been merely scraps of paper. This has not been the case where the Indians themselves have determined the forms of their own self-government.

Those Indians who have had experience in self-government will not need this guide. For many years, however, most of the Indian tribes have not only been denied the right to manage their own affairs, but have even been

3

denied a *voice* in those affairs. It thus happens that many Indians who are interested in the idea of self-government do not have very much practical knowledge or experience in the tasks of government. It is the purpose of this memorandum to help remedy this task.

SECTION 2

NAME OF ORGANIZATION

The choice of a name by any Indian group organized under the Wheeler-Howard Act is, of course, entirely a matter of choice by the group concerned. Ordinarily, it is expected that an Indian tribe, pueblo, band, or nation will continue to use its traditional name. If it becomes incorporated under Section 17 of the Wheeler-Howard Act, it may add the word "incorporated" before or after its traditional name, for example, the "Incorporated Pueblo of Picuris," or the "Eastern Band of Cherokees, Incorporated," or the "Papago Tribe, Incorporated." This, however, is not necessary, as federal corporations (such as the American Red Cross, the American Legion, and the District of Columbia) are not required by any law to use the words "corporation" or "incorporated" in their titles.

In some cases the organization affected under Section 16 of the Wheeler-Howard Act will not correspond exactly to any tribe or band. All the Indians of a given reservation may organize as a unit if they so desire, regardless of past tribal affiliations. In such cases the organization may either set itself up as a new tribe (under Section 19 of the Wheeler-Howard Act), choosing an appropriate name for the tribe, or use some other title such as "community," "reservation," "colony," "village," "pueblo," or "tribal association." The words "chartered" or "incorporated" may be added before or after any of these names if a charter of incorporation is granted under Section 17 of the Wheeler-Howard Act. The term "colony" might be appropriate for organizations developed on new lands outside of existing reservations, acquired under Section 5 of the Wheeler-Howard Act or under other statutory authority. The term "tribal association" would be especially appropriate where the Indian organization did not contemplate substantial political powers but proposed to set up simply as a business or social organization.

5

SECTION 3

STATEMENT OF PURPOSES

It is customary in drafting a written constitution to include a statement of the purposes to which the constitution is devoted. While such a statement of purposes is not absolutely necessary, it may be useful in the following ways: In the first place, it will help the constitutional convention or committee to keep in mind from the outset the purposes of its work. In the second place, it may help to make clear, to the Indians of the reservation concerned, what those who have drafted the constitution have tried to do and how far they have succeeded. In the third place, this statement of purposes may be a guide to the future officials of the tribe in matters which are not dealt with in detail in the laws of the tribe and may be a constant reminder to them of their responsibilities to the tribe. In the fourth place, a statement of general purposes may help judges and other officials to place a fair interpretation upon the language of the constitution and laws of the tribe, where the language cannot be properly understood without an appreciation of the general purposes of the tribal organization.

A statement of purposes may be included in the constitution as a "preamble" or as a separate section. Usually a preamble consists of a single sentence, so that if a very detailed statement of purposes is desired it would be better to include this statement in a separate section.

What are the fundamental purposes which an Indian tribe may seek to achieve through organization under a written constitution?

The purposes stated by the Commissioner of Indian Affairs in the circular letter of January 20, 1934, are

1. To establish Indian self-government and to promote a healthy and satisfactory community life.
2. To preserve and develop Indian lands in Indian ownership and to provide the opportunity of economic livelihood for all who choose to remain within the Indian community.

Other purposes, somewhat related, have been stated in various constitutions which have been adopted by Indian tribes or are now under consideration by such tribes. Some of those provisions follow. The following brief preamble is taken from a constitution proposed by Indians of the Pima Reservation:

> We, the people of the PIMA COMMUNITY OF ARIZONA, in order to establish justice, promote the general welfare, and secure the blessings of our heritage to ourselves and our posterity, do ordain and establish this Constitution for the Pima Community of Arizona.

Another very brief statement of purposes is found in the preamble of a constitution now being considered by the Sioux Indians of the Standing Rock Reservation:

> We, the Sioux of Standing Rock Reservation in the states of South Dakota and North Dakota, in order to re-establish our Tribal organization, to conserve our Tribal property; to develop our common resources, and to promote the welfare of ourselves and our descendants, do adopt and establish this Constitution.

In the constitution of the Oglala Sioux Tribal Council of the Pine Ridge Reservation, special reference is made to the treaty of 1868, which recognizes the rights of the tribe:

> *KNOW YE ALL MEN BY THESE PRESENTS*
> That, under and by virtue of the Treaty of 1868 we, the members of the Sioux Band of Indians duly enrolled on the Pine Ridge Indian Reservation in the State of South Dakota, for ourselves and successors do hereby pledge to organize under a Tribal Council; That, under and by virtue of Statutes of the United States of America granting such rights as pertains to Civil and Tribal authority of this reservation.

The constitution of the Klamath Business Committee contains a preamble which specifies such objects as higher education, good citizenship, and the honorable life:

> In order to secure to ourselves and our posterity the political and civil rights guaranteed to us by treaties and statutes of the United States, to obtain a higher education, to cultivate good citizenship, to build up an

independent and honorable life, to encourage and promote all movements and efforts leading to the good of the general welfare of our tribe, acknowledging Almighty God as the source of all power and authority in civil governments, the Lord Jesus Christ as the ruler of nations, and His revealed will as of supreme authority, we, the people, members of the several tribes of Indians enrolled on the Klamath Reservation, Oregon, in council assembled, hereby adopt this constitution and bylaws governing the election, duties, etc., of a business committee of the Lemath, Modos, and Yahooskin Band of Snake Indians of the Klamath jurisdictions.

Quite different from the objective expressed in the Pima constitution preamble "[to] secure the blessings of our heritage to ourselves and our posterity" is the preamble to a constitution offered in 1904 by the Menominee Tribe of Wisconsin, but never approved, which sets up as its main objective the destructions of the old tribal government:

Whereas, the government of the Menominee Tribe of Indians is not organized according to civilized principles, but is an old form of government which has existed from the earliest ages, in which the ruling power has been under the control of hereditary chiefs, as handed down from generation to generation from time immemorial to the present time; and our tribe being far enough advanced in civilization, in an age when this old system of government becomes inefficient for promoting the best interests and general welfare of the tribe, therefore:

We, the members of the Menominee Tribe of Indians in General Council assembled, believing that individual rights and interests as well as a closer tribal union and a more compact and substantial form of government will best conserve our common rights, privileges, and interest; ensure our protection and promotion; and better secure the blessings of civilization to ourselves and our posterity, do ordain and establish this Constitution for the government of our tribe.

Another constitution which abolishes older forms of tribal government that the Indians found inefficient under modern conditions is the constitution of the Seneca Nation of New York, adopted in 1848. This constitution contains the following preamble:

DECLARATION of the Seneca Nation of Indians, changing their form of Government, and adopting a Constitutional Charter.

We, the people of the Seneca Nation of Indians, by virtue of the right inherent in every people, trusting in the justice and necessity of our undertaking, and humbly invoking the blessing of the God of Nations upon our efforts to improve our civil condition, and to secure to our nation the administration of equitable and wholesome laws, do hereby *abolish, abrogate, and annul* our form of government by chiefs, because it has failed to answer the purposes for which all governments should be created.

- It affords no security in the enjoyment of property; it provides no laws regulating the institution of marriage, but tolerates polygamy.
- It makes no provision for the poor, but leaves the destitute to perish.
- It leaves the people dependent on foreign aid for the means of education.
- It has no judiciary, nor executive departments. It is an irresponsible, self-constituted aristocracy.
- Its powers are absolute and unlimited in assigning away the people's rights, but indefinite and not exercised in making municipal regulations for their benefit or protection.

We cannot enumerate the evils growing out of a system so defective, nor calculate its overpowering weight on the progress of improvement.

But to remedy these defects, we proclaim and establish the following Constitution or Charter, and implore the Governments of the United States and the State of New York, to aid in providing us with laws under which progress shall be possible.

A constitution considered by the Indians of Fort Belknap, but not yet voted upon, contains both a preamble and a special section stating the objectives of the organization more fully:

PREAMBLE
We, the duly enrolled members of the Fort Belknap Indian Reservation in the State of Montana, in order to secure to ourselves the benefits of self-government and the management of our own affairs without interference from other sources, and to perpetuate this reservation as an abiding place for all members of the Fort Belknap tribes, do establish this constitution of the FORT BELKNAP INDIAN TRIBAL ASSOCIATION.

* * * * *

Section 2. Objectives

A. To establish and maintain a form of self-government that shall promote the advancement and welfare of the Indians of Fort Belknap Reservation.

B. To establish and enforce such rules as may be necessary to safeguard Indian property for the use of future generations and to prevent the alienation of lands to white and non-members of this association.

C. To establish and maintain such rules of inheritance as will assure to all Indians of the present or future generations a share of lands upon which to establish a home.

The following preamble and statement of purposes is found in a constitution which is now being considered by some of the Indians of the San Carlos Reservation:

We, the Apache Indians of the San Carlos Reservation, wish to make use of the right of self-government in the United States and have herewith laid down, in the form of a Constitution, our resolutions thereon, adopted and confirmed by a general tribal vote, so anybody may know how the management of our own internal affairs shall be carried out.

Article I. Governing Body

We want the United States government to continue among us, for some time, such establishments as health and educational services, a superintendency, advisory officers, and other such connecting links with the federal government; but in our relation to it, similar to that of a town or a county to State and Federal Government, our own internal affairs shall be managed, insofar as not conflicting with United States laws or other governmental regulations, by a governing body which shall be known as the Tribal Council of the San Carlos Apaches.

A very detailed statement of objectives is found in the constitution of the Junior Yakima Indian Council, an unofficial organization of younger members of the Yakima Tribe:

The main objects of the organization are the protection and preservation of the Yakima Tribe of Indians and the American Indian race in general:

1. By practicing brotherhood among themselves in all dealings without regard to any racial, religious, or political differences;

2. By opposing any movement which may be regarded as detrimental to or against the peace and dignity of the Yakima Indian Tribe or to the American Indian race;
3. By presenting the true history of the Yakima Indian Tribe and the American Indian race, preserving the records and putting forth the true virtues, chief among which are honesty, truthfulness, and loyalty;
4. By promoting the study of the human and legal rights, privileges, and responsibilities and teaching and making known their true history among the members of the tribe;
5. By establishing new attitudes in life and devising things and enterprises for the individual and tribal betterment of the members, with the view of enabling them to adjust themselves happily to the social, spiritual, political, and economic requirements of the American people;
6. By encouraging attendance at school by Indian children;
7. By encouraging Indian women to help in the activities for the good of their children and the Indian people;
8. By establishing a legal department for the assistance and guidance of the members;
9. By directing the energies mainly to general principles and matters of interest and not allowing them to be used for any personal, political, or bureaucratic advantages, provided, however, that exceptionally meritorious individual cases shall be considered by the Board of Trustees before the council may extend any assistance;
10. By studying local conditions of, and possibilities for, the various Indian communities throughout the Yakima Indian Reservation, with a view of utilizing resources to the best advantage in creating self-supporting management of the properties of the individual Indian and of the tribe; self-supporting Indian homes and other enterprises, and the care and assistance of needy Indian members, and by these means prevent Indians from going to the county and state poorhouses and prisons;
11. By promoting, classifying, and protecting purchase, sale, trade, exchange, and distribution;
12. By verifying, determining, and rating values of lands, both individual and tribal, and liquidating credits, and to exchange needs, products, and services;
13. By establishing local councils or branches of the Junior Yakima Indian Council in all Indian communities and encouraging and promoting a more friendly relationship between its people;

14. By unifying the action of the local councils or branches of the Junior Yakima Indian Council, thereby ensuring uniform action in the work of the protection, preservation, and promotion of the welfare, management, control, interests, and such other matters as may be to their best interest and welfare;

15. And, to further transact, engage in, and perform any and all other things that may lawfully be done or performed by any person, tribe, association, or organization.

After considering each of the foregoing statements of constitutional objectives, those who are entrusted with the task of drafting a constitution will have to decide for themselves how far any of these objectives meets the needs of their own tribe and what other statements may be necessary.

SECTION 4

TERRITORY AND MEMBERSHIP

Following the statement of purposes it would be advisable to include in the tribal constitution a definition of the territory over which the constitution is to govern and of the individuals who are to be subject to the constitution.

The definition of territory over which the constitution and the laws of the tribe are to be in force will naturally be based upon the applicable treaties and statutes of the United States, and it may be advisable to recite these treaties and statutes. On allotted reservations the question will arise: Shall the tribe exercise jurisdiction over fee-patented lands within the original boundaries of the reservation, and shall it exercise jurisdiction over restricted allotments? No legal obstacle is seen to the exercise of tribal jurisdiction over such lands. That is to say, members of the tribe living on such lands will be subject to the same obligations toward the tribe and subject to the same jurisdiction on the part of the tribal courts as other members. Therefore, it would be proper for any tribe, if it so desires, to designate the original boundary of its reservation in defining the territory within which the tribal constitution and the laws passed under such constitution are to prevail. On the other hand, the tribe may find it advisable not to exercise any jurisdiction over fee patented land and may, accordingly, define its territory to include only land held in restricted Indian ownership.

Of course, the foregoing complications are irrelevant to reservations which have not been allotted.

The question of who is to be entitled to membership within the tribe and subject to the constitution and laws of the tribe will, on some reservations, prove very perplexing. It is impossible to lay down a general ruling on this subject applicable to all reservations.

There follow constitutional provisions showing how this problem has been dealt with by various Indian tribes.

A simple rule of membership, based upon enrollment but reserving the right of the Indians to add or subtract from the rolls for the purpose of

13

determining tribal membership, is found in an unapproved constitution of the Menominee Tribe, adopted in 1904:

Membership
Section 2. All persons whose names rightly appear on the present duly authenticated rolls of this tribe and their offspring shall constitute the Menominee Tribe of Indians. And the Business Committee hereinafter provided for shall have power to determine by resolution who are entitled to have their names continued thereon or added to said rolls from time to time.

A definite blood requirement is laid down in a constitution for the Fort Belknap Indian Tribal Association, now under discussion but not yet adopted:

Article II
Section 1. Eligibility
Only persons who have one-fourth degree of Indian blood or more and are dully enrolled members of the Fort Belknap tribes are eligible for membership or holding in this association.

Section 2. Election to Membership
Once each year, by a majority vote of the governing body of this association, new members may be admitted to membership in this association, provided they are eligible under Article 2, Section 1, hereof.

A more elaborate definition of membership, which considers the complications arising out of intermarriage, is found in the proposed constitution of the Pima Community of Arizona:

Article I. [Membership]
    Section 1. The Pima Community of Arizona shall consist of all Pima and Maricopa Indians of the Gila River Reservation and of the Salt River Reservation, both in Arizona.
    Section 2. All Pima and Maricopa Indians who have established or who may establish residence upon either of the above named reservations shall, while so actually maintaining residence upon either of said reservations, be considered members of the Pima Community of Arizona. A person must have lived upon the reservation at least six months to establish residence.

Section 3. All bona fide residents, as defined in Section 2 of this article, who have attained the age of twenty-one years, shall be entitled to participate in all matters affecting the Community.

Section 4. Indians of less than the half blood shall not be entitled to membership in the Community.

Section 5. Indians of other tribes, who can establish to the complete satisfaction of the Community Council, their possession of at least a one-half degree of Indian blood, and who are married to members of this Community shall be vested with full membership, provided they qualify in all other particulars, as specified in this Constitution.

Section 6. Mixed marriages between Caucasians and members of the Pima Community contracted prior to the date of the adoption of this Constitution shall be recognized by the Community, and the fact that one of the parties to such marriage is of Caucasian blood shall not constitute a bar to the membership of the Caucasian in the Community, provided all other particulars specified in this Constitution are fulfilled.

Section 7. Mixed marriages of any kind, contracted subsequent to the date of the adoption of this Constitution, will not be recognized by the Community, and any member of this Community entering into such mixed marriage contract shall forfeit membership in the Community, and shall not be entitled to continue to participate in communal affairs nor to reside on communal property.

The question may arise whether descendants of present members and possibly other Indians should be admitted to tribal membership automatically or should be required to pledge allegiance to the tribe and its constitution as a condition of membership. The Rules and Regulations for the Annette Islands Reserve in Alaska, promulgated by the Secretary of the Interior in 1915, which serve as a constitution for this reservation provide:

Article VI. Membership

Section 1. The act of March 3, 1891, reserves Annette Islands for the use of the Metlakahtlans who emigrated from British Columbia and such other Alaskan natives as may join them. Membership in the Annette Islands Reserve is therefore restricted to such persons as come within the purview of said act.

Section 2. Before exercising the right to vote for members of the council or otherwise to participate in the government of the Annette Islands Reserve, natives of Metlakahtla now 21 years old or over, all minors coming of age, and all other natives of Alaska who may be admitted to

membership in the Annette Islands Reserve by vote of the council, as hereinafter provided, shall subscribe to the following declaration:

DECLARATION
We, the people of Annette Islands Reserve, Alaska, do severally subscribe
to the following principles of good citizenship:

1. To be faithful and loyal to the Government of the United States of
   America.
2. To be loyal to the local government of our community, to obey its
   ordinances and regulations, and to obey the laws of the Territory of
   Alaska and the laws of the United States.
3. To cooperate earnestly in all endeavors for the education of our
   children, for the advancement of the community, and for the
   suppression of all forms of vice.

Section 3. All minor children of present or former members of the
Annette Islands Reserve shall be considered members of the reserve until
they reach their majority, at which time, in order to continue their membership, they must sign the declaration, as provided in Paragraph 3 of Section 4
of this article.

Section 4. A native of Alaska of indigenous race, over 21 years of age,
residing outside of the Annette Islands Reserve, hereafter desiring to
become a member of the Annette Islands Reserve, shall proceed as follows:

1. Make application in writing to the council of the Annette Islands
   Reserve, at Metlakahtla, Alaska, for admission to membership in the
   reserve.
2. If the council approves the application, by a vote of three-fourths of
   its entire membership, the applicant shall come before a mass meeting
   of the members of the reserve upon proper notice of the time and
   place of such meeting.
3. In the presence of the mayor, council, and the citizens of the reserve,
   the declaration in Section 2 of this article shall be read to the
   applicant, and he or she shall sign a copy of the declaration before
   two witnesses.
4. After the declaration has been duly signed and witnessed the mayor
   shall declare the applicant a member of the Annette Islands Reserve.
5. Minor children of persons so admitted shall be members of the
   reserve, but upon attaining their majority they shall, in order to

continue their membership, proceed as set forth in Paragraph 3 of Section 4 of this article.

Section 5. Continuous absence from the Annette Islands Reserve for two years or longer shall constitute forfeiture of membership in the reserve. The permit to occupy land held by any person whose membership shall so lapse may be canceled by the council, as provided in Article VII, Sections 1 and 6, of those rules and regulations. Such person may be readmitted to membership in the reserve, as provided in Section 4 of this article.

The constitution of the Junior Yakima Indian Council provides for two classes of members, active members and associate members, restricting the former class to those enrolled upon the reservation and providing that intermarried whites or Indians from other reservations may become associate members having all tribal rights except the right to vote, hold office, or receive tribal benefits.

Of course, it is not necessary to decide all questions of membership in the constitution itself. All that is necessary is that the constitution prescribe some definite method whereby any future dispute about membership may be settled. Thus, the constitution and bylaws of the Quechan Tribal Council, adopted by the Indians of the Fort Yuma Indian Reservation on February 27, 1934 (thus far not approved by the Indian Office), contains the following provisions:

RESIDENCE AND ENROLLMENT OF FOREIGN INDIANS

The council shall pass the necessary rules and regulations in conformity to the provisions of the Constitution whereby Indians from other reservations shall be permitted to secure enrollment and registration upon this reservation. Such rules and regulations shall protect in every manner the established rights and privileges of the members of this tribe.

The Council shall establish a minimum period of time, not to exceed five (5) years, in which such rights shall be granted. Such period of time shall date from date of such Indian's entry upon the reservation as a resident thereof. It shall further specify qualifications of character and of conduct which will ensure that such Indian so seeking registration and enrollment will be a proper and valuable member of the tribe. Provided that the full right of citizenship in this tribe, with right to require land through allotment, or to hold Tribal Office, shall extend only to those Indians from other reservations who shall marry members of this tribe, and that all other Indians (i.e., those who do not marry members of this tribe) shall be excluded from the benefits of Tribal allotments or other Tribal inheritance and shall not be entitled to hold any elective Tribal Office.

The effect of these provisions is to require the tribal council to pass detailed rules and regulations on the question of membership and to lay down certain general principles which the tribal council must follow in this task.

More detailed rules on membership or citizenship and the complicated problems arising out of intermarriage will be found in the written constitutions and laws of the Cherokee Nation, the Choctaw Nation, the Chickasaw Nation, the Muskogee (Creek) Nation, and the Osage Nation.

SECTION 5

OFFICES AND TITLES

On many questions which arise in the course of drafting a tribal constitution it will be necessary to choose between the older forms of tribal government and the forms of government which are customary in white communities. In making this choice wisely, each tribe must consider for itself how far it wishes to preserve its own ancient traditions of self-government. In many cases these traditions have been forgotten. But where they are still remembered they offer a very important source of knowledge and wisdom to those who are engaged in drafting a constitution, for it must be remembered that before the coming of the white man, each Indian tribe had its own governing officers, its own policemen if policemen were necessary, its own system of land holding and inheritance, its own laws of marriage and divorce, and its own code of crimes. Each tribe was organized for the purpose of dealing with the basic problems of the community as a whole, the problem of relations with other tribes, the problem of making a living, the problem of guiding and controlling the use of property so as to eliminate want and suffering within the tribe. All those problems remain, and the tribe that desires to achieve self-government must devise ways and methods of meeting those problems. In many cases the old methods will prove entirely satisfactory. This is particularly likely to be the case on those reservations which have never been allotted, where the Indian community is strong, and where the difficult problems of contacts between individual Indians and individual white men seldom arise. On the other hand, on those reservations where white men have entered in large numbers and where most of the Indians' troubles arise out of the activities of whites, the older methods of tribal government may be entirely inapplicable.

The choice between old ways and new ways must be made in the selection of titles, as well as in many more important questions. In the selection of titles it is possible to use such terms as chief, headman, principal men (principales), principal chief, subchief, cacique, and other words corresponding to

19

the native tribal titles. Where these titles are still held in respect among the Indians, the use of these titles may serve to remind the younger generation and future generations that the work of self-government was performed for many centuries by non-English speaking Indians who were not dependent in any way upon a Secretary of the Interior. The title of "principal chief" is still used, for instance, by the Eastern Band of Cherokee Indians, as a title for their highest executive officer. A constitution recently submitted for the consideration of the Indians of the Standing Rock Reservation uses the title of chief, first subchief, and second subchief and contains this provision: "The Chief shall be regarded by the Sioux of this Reservation in the same manner as were the Chiefs of the Tribe under our old Tribal life and government." (Article III, Section 3)

On the other hand, where the Indians have ceased to respect the native traditions or where white men who would not pay proper respect to officials in calling them chiefs or headmen are likely to be involved in Indian affairs, it may be advisable to use official titles similar to those used by the state or by the counties or municipalities of the region.

Thus, on those reservations where it is decided to center executive responsibility in a single official, it would be wise to call such official the governor of the tribe or reservation, or, if the reservation is a small one, the mayor. If any tribe achieves a large degree of self-government, so that its leader would actually perform most of the functions which are now performed by the Commissioner of Indian Affairs, it is suggested that such an official should be called the commissioner of the tribe or reservation.

On many reservations it will be found advisable not to have a single administrative head of the reservation with any independent powers. In such cases where the tribal council chooses a chairman he may be designated as the president or chairman of the tribal council.

The general representative body of the tribe may be called the tribal council, the executive council of the named tribe, the board of directors, the board of trustees, or the board of overseers. Where the powers of this representative body are strictly legislative, the body might well be called a tribal legislature or senate. Where two such bodies exist on a single reservation, they may be distinguished by such terms as senate and house of representatives, senate and assembly, senate and council, council and subcouncil, etc. The constitution of the Muskogee (Creek) Nation provided for a House of Kings and a House of Warriors.

The judicial officers of the tribe, if the tribe has independent judicial officers, may be designated as judges, justices, or justices of the peace. If there are separate judges in matters of inheritance, they might be called probate judges. Courts may be designated as tribal courts, reservation courts, or

Indian courts. In the Seneca Nation of New York the regular court is known as the Peacemakers Court. Where a system of appeal is provided from one court to another, the lower court may be designated as a district court and the upper court as a superior court or supreme court or court of appeals. Officers engaged in the administration of justice may have such titles as sheriff (or alcalde); marshal; constable; police commissioner; chief of police; police captain, lieutenant, or sergeant; or simply policeman. Among some of the Five Civilized Tribes of Oklahoma, the police force was designated as the Light Horse Company or Light Horsemen.

Other miscellaneous officers of the tribe may have such titles as secretary of the tribe, secretary of the tribal council, treasurer of the tribe, treasurer of the tribal council, sergeant at arms of the tribal council, assessors, highway commissioners, overseers of the poor, health officer, building inspector, cemetery warden, fiscales, tribal or national attorney or solicitor, mining trustee, director of a specified activity, or accountant.

Where special district officers or councils exist, it will be advisable to add the word "district" to those titles.

Each tribe should consider the propriety of having certain standing committees, boards or commissions to deal with the following subjects: (1) citizenship or membership, (2) finance, (3) education, (4) internal improvements, (5) judiciary, (6) claims. [The above committees are all provided for in the constitution of the Muskogee (Creek) Nation adopted in 1893.] The constitution of the Cheyenne and Arapaho Tribes adopted in 1934, but not officially approved, provided for committees on health, legislation and resolutions, budget and audit, and entertainment. Other committees or boards that might be established in a large enough tribe are a board or commission of elections, of lands, of public works, and of public welfare. The Constitution of the Seneca Indian Council of Oklahoma provides for a special "grievance committee" elected by the members of the tribe, which investigates complaints against the tribal council and call general meetings of the tribe when necessary.

No general rule can be given as to the number of offices that should exist within a given tribe. This will depend upon the population of the tribe,[*] the amount of time that a faithful officer can be expected to give to his tribe, the difficulties of transportation and communication among different districts, the qualifications and experience of available candidates for office, and many other factors, which all vary considerably among the different tribes.

---

[*]It has been recommended, for instance, that the 39 enrolled Indians who compose the population of Squaxin Island Reservation might be empowered to elect a justice of the peace and a constable.

SECTION 6

DISTRICT ORGANIZATION

The simplest form of government is centralized government. In a system of centralized government all the members of the community vote upon a single list of candidates for office, and each of the officers elected serves the entire community. On some reservations, however, there are two or more tribes which prefer to have separate elections and separate delegates to the general council of the reservation. Other reservations are so large that they contain many communities at considerable distances from each other, so that it would be impossible for a delegate elected from one community to know the wishes of people in other communities. In such cases it may be advisable to establish a form of district organization.

Such district organizations may be used in two ways:

1. Each district may elect its own delegate or delegates to the tribal governing body; or
2. Each district may elect local officials, as well as delegates to the central body.

In some cases the district is determined on purely geographical lines. In other cases the subordinate groupings are not geographic but based upon the tribe or band affiliations of individuals. The latter type of district organization might be more accurately called band organization.

On the Fort Belknap Reservation, for instance, there are two tribes approximately equal in numbers. Each tribe elects six members to the tribal council. The deciding vote in case of a tie is cast by the superintendent as ex officio chairman of the tribal council.

Similarly, the Shoshone and Arapaho tribal council consists of six representatives of each of the two tribes on the reservation. On the Uintah and Ouray Reservation, each of the three bands elects two members of the tribal business committee.

22

On the Colorado River Reservation, four council members were elected by one of the tribes on the reservation and four by each of two factions of the other tribe, but this system has been abandoned recently in favor of a single election. The experience of the Menominee Tribe in this connection may be instructive. The reservation covers about 350 square miles. Until now the tribal council has been elected as a unit. The superintendent of the reservation recently reported:

> It is further suggested that the Advisory Board should consist of members representing the various townships on the reservation rather than from those who are most popular as in the present case, [where they] are chosen largely from the industrial center at Heopit. This reservation consists of ten townships of land and approximately two thousand tribal members. The more desirable method of tribal representation would be similar to the congressional district representation such as is now used in the surrounding white settlement, apportionment being made on the basis of one representative to each two hundred members. I believe that the General Council which is called for September 22, 1934, will take tribal action to amend the present by-laws of the Advisory Board setting up the method of election as above stated.

In deciding whether representation should be by districts, it should be remembered that a representative is likely to think first of the interests of his constituency. Thus, district representation sometimes serves to aggravate factionalism.

On the other hand, where the reservation is large, it is hardly fair to have people vote upon candidates who are not known to them and who live so far away that the representative will seldom be able to discuss matters with the people he is supposed to represent.

If election districts are not too large, the representative of each district will be able to attend a mass meeting of the people of his district after each meeting of the tribal council. In this mass meeting he may explain what actions have been taken by the council and what measures have been proposed for future action. People of the district may then instruct their delegate how to vote at the next council meeting. In this way a close contact is maintained between the councilmen and the people they represent. This is the custom followed on the Navajo Reservation and on several other large reservations. A somewhat similar system is established by the constitution of the Hoopa Business Council. Along with the councilmen elected by a given district of the Hoopa Valley Reservation, certain subcouncilmen are elected. Each councilman must report to his subcouncilmen every month after the regular council meeting and must secure their approval on all important matters.

In the instances discussed above, district or band organization was used for purposes of representation on a centralized governing board. Some reservations, however, are so large that a centralized governing board cannot attend to all the tasks of government. It then becomes necessary to have district officers or band officers. These officers will ordinarily be elected by the people of the district.

In this situation it becomes important to make clear, in the tribal constitution, what the duties and powers of the district officers shall be. Otherwise, many disputes and difficulties are likely to arise, as they have arisen, for instance, in the United States where the conflict of authority between the federal government and the states has caused one Civil War and thousands of lawsuits.

The simplest way to ensure harmony within the tribal government is to provide that the district officers shall have no power to make laws of their own, but shall administer the duties assigned to them by the tribal council.

This form of government is established by the laws of the Choctaw Nation (1894), which provide:

Section II. District Chiefs
1. Be it enacted by the general council of the Choctaw Nation assembled: There shall be elected by the qualified voters of the Choctaw Nation, at the time and in the manner prescribed by the constitution, district chiefs in each district of this nation, who shall be commissioned by the principal chief, and shall continue in the office for the term of two years from the time of having been qualified unless sooner removed, and until their successors be duly qualified; and before they enter upon the discharge of their official duties, they shall take the oath prescribed in the constitution before the principal chief or any judge of the supreme, circuit, or county courts of the nation.
2. Each district chief within his district shall be a general conservator of the peace and shall see that the laws are faithfully executed by the proper officers, especially an act to prevent the introduction and use of intoxicating liquors in the Choctaw Nation, and report to the principal chief for the information of the general council, any failures occurring therein; and shall recommend to him from time to time any matter for the general good, and when the principal chief shall deem

it proper and expedient, and shall give them written notice of the time and place of meeting, they shall compose an executive council to furnish any desired information respecting their several districts; but said district chiefs shall in no manner interfere with the proper exercise of the duties prescribed by law of any officers of the nation.

3. Each district chief of the nation shall attend the circuit courts of his own district, and address the people on the importance of obeying and enforcing the law, and maintaining good order throughout the nation, and advocate the practice of temperance, industry, and morality; and their salaries shall be fifty dollars each annum, payable semi-annually on the certificate of the circuit judges at the terms of the circuit courts; but should any district chief fail or neglect to be in attendance at the said courts, to address the people as required of him by law, the circuit judge is hereby required to appoint some suitable person to perform the duties incumbent upon the district chief, and shall give the person performing the duties, a certificate for the sum of ten dollars, to be deducted from the pay of the district chief so failing.

The constitution of the Pueblo of Laguna, adopted in 1908, provides:

Section 10. Each officer in charge of a village is strictly subject to the orders of the Governor. He shall give no orders to the people of his village without first submitting same to the Governor, unless, however, he should have a standing order from the Governor to give certain orders or perform certain duties whenever he deemed it necessary. All cases of emergency excepted.

In considering the character of local groupings the following suggestions offered by Superintendent Roberts of the Rosebud Indian Reservation in South Dakota may prove helpful on some reservations:

An obstacle of serious proportions in any community consideration of Indians here lies in the fact of the scattered population of the Rosebud people. The Rosebud Reservation is about 150 miles long and 50 miles wide, with Indian people scattered throughout the territory. At no point on the Reservation is there a compact, closely knit community. Rather, communities are scattered over a considerable territory. For instance, a Grass Mountain gathering will have an attendance with some Indians from twenty-five or thirty miles away; others in the congregation will live ten or fifteen miles; some as close as one or two miles. This is typical of the Rosebud country.

* * * * *

It seems most likely, therefore, in setting up a community enterprise, that the best nucleus may be built around the local community halls (dance halls). As a definite illustration, consider

> *The Grass Mountain Dance Hall*: The analysis of the attendance at a typical Grass Mountain dance will be found to consist of people from several communities, so far as topography is concerned. This affiliation follows those natural tendencies of the Indians, which makes them desire to affiliate with one another at that particular place. It is quite likely that on the same night people living within two or three miles of the Grass Mountain Hall will be found in attendance at the Hollow Horn Bear Hall, fifteen miles away. This is explained by the fact that their natural tendencies out of past inheritances, or out of religious beliefs, or out of some other reason, cause people to select a meeting place not necessarily the nearest to their houses.

Assuming, therefore, that the community dance hall is the proper place from which to start, that the best approach seems to lie in the following type of organization:

1. That those people who voluntarily gather at a given hall should be the representative community insofar as organization is concerned; that the numbers should be developed through the voluntary and spontaneous desire of those particular people who gather at that hall; that those members should be recorded and from it a governing function evolved.

2. The community members of a hall should first, voluntarily, from its group, choose three persons to act as a standing committee, for a length of time equitable to the community (probably one year). This committee would have the following duties:

    (a) Set the time and frequency of the native Indian dances.

    (b) Set the time and frequency (in collaboration with the Extension Division) of the farm clubs, stock associations, cooperative groups, and the like.

    (c) Arrange for other Indian celebrations, rodeos, gatherings, and the like.

    (d) Cooperate with the Extension Division in such projects as 4-H Club work and the organization of industrial enterprises such as livestock associations, community gardens, and the like.

(e) Cooperate with the school groups to promote better attendance of pupils; to develop parent-teacher associations; to assist in such matters as truancy, tardiness, and absence; and in general to promote a better school program.

(f) Cooperate with the administration in maintaining desirable moral standards, promoting better observance of law and good order, and assisting all officials in better relationships with the people in the community.

(g) Assist in determining real wants and needs in a community and developing ways and means to prevent[such wants and needs.]

* * * * *

After the above-defined community shall have organized, it shall be empowered to select the representation of that community in the general assemble of the council.

SECTION 7

FORM OF GOVERNING BODY

The simplest form of representative government is unified government, that is to say, government by a single body of representatives clothed with comprehensive powers. These representatives may choose special officials or committees for tasks which cannot be efficiently carried out by the governing body as a whole.

The administration of justice, for instance, may be such a task. If offenses and disputes are so numerous that too much of the time of the governing body would be taken up with those matters, or if the law to be applied is so complicated that the elected representatives of the people are incapable of administering justice, the governing body may appoint judges for this special task. Similarly, if the task of planning the use of land is too large a task or too difficult a task for the governing body to undertake itself, this body may appoint a board of land commissioners, or a land committee, either from its own membership or from outside its membership, and delegate to this board or committee sufficient power to perform the necessary tasks. In every case the central governing body of the community will supervise all the special tasks that must be done by special officials, will require regular reports from those officials, and will have the power to remove those officials if they neglect their duties or fail to carry out the policies approved by the governing body. While the governing body is not in session, it may delegate the task of general supervision over governmental activities to its chairman or president or to an executive council or committee. Such officers would, of course, be responsible to the governing body and would be bound by the laws and resolutions of that body. The simple principle underlying the system of unified government is that *all* powers of government are vested in a single governing body, which may delegate to subordinate officials such powers as it thinks proper.

This form of government was enjoyed by practically all Indian tribes before the coming of the white man, and it persists in the most successful self-governing Indian committees today, with only slight modifications.

Under the bylaws and constitution of the Laguna Pueblo Indians, adopted January 1, 1908, all powers of government are vested in a court consisting of eight officers, including the governor. Section 3 of the constitution provides:

> The Governor with the other seven court officers shall have the power to decide all matters of business that come before the court. After they have examined all witnesses and ascertained full details of the case, and, in their opinion, it has been sufficiently commented upon, they shall then retire to a private place to make their decision. If they cannot all agree upon a decision, the case shall be decided by a standing vote of all the officers except the Governor, and the majority shall rule. The Governor not having a vote, it shall be his duty and privilege to instruct the other officers regarding his views in the case before a vote is taken.

Another section provides that the governor shall be the supreme ruler, but it is understood that all his orders are subject to the will of the tribal court. Thus, Section 2 of the constitution provides:

> The Governor shall be the supreme ruler, and his orders must be obeyed by the people in general. It is understood, however, that if any person considers that the ruling of the Governor is unjust, and that he is being imposed upon by his order, he shall perform the duty as ordered under protest, and then he shall have the right to demand that the matter be brought before the court officers for adjudication at the next meeting of said officers.

A possible model for a system of unified government is contained in the following provisions from a draft of a constitution under consideration on the Fort Belknap Reservation:

> *Article II. Powers of the Council*
> The government of the Fork Belknap Indian Community shall be entrusted to a Council, consisting of _____ members elected for a period of one year, and to such officials as the Council may select. All powers of government not otherwise provided for by this constitution may be exercised by the Council or delegated by the Council to agents or officials. The Council may pass, repeal, or modify ordinances or resolutions by a majority vote, but except in case of emergency, general ordinances shall not take effect until twenty days after the date of passage.

* * * * *

Article V. Election of Officials
Within one week after induction into office, the Council shall meet under the temporary chairmanship of its oldest member and shall forthwith proceed to elect the following officials:
> Governor
> Secretary
> Treasurer
> Three Judges
> Three Policemen
> Three Commissioners of Lands
> Three Commissioners of Public Works
> Three Commissioners of Elections
> Three Commissioners of Public Welfare

and such additional officials as may be needed to perform the duties of government.

Any official may be removed by a majority vote of the Council, but no official shall be removed until he has had notice of the reasons for which his removal is sought and an opportunity to hear the evidence and confront the witnesses testifying against him, and to speak in defense of his actions and policies.

The Rules and Regulations for the Annette Islands Reserve in Alaska provide:

Article II. Local Government
  Section 1. The local government of the Annette Islands Reserve shall be vested in a council consisting of twelve members, all of whom shall be members of the Annette Islands Reserve.
  Section 2. The officials of the Annette Islands Reserve shall be a mayor, a secretary, and a treasurer.
  Section 3. The members of the council and the officials of the Annette Islands Reserve shall be elected by ballet, printed or written, on the Tuesday last proceeding December 25 in each year. . . .

Article III of those Rules and Rregulations confers full power upon the council to make and enforce laws and to punish disobedience. Under those Rules and Regulations the mayor presides over council meetings, but has no vote power over legislation and no administrative or executive powers, except such as may be assigned to him from time to time by the council (Article IV). Thus, all responsibility is centered in the council.

A somewhat similar arrangement is provided by the drafted constitution for the Pima Community of Arizona now under consideration. This constitution provides:

> *Article II.* [Legislative Department]
> *Section 1.* All legislative powers herein granted shall be vested in a Pima Community Council.
> *Section 2.* The Pima Community Council shall be composed of ten members chosen every second year by the people of the several districts. North Blackwater and Blackwater shall constitute District Number One and shall be entitled to one member in said Council. . . . Casa Blanca shall constitute District Number Three and shall be entitled to two members. . . .
> *Section 4.* The Community Council shall choose from outside their number a President who must possess all the qualifications necessary to membership in said Council. Said President shall preside at Council meetings, shall be permitted to participate in debate, and shall be entitled to vote only in case of tie. . . .
> *Section 17.* The Council shall appoint all Community Judges and all Community Police whose duty it shall be to enforce, under the direction of the President, all applicable federal statutes and all laws and ordinances enacted by the Council. Judges and Police shall be appointed for terms of five years.

Opposed to these comparatively simple forms of government are those forms of government which attempt to distribute various powers among various governmental bodies, none of which is supposed to be superior to any other body.

An example of this is found in the distribution of legislative power between two separate bodies. This system was adopted by the United States partly because of the necessity of reaching a compromise between two different theories of government, the theory that the United States was a group of independent states, each of which ought to have equal representation, regardless of population, and the theory that the United States was a single nation in which representation should be allocated to localities according to population. As a compromise measure, *both* forms of representative body were established. It is possible that a similar situation may exist on some reservations in that the older members of the tribe may want a system of government by chiefs, and the younger members may want government by representatives elected for short terms. If no other compromise can be effected, a legislature consisting of two bodies might be adopted. This system, however, as tried out upon the Rosebud Reservation, which is governed by a council of seventy-four members and a Board of Advisors of twenty elected chiefs, has not been very successful.

A two-chambered legislature was adopted by four of the Five Civilized Tribes, that is, the Cherokee Nation, which under its constitution had a National Committee and a National Council; the Muskogee (Creek) Nation with a House of Kings and a House of Warriors; the Chickasaw Nation with a Senate and a House of Representatives; and the Choctaw Nation with a Senate and House of Representatives. In each case this plan was adopted because of admiration for the United States Constitution rather than because of any consideration of the special needs of the Indians concerned.

Except in very unusual circumstances, there can be no justification for having two distinct legislative bodies in a single tribe. The extra expense; the duplication of effort when two independent bodies have to consider the same matters separately; the consequent delay, friction, and inefficiency; the divided responsibility; the temptation of each house to blame the other for what goes wrong instead of trying to cure the wrong, all these consequences make a two-chambered legislature highly inadvisable for any Indian tribe.

The same difficulties attending a two-chambered legislature are likely to arise if powers of government are divided up among separate coordinate "departments," for example, an executive, legislative, and judicial department. Under such a "separation of powers" there is bound to be friction, delay, and uncertain responsibility. This is especially likely to be the case if the executive and the judicial departments are given the power to veto laws which they regard as unconstitutional or unwise. Such a system of government makes change very difficult. The executive and judicial departments can stop the car but they cannot make it go.

For these reasons it is recommended that an Indian tribe, if it desires to establish an independently elected president or governor, should not give this officer the power to vote laws,[*] but should require him to carry out the laws passed by the council in such manner as the council may direct. So too, if courts are established, the decisions of these courts, at least on very important questions, should be reviewable by the council, or by the people at large.

---

[*]Such veto power is assigned by Article II of the Constitution and by Section 13 of the Charter of the Eastern Band of Cherokees in North Carolina.

SECTION 8

RELATION OF THE INDIAN SERVICE
TO TRIBAL GOVERNMENT

Three levels of self-government may be distinguished. In the first place, the governing body of the Indian tribe may be empowered to act only with the approval of the Indian Office. A more advanced constitution would provide that certain acts of the tribal council should not require such approval. The greatest degree of self-government that could be attained under existing law would give the tribal government complete independence of the Interior Department. Even in this case, however, it must be remembered that Congress would retain the power which it now has to nullify any tribal ordinances or resolutions. No constitution or charter could take that power away. Even Congress could not deprive itself of that power.

Which of these levels of self-government a tribe will achieve through its constitution must depend upon the desires, capacities, and experience of the Indians themselves.

Under the most elementary form of self-government it will be necessary to submit all resolutions or ordinances of the governing body of the tribe to officials of the Interior Department for approval. In order to save time in this process, the constitution of the tribe might provide that the superintendent of the reservation, or some other local employee of the Indian Service, should be an ex officio member or officer of the tribal council. A constitutional provision might then assign to such employee the power to approve the veto acts of the council and allow a right of approval by the council from any such veto to the Commissioner of Indian Affairs or to the Secretary of the Interior. Under an alternative arrangement, the superintendent or other local agent would have merely the power to "suspend" acts of the council for a given period, during which time the act may be passed upon by the Commissioner of Indian Affairs or by the Secretary of the Interior. Such an arrangement is found in Article VIII, Section 1, of the Rules and Regulations for the Annette Islands Reserve, providing:

The person in charge of the work of the United States Bureau of Education at Metlakahtla shall have a seat in the council and all the privileges of a member of the council, except that he shall have no vote. He shall have authority to suspend the operation of any ordinance of the council whenever he feels that such action is for the best interests of the reserve, but he shall immediately report his action in the matter, with his reasons therefore, to the district superintendent of schools, who shall refer the matter to the Commissioner of Education for decision, with his recommendation thereon. With the approval of the Secretary of the Interior, the Commissioner of Education may declare null and void any ordinance passed by the council.

It may be noted that since the promulgation of this provision in 1913, the power to suspend ordinances has been exercised only once, and then in a minor matter.

A somewhat similar arrangement is found in a draft constitution which is now being considered by the Indians of the Fort Belknap Reservation. This constitution provides that the superintendent, appointed with the approval of the tribal council, shall be the executive head of the reservation, enjoying full veto power over acts of the council. Article IV of this constitution provides:

1. The Reservational Superintendent shall be the executive head of the entire jurisdiction and be responsible only to the Tribal Council and the Government of the United States. He shall carry out all rules, regulations and ordinances legally passed for the Government of this jurisdiction and may appoint duly authorized employees to act for him.

2. Every measure or resolution which shall be passed by the council, before it becomes effective, shall be presented to the Reservation Superintendent; if he approves, he shall sign it, but if not, he shall return it with his objections to the council, who shall enter the objections at large on their records and proceed to reconsider it. If, after consideration, two-thirds of the council agree to pass the resolution, it shall be referred to the legal voters of the Association and must be carried by a two-thirds vote of all adult members having the qualifications hereinbefore set forth. If any resolution shall not be returned by the Superintendent within thirty days (Sundays excepted) after it shall have been presented to him, the same shall become effective, in like manner as if he had signed it. Return of resolution to the Secretary of the Council shall be deemed legal notice.

3. The Reservational Superintendent shall act as Disbursing Agent for the Association and may be required to furnish bond for the proper performance of his duties. He shall refuse to make any disbursements which in his opinion are illegal until authorized to do so by the Commissioner of Indian Affairs.

4. The Reservational Superintendent shall have power, by and with the advice of the council, provided two-thirds of the council present shall concur, to establish needful positions, and shall nominate and, by and with the advice and consent of the council, appoint employees to these positions, but the council by resolution may vest the appointment of such inferior employees as they think proper in the Superintendent alone.

5. The Superintendent shall from time to time give to the council information as to the state of the Association and recommend for their consideration such measures as he shall judge necessary and expedient.

It may be doubted whether an Indian tribe would want to give its superintendent such large powers over its own government unless the superintendent were appointed with the approval of the tribal council. Under existing law the choice of a reservation superintendent cannot be left with the tribal council, and a constitutional provision requiring such approval would be invalid. It would, however, be possible to provide in the constitution that a superintendent, if approved by the tribal council, should have powers such as those specified above.

The plan of general review by the Interior Department over all acts of the tribal council, which is employed in the constitution above cited, is the least measure of self-government that any Indian tribe can demand.

On the other hand, complete freedom from Indian Office supervision may be secured by a tribe which demonstrates its capacity to care for its own affairs. Such a tribe might incorporate in its constitution a provision such as the following, which is modeled after the federal statute providing for the government of the Territory of Alaska (U.S. Code, Title 48, Sections 88 and 90):

The governor of the _____ Tribe shall, within _____ days after the enactment of any ordinance or resolution, transmit to the Commissioner of Indian Affairs a copy of such ordinance or resolution, certified to by the secretary of the council, with the seal of the tribe attached. All such ordinances and resolutions shall be submitted to Congress by the Commissioner of Indian Affairs, and, if disapproved by Congress they shall be null and of no effect.

Intermediate between those two levels of self-government is the level which requires discrimination between certain powers which the tribe may exercise in its own right, without securing the approval of the Indian Office, and other powers which may be exercised only with the consent of the Indian Office. This type of arrangement offers the greatest difficulties in the drafting of a constitution. No general rule can be laid down as to the distinction between the two kinds of tribal power. Each type of activity must be considered in the light of the experience and qualifications of tribal officials entrusted with the given task, the temptations that may boost them, and the needs of future generations. In the light of this study the statement of tribal powers included in the constitution, which is discussed below, should be followed by the statement that such and such powers may be exercised only with the consent of the Commissioner of Indian Affairs or only with the consent of the Secretary of the Interior.

SECTION 9

PLACE OF CHIEFS IN TRIBAL GOVERNMENT

The place of traditional chiefs, headmen, or other officers (such as the caciques of the pueblos) in tribal government presents a vary delicate problem on certain reservations.

Where these titles are generally recognized by the members of a tribe, the Indian Office will not object to any constitutional provision assigning such individuals regular governmental powers.

It is necessary, however, that the constitution show exactly who are entitled to be recognized as chiefs, headmen, caciques, etc. Unless the constitution contains specific provisions on this point, it is impossible to guarantee the continued recognition of the traditional powers of such tribal officials.

Where there are a number of recognized chiefs or headmen in a given tribe, these individuals may constitute a second legislative body, coordinate with the regularly elected legislative body, as has been suggested in Section 7 above. This was attempted at the Rosebud Reservation in South Dakota, but it is reported that the Advisory Board, which was supposed to be elected from among the recognized chiefs, now contains many members who are not chiefs. A more simple arrangement would be to assign to the recognized chiefs a regular life tenure in the tribal council. This was done in the early organization of the Metlakahtla Indian Community, which was at first governed by a council of thirty people composed of ten chiefs, enjoying life tenure, and twenty elected members, enjoying terms of one year. In later years, when all those chiefs had died, the council was purely elective. Another possible arrangement would be to establish a council of chiefs with certain specified powers which would not conflict with the powers of the regular tribal governing body. Such a council of chiefs might be given the power to *suspend* acts of the tribal council that are thought to be detrimental to the best interests of the tribe and to require that such acts be put to a popular vote of the tribe. (See "Articles of Incorporation" of the Oglala Tribal Council of the Pine Ridge Reservation, Article IV.) Such a council of chiefs might be given the power to select the chairman of the tribal council from among the elected councilmen or else from among its own number. Finally, such a council might constitute a court of appeals or supreme court to review decisions of the ordinary tribal courts.

Where the Indians of the reservation are divided into several communities, each with its own recognized chief, the chiefs might be made leaders of their districts subject to the orders of the central governing body. (The practice at Hopi may be instructive on this point).

Where there is a single recognized chief on a given reservation, he may be assigned the position of chairman of the tribal council (as in the Fort Bidwell Indian Colony) for life or for a term of years, or he may be given the power to select such a chairman from the elected council members, or he may be given the power to nominate officers at all elections. A typical pueblo constitution might confirm the power of the cacique or caciques of the pueblo to nominate pueblo officials. The nature of this power may vary as the custom of the pueblo now varies. The nominating power might be exclusive or it might be jointly exercised either with the ex-officers of the pueblo known as "principales" or with the council or with the people of the pueblo. Under the first procedure, the caciques would make all nominations to tribal office. Under the second procedure, the caciques would agree on nominations with the principales, or, in case of disagreement, the caciques would nominate one set of candidates and the principales would nominate additional candidates. Under the third suggested procedure, the caciques would agree with the council on nominations, or else two sets of nominations might be made. Under the fourth procedure, the caciques would present candidates, and other candidates might be nominated by the people assembled for the election.

It is plain that the constitutional definition of traditional tribal powers is a task that requires careful analysis of the social heritage of living Indians. The foregoing suggestions are probably entirely inapplicable to most Indian groups. They are offered as examples of the way in which ancient powers may be given modern names that a white man's court and white officials are likely to respect.

Even more difficult than the task of assigning governmental powers to chiefs or caciques is the task of determining who is a chief or cacique. Unless this can be determined under the constitution, there is no way of protecting the traditional system of government against dissolution. Sooner or later a discontented group will arise to challenge the authority of those who claim the traditional titles and perhaps to advance the claim of some new men to such titles. In order to obviate this possibility before it becomes actual, it would be desirable to insert a specific provision in the tribal constitution governing the right to these traditional titles.

In the first place, the names and titles of those recognized at the time of the adoption of the constitution should appear in the constitution itself. This may be done by inserting a special provision to the effect that:

> The following members of the _____ Tribe are recognized as chiefs (or headmen, caciques, etc.) of the tribe, entitled to exercise the following powers: . . . .

Another way of dealing with this matter would be by having the written constitution signed by the chiefs of the tribe before being submitted for the approval of the Secretary of the Interior or perhaps before being voted on by the tribe itself. The signatures would then be a permanent record of those recognized as chiefs.

Where the methods of appointing new chiefs or deposing old chiefs have been forgotten by the tribe or are no longer practicable under modern conditions, one of two courses of action may be taken. Either the roll of chiefs may be closed forever with no provision for new enrollments (an account of the transition from rule by chiefs to rule by council is found in the answer to Questionnaire S7126 from Pyramid Lake Indian Reservation), or else a method may be worked out whereby the tribal council or the people at large shall appoint new chiefs or remove old chiefs on the basis of their achievements and their contributions to the welfare of the people. It is believed that among most tribes chieftainship was reward for recognized merit and leadership in defending the interests of the tribe as a whole. Although some of the ways of showing such merit and leadership, such as proof by battle, may be obsolete today, other methods of proving merit and demonstrating capacity for service to the tribe remain.

Where the traditional methods of appointing new chiefs or removing old chiefs are still known and respected and are still practicable, it should be possible to state in the tribal constitution in simple language what this method is. If this method involves secret matters, it would be enough to provide that the chiefs or caciques should be chosen or deposed according to the ancient customs of the tribe, and that any dispute that may arise over those matters should be finally settled by the tribal court, by the tribal council, or by some other designated body.

SECTION 10

CONDUCT OF ELECTIONS

One of the matters that should be set forth very clearly in any Indian constitution is the manner of electing officers of the tribe. This may be a very simple matter on a small reservation where everyone can meet together on the date set for elections and proceed to elect the officers by a standing vote. On a larger reservation, where many polling places are needed, the procedure must be more complex.

Each Indian constitution should specify whether candidates for office should be required to announce their candidacy a certain period of time in advance of the election and how such announcements should be made, what the manner of balloting should be (whether by rising vote or by secret ballot, whether by proportional representation, etc.), what officers should be in charge of the voting and the counting of votes, when elections should be held, and what the qualifications of voters should be.

Some useful suggestions for the drafting of constitutional provisions on these subjects may be found in the following extracts from various Indian constitutions.

A very simple provision suitable for a small reservation is found in the Rules and Regulations for the Annette Islands Reserve in Alaska:

> The members of the council and the officials of the Annette Islands Reserve shall be elected by ballot, printed or written, on the Tuesday last preceding December 25 in each year, at which election all male members of the Annette Islands Reserve above the age of 21, and not in arrears for nonpayment of taxes, fines, or fee for a permit to occupy a lot or tract of land, shall have the right to vote.
>
> At each election, after the first held under these rules and regulations, each male voter may be required to present his receipt for taxes, fines, or fee for a permit to occupy a lot or tract of land, as evidence that he is entitled to vote. (Article II, Section 3)

The council shall prescribe rules regarding the place and conditions of the annual election. Notices of said election shall be posted in three or more public places in the reserve at least 10 days prior to such election. (Article III, Section 10)

The following provisions, taken from a draft constitution now being considered by the Indians of the Fort Belknap Reservation and dealing specifically with the question of nominations and voting qualification, deserve consideration:

Article III
Section 3. Elections

A. to membership on the tribal council shall be held the first Tuesday in December of every second year. Duly elected tribal councilmen will take office on January 1 of the succeeding year.

B. Elections shall be taken by ballot, and polling places in each district shall be established by the council. The council shall appoint three election judges.

C. Candidates for election to membership on the tribal council shall give public notice of such intention at least thirty days prior to the election date, and at the same time file with the secretary of the council a certificate of such intention endorsed by five duly qualified electors, other than immediate relatives.

D. All persons of either sex, over the age of 21 years, and duly qualified members of this association, are entitled to vote, provided they have registered as such at least sixty days prior to the election.

A more detailed provision on election procedure is found in the Klamath Constitution adopted in 1929, which provides:

Article 19. The election shall be conducted at one or more polling places under the direction of the Superintendent of the reservation, who shall appoint a board of election for each polling place, such board to consist of three adult persons, carefully selected for known good character and ability to perform the duties required. It shall be the duty of the election board to provide the ballots, to carefully and truthfully interpret the ballots to such voters as are unable to read, and to count the ballots at the close of the election, *provided* that whenever an election of members of the business committee is held, under the provisions of this constitution and bylaws, each candidate, or his authorized agent, shall have the right to be present in any polling place during the balloting, and at the counting of the ballots there-after, in order that he may be in a position to detect any irregularities and report them to the Superintendent or to the Commissioner of Indian Affairs.

All ballots after being counted shall be carefully preserved by the Superintendent of the reservation until the term of office of the members elected by them has expired.

Another example of constitutional regulations covering election proce-dure is found in the constitution of the Menominee Indians, as amended in 1928:

2. The method of selection shall be as follows: All nine members shall be elected by the adult members of the tribe in the manner hereinafter described: Those desiring to be candidates shall, not less than ten days before election day, file their names in the office of the Superintendent of the Reservation, supported by a petition signed by not less than twenty-five qualified voters of the Tribe. The Superintendent shall prepare a ballot containing the name of all the nominees so filed. Election shall be held on a day in September to be designated by the Superintendent and properly advertised for not less than thirty days prior thereto. An election board shall consist of an Inspector, Clerk, and Ballot Clerk, to be selected by the bystanders at the time designated for the opening of the polls, and who shall immediately thereafter declare the polls open. Polls shall be open at 9.00 a.m. and remain open until 5.00 p.m. Each voter shall obtain from the ballot clerk an official ballot, which shall bear the endorsement of the bal-lot clerk. The voter shall immediately mark his choice of nine from the list of candidates and deliver the ballot to the inspector who shall deposit same in the ballot box and announce to the clerk the name of the voter, which shall be written on the polling list by the clerk. In case any voter is not able to prepare his ballot, he may call upon any member of the election board to assist him. Immediately after the closing of the polls, the ballot box shall be opened and the votes counted by the election officers. The ballots and tally sheets shall then be delivered to the Superintendent, who, with the two judges of the Indian Court of the Menominee Reservation, shall con-stitute the canvassing board. The nine candidates receiving the highest number of votes shall be declared elected.

If it is necessary to provide, in even further detail, for the manner of casting and counting ballots, etc., an available model is the set of rules promulgated by the Interior Department, dated March 8, 1934, for the Osage Nation, designated as "Rules Governing Osage Election."

On some reservations it may be thought wise simply to provide that the procedure followed in state elections shall likewise be followed in tribal elections. Such a provision was contained in an earlier constitution of the Neah Bay Village. Where elections are to be held by districts, the following provisions from Article II of the constitution of the Pima Community may prove to be useful models:

> *Section 10.* In case an election is due in any District, it shall be the duty of the Community Council to call the attention of the residents of said District to such fact at least two weeks prior to the date of such election, naming the date on which said election is to be held, also naming the place of said election, which place shall be within the District and at some central location most convenient to the residents of the District. On the date and at the place named, the legal voters of the District shall assemble and the outgoing member representing said District, if present, shall act as temporary chairman. At once, a permanent chairman shall be chosen and three tellers who shall be officers and judges of election. The assembled legal voters of the District shall then proceed to transact the business for which they have been assembled. Nominations shall be the first thing in order. This having been completed, and the nominations having been declared closed, the election shall take place, the wishes of the voters being ascertained by means of a rising vote. The nominee receiving the majority of all votes cast shall be declared elected. The newly elected member shall be furnished with a certificate of his election, to be signed by the permanent chairman and the three tellers.
>
> *Section 11.* The Community Council shall be the judge of the validity and authenticity of the Certificates of Election presented to it.

A more complex arrangement is that provided by the constitution of the Laguna Pueblo Indians for the election of the pueblo governor. Section 1 of the constitution adopted in 1908 provides:

> *Section 1.* An election shall be held on or near the first day of each calendar year, in which the following officers shall be chosen to serve the ensuing year; all officers being elected by a standing vote of the general pueblo:

*One Governor	*One Secretary
*One 1st Lt. Governor	One Treasurer
*One 2nd Lt. Governor	*One Interpreter
*One Fiscal	One Capt. of War

*One 1st Lt. Fiscal	One 1st Lt. Capt. of War
*One 2nd Lt. Fiscal	One 2nd Lt. Capt. of War

*These eight (8) officers shall be termed the "Court Officers" and shall be the sitting jury in all cases coming before the court.

Any number of Mayordomos that the Pueblo deems advisable may be chosen."

The following amendments to this section have recently been adopted:

Section 1. No elections shall be held on a Sunday nor New Year's Day; date of the general election to be set by the Governor and his official staff. Members employed at Gallup and Winslow to vote as in the past through an authorized representative. . . .

Clause 2. Time of service of officers elected limited to *two* consecutive years only.

Clause 3. Method of Election. Through preliminaries to be held at each village a month or so prior to a general election to be held on or near the first day of each calendar year; Exact date of general election to be set as above provided in Clause 1.

At a General Assembly prior to said general election, all candidates chosen at the different villages to run for Governor are to undergo a process of elimination by the Principals to *two* candidates for the said office of Governor, and which *two*, after their selection as candidates, shall at the general election be voted on, the one receiving the majority of standing votes shall be declared Governor.

Clause 4. Physical qualifications of each candidate to be considered.

Clause 5. In case of death, prolonged sickness, disabilities resulting from any cause, which would render the Governor-elect incapable of further discharges of his official duties, the 1st Lt. Governor to succeed automatically. This would also apply to War Captains so elected to such office.

Clause 6. Absentee candidates elected to office shall under this law be expected to serve, providing such candidates so elected meet physical qualifications.

Clause 7. Cases where a candidate for the office of War Captain has been successfully elected and has taken the "Oath" of said office, when upon his arrival home where opposition is shown by his wife or other members of his immediate family to his successful election, such members of his family are to be approached in a kind manner, with due explanations made to them, of the importance of said office, and inducements stressed on honoring his election. Methods of compulsion are not to be resorted to, as this would be contrary to the state laws governing "Private and Personal Rights of Individuals."

Clause 8. The "Oath"of officers elected shall be administered by one of their own choice, or by anyone whom the Principals may name, to administer such "Oath" to such newly elected officers.

In some cases elections will be in accordance with ancient customs. The Articles of Incorporation of the Oglala Tribal Council of the Pine Ridge Reservation provide, under the bylaws:

Chief. The election of and the appointment of Chiefs and Sergeant at Arms shall be made in accordance with the custom of the Tribe (Sioux) and it shall in no way be arranged by the Council.

If it is deemed advisable to provide in the constitution itself for an immediate election, the following provision taken from a constitution drafted for the Indians of the Standing Rock Reservation, but not yet approved, may be looked to for guidance:

Section 3. The first election of Headmen shall be held on call of the Provisional Committee which shall consist of _____, _____, and _____, which Provisional Committee is hereby authorized to call and to supervise the election of Headmen within thirty (30) days after this Constitution is approved by the Secretary of the Interior. The Provisional Committee shall issue its certificate of election to the persons receiving the highest number of votes in each district in accordance with the quota assigned hereby to each said district and the Headmen so elected and certified shall take office at once and shall meet at the Agency and organize for business. (Article II, Section 3)

In selecting a day for elections it is important, of course, to select a time at which the largest possible number of people in the reservation may come together. At Fort Peck this problem has been solved by selecting the day on which per capita payments are made for the holding of elections.

Not only should the election be fixed at a time when people can conveniently come together, but it should also be at a time when the officers of the tribe have completed most of their important work for the year. Thus, where the midwinter represents a period of comparative inactivity, the late fall or early winter would be a convenient time for elections. It would be unfortunate to interrupt the duties of elected officials in connection with the management of farming and grazing lands, for instance, by holding elections at a time when such work has not been completed for the year. Most tribal elections are now set at dates between September and February.

SECTION 11

TENURE OF OFFICE

The question of tenure of office is bound up with the whole question of what rate of change in existing conditions and customs is necessary or desirable. Short terms of office, with easy means of removing unsatisfactory officials from office, make it easier to effect basic changes and will appeal to those tribes that look forward to rapid progress under the program of self-government. On the other hand, those tribes that want, above all, to perpetuate their present system of government and property relations, without any basic changes, may well prefer to elect leaders for long terms or even for life or good behavior and to make the removal of such officials from office very difficult.

This is a matter which each tribe must decide for itself.

Tenure of office for life or good behavior was customary among most Indian tribes in earlier days. It still prevails in certain tribal governments, e.g., the Seminoles of Florida, the Utes of the Consolidated Ute Agency, the Lummi of Washington, and the Apaches of Fort Apache. Where life tenure continues to exist, the young people of the reservation frequently object to it as "un-American." It may be remembered, however, that the judges of the United States courts, who have the power to nullify state and federal laws, are also selected for life.

Among most tribes which have adopted more modern and democratic methods of government, the tenure of all offices is fixed at one, two, three, or four years.

A provision recently added to the Laguna Constitution of 1908 prohibits reelection to any office for a third consecutive term.

The following provisions on removal from office may serve as useful models. The Constitution of the Tongue River Tribal Business Committee provides:

Article IX. Removal. Any member who shall be guilty of conduct which will bring the Tribal Business Committee into disrepute may be expelled by a majority of two-thirds of the members of the Tribal Business Committee, but no member shall be expelled until he shall have been notified and given an opportunity to appear in his defense. Any member of the Tribal Business Committee found guilty of signing petitions or documents which are injurious to individual members of the tribe without first securing consent of the Ttribal Business Committee shall be automatically expelled.

The same constitution provides for the filling of vacancies in the following terms:

Article VII. Vacancies. Any district whose representative has been expelled shall be notified in writing and shall be requested to elect a new representative, the said representative to be present at the next regular meeting. Election shall be by ballot of the district. Failure to comply with the request will authorize the Tribal Business Committee to elect a representative from the district in which the vacancy occurred.

The constitution of the Cheyenne River Sioux Indians, adopted in 1925, provides:

Article XI. Any or all officers of this Council may be removed from his office if convicted of the violation of any State or Federal law; for any violation of any regulation of the Indian Office; for taking charge of any matters or correspondence affecting the Tribe without the full knowledge and consent of the Council, or for absenting himself from two successive Councils without good and sufficient reasons, the Council to be the judge of the reasons offered.

A constitution recently drafted by Indians on the San Carlos Reservation, but not yet adopted or approved, provides:

Article IV
Section 5. Forfeiture of Office
a. If a member of the Council fails or refuses to attend two regular
    meetings in succession, if not too sick to attend or otherwise
    prevented by circumstances for which he cannot be held responsible,
    his office shall be forfeited, and a special election shall be held to
    replace him.

b. If a Council officer shall fail in the performance of the duties assigned to him, or by giving public offense become subject to action of the law, as imprisonment, his recall from office shall be a matter to be taken up by the Council and be acted upon by the vote of his District; if the chairman shall be involved, by the Tribal vote. If the representative of the U.S. government prefer charges against a member of the Council, the Council shall investigate the matter, and when unable to settle it, submit it to the Tribal vote.

The Rules and Regulations for Annette Islands Reserve provide:

Article III

Section 11. The council may, by the vote of three-fourths of its entire membership, remove the mayor, secretary, treasurer, or other official upon sufficient evidence that he is unworthy to hold office; and the council may, by the vote of three-fourths of its entire membership, expel a member of the council.

Section 12. When a vacancy occurs in the membership of the council or in any office, the council may, until the time of the next annual election, temporarily fill such vacancy by a two-thirds vote of the membership and provide for the induction into office of the person so elected.

A provision giving more power than any of the foregoing provisions to the Commissioner of Indian Affairs is the following provision taken from the Yankton Sioux Constitution now in force:

Article 13. Any member of the Tribal Committee shall be subject to recall from office for reasonable cause, upon investigation by the Commissioner of Indian Affairs or his representative.

The Tribe also shall have the right, by petition of over fifty (50) per cent of the adult resident members, to demand the removal of any committeemen for cause. The Commissioner of Indian Affairs shall act thereon in his discretion.

SECTION 12

POPULAR INITIATIVE AND REFERENDUM

A principle of representative government which was established in the traditional governments of many Indian tribes is the principle that matters of great importance should not be decided by the governing body of the tribe without being first referred to the popular vote of the members of the tribe. The chiefs or councilmen were considered to have no authority to oppose the majority will of the tribe itself. As an old-time Indian of the Fort Belknap Reservation declared: "They are merely the Voice or Interpreter of the wishes of the people."

This principle was laid down in the Great Binding Law of the Iroquois Confederacy (Gayaneshakgowah):

> *93.* Whenever a specially important matter or a great emergency is presented before the Confederate Council and the nature of the matter affects the entire body of Five Nations, threatening their utter ruin, then the Lords of the Confederacy must submit the matter to the decision of their people and the decision of the people shall affect the decision of the Confederate Council. This decision shall be a confirmation of the voice of the people.
>
> *94.* The men of every clan of the Five Nations shall have a Council Fire ever burning in readiness for a council of the clan. When it seems necessary for a council to be held to discuss the welfare of the clans, then the men may gather about the fire. This council shall have the same rights as the council of the women.
>
> *95.* The women of every clan of the Five Nations shall have a Council Fire ever burning in readiness for a council of the clan. When in their opinion it seems necessary for the interest of the people they shall hold a council and their decision and recommendation shall be introduced before the Council of Lords by the War Chief for its consideration.

96. All the Clan Council Fires of a nation or of the Five Nations may unite into one general Council Fire, or delegates from all the Council Fires may be appointed to unite in a General Council for discussing the interests of the people. The people shall have the right to make appointments and to delegate their power to others of their number. When their council shall have come to a conclusion on any matter, their decision shall be reported to the Council of the Nation or to the Confederate Council (as the case may require) by the War Chief or the War Chiefs. (The Constitution of the Five Nations, edited by Parker.*)

A somewhat similar provision is to be found in the constitution of the Laguna Pueblo Indians adopted in 1908:

> *Section 7.* In *special* matters of business in which all of the people are equally interested, the Governor shall send a request to the Pueblo in general for their presence at the time such business is to be transacted. The Governor shall also have the right to summon any of the principal men to be present at any of the meetings, when in his opinion, their presence is needed; and in case any one of them cannot come when summoned, he shall furnish the Governor with his reasons for not being present, who shall excuse him if his reasons appear justifiable. But the general pueblo shall not be requested to appear, nor the principal men summoned unless their presence is absolutely necessary or very important.

A similar provision is found in the Klamath Constitution now in force:

> *Article 20. Reference to General Tribal Council*
> Matters of great importance to the tribe and which the business committee believes should be referred to a general tribal council, may be so referred by a vote of at least five (5) of the members of the business committee, provided that such general council of the tribe shall be called by the Superintendent at such time as he may deem proper.

The constitution of the Yankton Sioux provides for the calling of a referendum election either by the tribal committee or by the Commissioner of Indian Affairs or by popular petition:

---

*Arthur C. Parker, "The Constitution of the Five Nations," *New York State Museum Bulletin* 184 (1916), 7–158.

Article 14. Matters of great importance to the Tribe which the Commissioner of Indian Affairs or the Tribal Committee believe should be referred to a general Tribal Council shall be so referred.

Or a Tribal Council shall be called upon petition to the Commissioner of Indian Affairs signed by not less than ten (10) per cent of the adult members of the Yankton-Sioux Tribe resident in Charles Mix County, South Dakota.

A similar provision is found in the constitution of the Hoopa Business Council, now in force:

Article 14. Matters of great importance to the tribe, which the Commissioner of Indian Affairs, superintendent, or the business council believes should be referred to a general tribal council, shall be so referred.

A narrowly limited veto power over tribal council acts is provided by the constitution of the Quechan (Fort Yuma) tribal council, recently submitted for approval:

Article 15. Power of Veto
(1) The members of the Quechan Tribe shall have and may exercise the power of "veto" over any decision of the Quechan Tribal Council and such veto may be exercised in the following manner:
(2) When members of the Quechan Tribe are dissatisfied with any decision or ruling of the Tribal Council and desire to veto same, they may circulate a petition amongst the regularly and legally enrolled adult members of the Quechan Tribe and such petition shall state and set forth fully the ruling or decision to which objection is made and the reason for their objection thereto.
(3) If 100 regularly and legally enrolled adult members of the Quechan Tribe shall sign such petition and shall then file such petition with the Tribal Secretary or with the President or in his absence with the Vice-President of the Tribal Council, then said Tribal Council shall forthwith call an election of the adult members of the Quechan Tribe in the regular manner.
(4) If upon balloting, three-fourths (3/4) of the adult members of the Quechan Tribe shall vote to sustain such veto, then and in that event, the ruling or decision so vetoed shall be declared by the Tribal Council to have been vetoed and said ruling or decision shall thereafter have no force or effect.

A draft constitution now under consideration by the Indians of the Fort Belknap Reservation contains a general provision covering initiative, referendum, and recall in the following terms:

Article XVII. Initiative, Refernedum, and Recall
Any official may be recalled, any new official may be elected, any ordinance or other act of the Council may be revoked, and any ordinance may be promulgated by a popular vote of the members of the Fort Belknap Indian Community. Upon the presentation to the Commissioners of Elections of a petition signed by one-fifth of the number of voters who voted at the most recent regular election it shall be the duty of the said Commissioners to hold a special election. The subject matter of such election shall be announced as indicated in the petition. At such election each voter shall vote yes or no on the subject of the petition and the decision of the majority shall be the law.

Another draft constitution under consideration upon the same reservation provides that some but not all of the powers of the tribal council shall be subject to a referendum vote. In the enumeration of the powers of the tribal council, qualifying clauses are added to certain statements of power, as for instance in the following provision (Article III, Section 5, Paragraph Q):

Q. To enter into negotiations for leases, disposal of timber, minerals, or other natural resources of the tribe, and to approve such leases or other agreements, provided that this action may become a referendum measure should a petition signed by five percent of the legal voters be presented to the Tribal Council within thirty days after such action has been authorized.

Another constitutional provision for a referendum vote on certain designated questions is found in the draft constitution under consideration on the San Carlos Reservation, which provides in Article III, Section 1:

(b) Any sale, grant of any portion of the reservation, or the granting of any rights as to the use of any land, or the granting or relinquishment of any water rights, of the Indians of this reservation, is hereby expressly and exclusively withheld to the Indians of this Reservation and shall in no way be delegated but by a three-quarter majority of the Tribal votes cast on the matter after it has first been unanimously approved and recommended by the Council at least thirty days prior to the taking place of the Tribal vote on the matter, duly called for that purpose; and the total vote cast on the matter must represent at least three-fifths of the tribal voting population.

In connection with these referendum provisions, it must be remembered that any rule or provision which is included in the constitution or the bylaws of the tribe may be amended only by a referendum vote in accordance with Section 16 of the Wheeler-Howard Act, which provides:

> Amendments to the constitution and bylaws may be ratified and approved by the Secretary in the same manner as the original constitution and bylaws.

Under this section it is necessary, in order to amend the constitution or bylaws, to secure a majority vote of all the adult members of the tribe or community.

Matters of minor importance and matters which ought to be subject to change with changing conditions may take the form of "ordinances" or "resolutions" rather than constitutional provisions or bylaws. Referendum provisions with respect to ordinances, resolutions, or other acts of the tribal council are not controlled by the provisions of the Wheeler-Howard Act. It is for each tribe to decide whether such acts of the tribal council should be subject to referendum, and what the mode of such referendum should be.

SECTION 13

POWERS OF TRIBAL SELF-GOVERNMENT

Perhaps the most important part of any Indian tribal constitution is that which specifies the powers that may be exercised by the governing body of the tribe. It is very important that those powers be stated clearly, distinctly, and comprehensively. In effect, this statement will be a declaration of independence for the Indian tribe.

The whole history of the Indian Office has been one of continued encroachment upon the affairs of the tribe. One after another, the powers exercised by the authorities of the tribe for the government and guidance of their people have been taken over by the Indian Office, sometimes in accordance with treaties or legislation, but more often without any such authority. It will be one of the chief functions of any tribal constitution to reassert and reestablish the ancient powers of the tribe except insofar as those powers have been definitely ended by federal law or have become utterly inapplicable in modern life.

If simplicity and brevity of language were the chief considerations in drawing up an Indian constitution, it would be enough to provide briefly that:

> The tribal council shall exercise all powers of government over the members of the _____ Tribe except in so far as such powers are limited by the laws of the United States or the provisions of this constitution.

To this there might be added the general statement found in a constitution drafted by Indians of the San Carlos Reservation, providing:

> The Council shall have authority to represent and speak for the San Carlos Apache Indians; they shall act in all matters that concern the welfare and are for the good of the tribe and shall make decisions in this regard that do no go beyond the limits set by this constitution. (Article III, Section 1a)

But those general statements, although legally sufficient, would not be effective either to educate the members of the tribal council in their new powers and responsibilities or to impress upon officials of the Indian Service the new limitations upon the power of such officials. A constant trespassing upon the field of Indian self-government can be stopped only by a strong fence with many posts set close together.

There follows a list of specific powers which may be affirmed by an Indian tribe and delegated by the tribe to its proper governing body. The Indian Office does not recommend that each of the powers here enumerated should be exercised by every Indian tribe. What follows is a complete, or nearly complete, list of the powers which an Indian tribal council may have if the people of the tribe so desire. Any of these powers may be denied to the tribal council by the people of the tribe. Any of these powers may be qualified in such manner as may seem proper to the Indians concerned. Thus, it has been noted in the preceding section that certain statements of power in the draft constitutions of the Fort Belknap and Fort Yuma Reservations provide that certain powers may be exercised by the tribal council only with the affirmative approval of a large majority of the people of the tribe, or else subject to veto by the tribe. Unless these provisions are made general and applicable alike to all tribal powers, consideration should be given to each of the enumerated powers of the tribal government with a view to qualifying those powers that ought to be exercised only with the consent of the numbers of the tribe.

The Wheeler-Howard Act specifically grants certain powers to organized Indian tribes in the following language:

> In addition to all powers vested in any Indian tribe or tribal council by existing law, the constitution adopted by said tribe shall also vest in such tribe or its tribal council the following rights and powers: To employ legal counsel, the choice of counsel and fixing of fees to be subject to the approval of the Secretary of the Interior; to prevent the sale, disposition, lease, or encumbrance of tribal lands, interests in lands, or other tribal assets without the consent of the tribe; and to negotiate with the Federal, State, and local Governments. The Secretary of the Interior shall advise such tribe or its tribal council of all appropriation estimates or Federal projects for the benefit of the tribe prior to the submission of such estimates to the Bureau of the Budget and the Congress. (Section 16)

There follow statements suitable for adoption in a tribal constitution affirming these powers. These statements might be preceded by the general formula:

The council (or senate, legislature, etc.) of the _____
Tribe shall exercise the following powers subject to any limitations imposed
by the laws or the Constitution of the United States and subject further to all
express restrictions upon such powers contained in this constitution:

1. Control over Tribal Property

*To approve or veto any sale, disposition, lease, or encumbrance of tribal
lands, interests in lands or other tribal assets, which may be undertaken by
the Department of the Interior or by Congress or by any other agency or
individual.*

This section is broad enough to cover all use of tribal lands, including
the issuance of grazing permits, fishing and hunting permits, agricultural
and mining leases, permits for prospecting, grants of rights of way, and
assignments of tribal land to individual Indians. It also includes all use of
tribal moneys, whether used for administrative purposes, for the making of
reimbursable loans, for per capita payments, or otherwise.

It will be seen, however, that this power, by itself, is only a veto power
and does not give the tribe any authority to act without the approval of Congress or the Secretary of the Interior. Such power may be granted by other
clauses, which will be discussed later.

The power of veto and approval in matters affecting tribal property may
itself be limited in the constitution so as to prevent future dissipation of
tribal property. Thus, the Constitution drafted for the San Carlos Reservation (but not yet adopted) limits the power of the tribal council to approve
expenditures of tribal funds by the following provisions:

Section 2. Expenditures
The Council shall have power to permit, in connection with the U.S.
Indian Departmental authority, expenditures from the Tribal fund, provided that the expenditures do not go beyond Five Thousand Dollars
($5,000). For the allowance of expenditures from the Tribal fund beyond
this sum, permission must be granted by a vote of the qualified voters of
the Tribe at a special election called for that purpose as hereinafter provided; and a two-thirds majority of the aggregate votes cast as such an
election shall be required to confer the permission of such expenditure
with Departmental authority. (Article III)

The same constitution forbids the tribal council from ever agreeing to
any future allotment of tribal lands, so that, even if Congress should repeal

the provision of the Wheeler-Howard bill which forbids future allotments, the constitution of the tribe would continue to prohibit allotment of the tribal land. The provision in question follows:

> *Section 2. Reservation Land*
> The reservation land shall as a whole remain Tribal property and shall not be divided by allotment of any parts to individuals or groups of individuals as private property that could be sold at will; but assignments of land for private use may be made, provided the rights of all members of the Tribe be not violated, and long-established allocations or dwelling places and improvements made by individuals or families are accordingly to be recognized. (Article VI)

A second specific power granted by the Wheeler-Howard Act may be expressed in the following terms:

2. Advisory Power on Appropriations

To confer with the Secretary of the Interior upon all appropriation estimates or federal projects for the benefit of the tribe prior to the submission of such estimates to the Bureau of the Budget and the Congress, and to make prompt recommendations to the Secretary of the Interior or to the proper committees of Congress with respect to all such estimates and appropriations.

It will be noted that this power is merely advisory and that it extends to gratuity appropriations, that is, appropriations not made out of tribal funds nor in pursuance of treaty obligations. The following provision of a drafted constitution for the Fort Belknap Reservation stresses this point in the following language:

> To seek grants of money through Government channels for tribal support, reimbursable assistance, reservational improvement, health, education, and other necessary activities looking toward the advancement of the members of this association, and to authorize the expenditures of these funds, when and if allotted, in accordance with approved budget recommendations. (Article III, Section 5, H)

A third power specifically mentioned in Section 16 of the Wheeler-Howard Act may be affirmed in the following language:

3. Employment of Counsel

To employ legal counsel for the protection and advancement of the rights of the tribe and its members, the choice of counsel and fixing of fees to be subject to the approval of the Secretary of the Interior.

It may be advisable to add to such a statement a definition of the type of suit or legal proceeding which the tribal council may undertake.

A fourth power, specifically affirmed in Section 16 of the Wheeler-Howard Act, may be stated as follows:

4. Power to Represent Tribe in Negotiations

To negotiate with the federal, state, and local governments on behalf of the tribe.

The constitution drafted by Indians of the Fort Yuma Reservation makes the scope of this power more definite:

(13) It shall have the right to negotiate with the Commissioner of Indian Affairs or with the Bureau of Indian Affairs and shall have the right to conclude and approve such negotiations [on the part of the Quechan Tribe] whereby the Bureau of Indian Affairs may assist, according to the terms of such negotiations, in carrying on hospitalization, education, or financial assistance necessary to best promote the advancement and cultural development of the members of the Quechan Tribe, whereby they may reach a high stage of cultural development and economic security. (Article III)

Negotiation sometimes involves the choice of delegates. The following provision on the choice of delegates, taken from the constitution of the Winnebago Indian Tribal Council, adopted in 1929, may serve as a model:

Article VII

Section 1. The Council shall have the power and authority to select from their own members or from the qualified electors of the tribe, or partly from each, delegations to send to Washington or other place or places as tribal representatives in behalf of said tribe, at any time occasion may justify, and when approved by the Superintendent and Interior Department cause their expenses to be paid from tribal funds.

Section 2. The Council shall issue credentials to all duly appointed delegates, which credentials shall show that they are the duly appointed delegates and that they have been duly authorized to represent the tribe.

The power to conduct negotiations carries with it the power to offer recommendations on many matters which are now entrusted to the Interior Department. It may be thought useful to list these matters in the following terms:

To pass upon and make recommendations concerning:
a. Issues of rations
b. Applications for enrollment
c. Applications for government loans
d. Granting of fee patents on reservation lands
e. Exchanges of restricted allotments
f. Approval of wills
g. Approval of any partition of heirship lands
h. Location and construction of roads
i. Acquisition of land for the benefit of the tribe under the Wheeler-Howard Act
j. Appointment of nonservice employees
k. Appointment and tenure of other employees
l. Drafting and advancement of legislation affecting the tribe
m. Education
n. Social welfare activities of the Indian Service

With respect to the selection of Indian Service and other employees, it may be noted that the Wheeler-Howard Act, as finally passed, does *not* give the Indian tribe or community any right to remove federal employees. The only power which can be exercised is that of advising with the superintendent or the Commissioner of Indian Affairs on questions of appointment and removal.

With respect to each of the foregoing advisory powers, more-detailed provisions may be adopted in the bylaws of the tribe. Since these powers are only advisory, it is not necessary to elaborate on them in that part of the constitution which deals with the grant of tribal powers.

All of the powers already discussed are expressly referred to in Section 16 of the Wheeler-Howard Act as proper powers of an organized Indian tribe, but those powers expressly mentioned in the act do not purport to be a complete list of tribal powers. Section 16 of the act provides that the powers therein specified shall be "in addition to all powers vested in any Indian tribe or tribal council by existing law." What powers are vested under existing law is a matter discussed in great detail in a recent opinion of the solicitor of the Interior Department, approved October 23, 1934 (M-27781), which may be obtained from the Indian Office upon request. For the present, the main conclusions of this opinion are employed in the following series of constitutional clauses assigning specified powers to the tribal council or other governing body.

5. Appointment of Officials

To appoint subordinate officials not otherwise provided for in this constitution, and to prescribe their tenure and duties.

A provision similar in effect is found in Article III of the Rules and Regulations for Annette Islands Reserve, providing:

> *Section 9.* The council may create such additional offices, not in conflict with these rules and regulations, as it may deem necessary for the effective administration of the local government, provide for the filling of such offices, define the duties of the same, and fix the amount of remuneration, if any. (Article III)

Where the constitution does not specifically provide for the type of district governments to be established, the following clause taken from a draft constitution under consideration on the Fort Belknap Reservation may be useful:

> *Section 5. Council Powers*
> The council shall have power to establish district or community governments inferior to the reservational government and authorize such governments to pass local ordinances which would specify punishment for misdemeanors, such as drunkenness, disorderly conduct, dishonesty, etc. (Article III)

The propriety, however, of granting to a district government the power to promulgate ordinance, may be seriously questioned.

6. Control over Election Procedure

To provide for the manner of election and removal of tribal officers.

This clause will be unnecessary if the constitution itself prescribes all the details of election and removal procedures. If the constitution simply lays down certain general principles on this subject, leaving other matters to be determined by the tribal council, some such clause as the following, taken from the Rules and Regulations for Annette Islands Reserve, might be included in the list of tribal council powers:

> *Section 10.* The council shall prescribe rules regarding the place and conditions of the annual election. Notices of said election shall be posted in three or more public places in the reserve at least 10 days prior to such election. (Article III)

7. Power to Regulate Procedure

To prescribe the procedure of the tribal council and all subordinate committees or commissions.

Again, this clause will be unnecessary if the constitution or the bylaws deal with this subject in a comprehensive fashion.

8. Power to Appropriate

To provide for the salaries or expenses of tribal officers, and other expenses of public business, by appropriating funds within the control of the tribe, or by recommending the appropriation of tribal or other funds within the control of Congress or the Secretary of the Interior.

It has already been noted that this particular power is one which may well be made subject to a referendum whereby the wishes of the entire tribe may be entertained.

9. Control over Membership

To provide the conditions of tribal membership, to prescribe rules governing adoption and abandonment of membership, and to make all other necessary rules and regulations governing membership in the tribe so far as may be consistent with existing acts of Congress controlling enrollments and the property rights of enrolled members.

It will be noted that enrollment acts and other acts of Congress guarantee to members of the tribe certain individual property rights regardless of their continued participation in tribal affairs. This is a limitation which the tribal government cannot overthrow. Nevertheless, the tribal government will have complete authority to determine tribal membership for all other purposes, e.g., for the purpose of voting or receiving assignments of tribal land. If any qualifications are to be set upon the power of the tribal council to deal with questions of membership, they should be set forth clearly and distinctly in the constitution. Some of the problems arising in this connection have already been referred to in Section 4 of this memorandum. The legal status of membership rights is discussed in the opinion of the solicitor already referred to (M—27781), at pages 28 to 40. The discussion includes numerous references to Indian tribal laws governing the acquisition and loss of membership.

10. Determination of Voting Qualifications

To prescribe and pass upon qualifications for voting in all matters as to which the Wheeler-Howard Act does not control.

It will be observed that the Wheeler-Howard Act prescribes qualifications for voting upon the referendum on the application of the act, upon the adoption and amendment of a tribal constitution, and upon the ratification of a tribal charter. In these elections, women, as well as men, may vote, and the age of majority is set at 21 years. In these elections the definition of Indians entitled to vote is either contained in the act or left to the Secretary of the Interior. In all other elections, however, the question of eligibility to vote is left to the Indians to determine. Thus, with respect to elections of tribal officers, the recall of such officers, referendum elections on tribal ordinances, and many other matters on which elections may be held, the Indian tribe may or may not adopt women suffrage; it may, if it chooses, set the age of majority lower or higher than 21 years; it may prescribe specific qualifications of residence, tribal affiliation, and degree of blood or character as voting qualifications.

11. The Control of Domestic Relations

To regulate the domestic relations of members of the tribe by prescribing rules and regulations concerning marriage, divorce, legitimacy, adoption, the care of dependents, and the punishment of offenses against the marriage relationship, and to provide for the issuance and registration of marriage licenses and decrees of divorce.

Under this power, as under other powers, the tribal council might either adopt and reaffirm the laws of the state in which the reservation is situated, or establish ordinances of its own.

12. The Appointment of Guardians

To provide for the appointment of guardians for minors and mental incompetents.

The following provision of the proposed bylaws of the Quechan (Fort Yuma) Tribal Council may be used as a model:

Guardianship of Minors and Incompetents
The Council shall pass all necessary rules and regulations, consistent with the Constitution, whereby the rights of minors and incompetents shall be properly safeguarded and shall assume control over and administration of such funds and other assets as shall belong to same and which shall not be otherwise allocated or properly safeguarded and such control or administration shall be for the exclusive benefit of such minors or incompetents and for no other purpose whatsoever. It shall be the duty of the Council to make semi-annual reports concerning all such guardianship funds or assets and such reports shall be matters of public record.

In this connection it must be noted that U.S. Code, Title 25, Section 159, specifically recognizes the power of an Indian tribal council to appoint guardians for incompetents and minors, but deprives such guardians of the power to administer federal trust funds. (See Solicitor's Opinion, "Powers of Indian Tribes" (M—27781), at page 41.)

13. The Control of Inheritance

To prescribe rules of inheritance.

On allotted reservations it will be noted that state inheritance laws are applicable to the descent of allotted lands. This cannot be changed by a tribal constitution. However, the descent of personal property and of interests in tribal lands will be governed by the laws of the tribe. (See Solicitor's Opinion, "Powers of Indian Tribes," pages 45–50.)

14. The Taxing Power

To levy dues, fees, assessments, or taxes upon the members of the tribe and upon nonmembers trading or residing within the jurisdiction of the tribe.

The legal authority supporting this power of taxation is analyzed in the Solicitor's Opinion on "Powers of Indian Tribes," at pages 51–54.

A typical grant of powers of taxation is found in the constitution of the Osage Nation, Article III, Section 18, which provides:

> The national council shall have power to make laws for laying and collecting taxes for the purpose of raising a revenue.

A similar provision is found in the Articles of Incorporation of the Oglala Tribal Council of the Pine Ridge Reservation, which provides:

> *Article Seven.* The Council is hereby authorized to assess funds against members of the organization to carry out the requirements of this Constitution and Bylaws. Any funds assessed or contributed to funds of this organization shall not be withdrawn for any purpose except when appropriated by the Council. No part of funds in the Treasury of the Council shall be loaned or borrowed.

The taxing power is necessarily a disagreeable power to contemplate, and some constitutions have attempted to restrict the taxing power in various ways. The Rules and Regulations for Annette Islands Reserve provide:

> *Section 2.* The council is authorized to levy an annual tax of three dollars ($3), or of such a sum as it may deem necessary, not exceeding three dollars ($3), upon each able-bodied male member of the Annette Islands Reserve between the ages of 21 and 60, said tax to be collected by the secretary and expended for public purposes, as the council shall direct. The council may, by a two-thirds vote of its membership, remit the annual tax of any individual who because of continued sickness, poverty, or physical or mental disability is unable to pay said tax. (Article III)

15. The Power of Exclusion

To remove or to exclude from the limits of the reservation nonmembers of the tribe, excepting authorized government officials and other persons now occupying reservation lands under lawful authority, and to prescribe appropriate rules and regulations governing such removal and exclusion, and governing the conditions under which nonmembers of the tribe may come upon tribal lands or have dealings with tribal members, providing such acts are consistent with federal laws governing trade with the Indian tribes.

The legal authority for this power is analyzed in the Solicitor's Opinion on "Powers of Indian Tribes," pages 55–56. Detailed constitutional provisions on this point are found in the bylaws of the Quechan (Fort Yuma) Tribal Council, which provides:

Solicitation and Endorsement
The Council shall pass necessary regulatory rules and regulations by which to control problems arising from the practice of soliciting, peddling, or vending upon the reservation and shall require a license or permit be issued to all who shall engage in such activities upon the reservation. It shall make a thorough investigation before issuing such license or permit or before giving to any individual, form, or association an endorsement or approval of any nature. It shall prevent the unauthorized soliciting or vending of any articles, commodity or thing upon the reservation on so far as it is able so to do.

Unauthorized Practice of Medicine upon the Reservation
The Council shall prevent by ordinance or otherwise the unauthorized practice of medicine upon the reservation and shall require that any nonmember of the tribe who seeks to so practice medicine upon the reservation or to deal in drugs or medicinal supplies shall prove to their satisfaction that he is qualified and recognized so to do by the laws of the State of California or of the Federal Government. Nothing in this section, however, shall serve to apply to or to interfere with those members of the tribe who seek to use native remedies or practices in curing illness or disease.

* * * * *

White Residents of the Reservation
The Council shall have the duty of passing rules and regulations for the control of white residents of the reservation other than government or state employees, and such rules and regulations shall be consistent with and not in conflict with such Federal laws, rules, or regulations which are now or may be hereafter passed, . . . concerning such white residents of the reservation, nor with the laws of the State of California or of any political subdivision thereof, insofar as the same may apply to such white residents of the reservation.

16. Prescription of Communal Duties

To require members of the community to contribute labor towards the maintenance of public works and public enterprises.

The power to require members of the community to take part in community enterprises is not essentially different from the power to tax. The following provision found in the Rules and Regulations for Annette Islands Reserve may serve as a guide:

> *Section 3.* The council shall have the authority to direct, by its ordinance, that every able-bodied male resident of Annette Islands Reserve shall perform, without reservation, in each calendar year not more than two days' labor of eight hours each on the streets, roads, wharves, public buildings, or other public improvements within the Annette Islands Reserve undertaken by order of the council.
>
> The Secretary shall keep a record of the labor thus performed, showing the dates, the number of hours, and the character of the service rendered by each person. (Article III)

The proposed constitution of Quechan (Fort Yuma) Tribal Council contains the following clause:

> It shall have the right when just cause or extreme emergency exists, which shall create a hazard to the peace and safety of the tribe as a whole or to the individual members thereof, to require the individual members of the Quechan Tribe or other residents upon the reservation so assist in community labor. (Article III)

17. Administration of Tribal Property

To administer all tribal lands and property of every description.

This power includes the power to make assignments of tribal land to members of the tribe; to issue permits for grazing, prospecting, quarrying, hunting, fishing, the cutting of timber; to regulate the use of all tribal lands; and to invest or disburse tribal funds. Such powers are subject to the consent of the Secretary of the Interior insofar as they may involve the disbursement of funds or the disposition to outsiders of lands held in trust by the United States government. A draft constitution under consideration on the Fort Belknap Reservation lists, among the powers of the tribal council, the following:

> *Q.* To enter into negotiations for leases, disposal of timber, minerals, or other natural resources of the tribe, and to approve such leases or other agreements, provided that this action may become a referendum measure

should a petition signed by five per cent of the legal voters be presented to the tribal council within thirty days after such action has been authorized.

    R. To collect and disburse tribal or individual income from such leases, timber sales, royalties, or other sources, in accordance with government regulations now in effect. (Article III, Section 5)

18. Control over Individual Property

To regulate the use and disposition of the property of the members of the tribe.

This includes the tribal power to regulate grazing, even on individual allotments; to regulate or prohibit the leasing of restricted lands to non-Indians; to determine the form of leases and permits of individual lands; to prohibit the maintenance of nuisances; and to undertake any other form of regulation in the public interest which a state or municipality is ordinarily empowered to undertake. Legal authorities indicating the scope of such power are collected in the Solicitor's Opinion, "Powers of Indian Tribes," pages 50–68. The following provisions from the Fort Belknap constitution, noted above, may offer useful models:

> To prohibit the sale, mortgage or in any way the disposal of the individual Indian or Tribal lands to persons other than duly enrolled members of this Association. To prohibit overgrazing of lands, excessive sale or slaughter of cattle, or other depletion of the capital or natural resources of the community and the Association.
>
> * * * * *
>
> To establish laws relating to inheritance, assignment, use, or transfer of allotted or tribal lands within the jurisdiction. (Article III, Section 5)

19. Condemnation of Property

The power to condemn land or other property for tribal purposes.

A recent opinion of the solicitor holds that an Indian tribe may exercise condemnation proceedings against the restricted property of members of the tribe before tribal courts, provided, however, that the transfer of property held by the United States in trust for an individual Indian can be effectuated only if the Secretary of the Interior approves the transfer. With respect to property of nonmembers and fee-patented land of members of the tribe, condemnation proceedings may be instituted by the tribe but must be in accordance with state laws and must be brought before state courts.

The power of condemnation is one of the most important powers of any community. It is, as the Supreme Court of the United States declared, "one of the powers vital to the public welfare of any self-governing community." The Wheeler-Howard Act contemplates the development of progressive, economically independent communities on many of the existing reservations. This will entail the construction of roads, trails, bridges, and public buildings; the development of municipal water and sewerage systems; the erection of sawmills, power plants, and other public utilities; the building of dams and levees to curtail erosion; and the development of irrigation projects. It is believed that such a program can be undertaken only by a community which has the right to condemn land when other means of acquiring property fail. Of course, it will be for each community to decide for itself upon the purposes for which powers of condemnation may be used. If, for instance, an Indian tribe does not wish to permit condemnation proceedings in the building of roads, it may so provide in its constitution. Likewise, if an Indian tribe wished to include the establishment of a tribal grazing range among the public purposes for which condemnation proceedings may be invoked, it has full liberty to do so. The following provision on condemnation is found in the constitutional charter of the Eastern Band of Cherokee Indians, a legislative charter enacted by the State of North Carolina:

> *Section 28.* That whenever it may become necessary, in the opinion of the council, to appropriate to school, church, or other public purposes, for the benefits of the band, any of the lands owned by the Eastern Band of Cherokee Indians, as a corporation or tribe, and occupied by any individual Indian or Indians of the band, the council may condemn such land for the aforesaid purpose only by paying to the occupant of such land the value of such improvements and betterments as he may have placed or caused to be placed thereon, and the value of such improvements or betterments shall be assessed by the jury of not less than six competent persons, who are members of the band, to be summoned by the marshal of the band, under such rules and regulations as may be prescribed by the council. *Provided* that either party to such condemnation proceedings may appeal from the judgment rendered therein without bond to the superior court of the county in which such lands lie, but such appeal shall not stay execution, and the judge of the superior court to which such appeal is taken may, in his discretion, require either party to give such bond, either before or pending such trial, as he may deem fair and reasonable.

It will be noted that the provisions in this section for appeals to state courts would be possible only where the state enacted appropriate legislation. Likewise, there can be no appeal to federal courts on condemnation matters or any other matters under the present state of the law.

20. Control over Other Tribal Organizations

To charter subordinate organizations and to regulate the activities and operations of all associations or corporations of members of the tribe within the jurisdiction of the tribe.

The power to regulate the activities of such organizations is incidental to the general power to regulate personal conduct of members of the tribe to control the use and disposition of property. Without some such power to control other organizations there is always danger that the democratic organization of the people of the tribe may become subordinate to powerful undemocratic organizations that seek to exploit the resources and the members of the tribe.

It will often be necessary, however, to qualify the foregoing statement of powers so as to guarantee the proper continuance of cooperatives and other useful organizations.

The following provisions are contained in the constitution noted above, proposed for the Fort Yuma Reservations:

> It shall have the right to form any association, company, organization, or corporation having for its purpose and sole objects the benefits of the members of the Quechan Tribe.
>
> Any such association, company, organization, or corporation shall be for the benefit of the Quechan Tribe as a whole and not for the exclusive benefit of any individual member or members thereof, in whole or in part, except as such individual member or members shall benefit through the tribe as a whole. Such association, company, organization, or corporation shall have the right to engage in collective or cooperative bargaining and in collective or cooperative marketing or purchasing of supplies, crops, equipment, seeds, machinery, building or livestock, etc.
>
> It shall have the right to establish rules and regulations covering the activities and operations of such other organizations, associations, companies, or corporations of a cooperative nature as shall be formed amongst the members of the Quechan Tribe on the Fort Yuma Indian Reservation, and to enforce the observance of such rules and regulations by such other organizations, associations, companies, or corporations. (Article 3)

21. Promotion of the Public Welfare

To protect the public health and morals and to provide for the public welfare. Some such general phrase as that above noted should be used to cover the various services than an enlightened community may render to its members outside of the of the strictly governmental functions already noted. In this connection, the following provisions of the constitution proposed for the Fort Yuma Reservation deserve attention:

> It shall recognize the responsibilities of tribal self-government and shall at all times determine in a careful manner what constitutes just cause for charity or financial aid or assistance to the individual indigent members of the Quechan Tribe and shall make recommendations to proper agencies for the relief thereof.
>
> It shall, at all times, endeavor to decrease and eliminate the cause for indigency among the members of the Quechan Tribe by exercising a wise and judicial supervision and management of tribal affairs and finances, and insofar as is possible, the affairs and finances of individual members of the tribe to the end that want, privation, and financial distress may be entirely eliminated from amongst the members of the Quechan Tribe.
>
> It shall make a careful and detailed study and analysis of the problem arising from heirship and allotment matters, and shall endeavor to eliminate the abuses and inequalities that now exist at the earliest possible date. It shall, from time to time, make a full and detailed report of its findings and decisions in such matters to the members of the Quechan Tribe and shall also transmit, to the office of the Commissioner of Indian Affairs, true and exact copies of all such findings and reports, together with necessary recommendations for the amelioration of such unfavorable conditions as maybe be found to exist. (Article 3)

22. Supervision of Indian Service Employees

To direct the employment of employees of the Interior Department where the Secretary of the Interior agrees to delegate such powers to the tribal council.
The power of the Secretary of the Interior to require employees to follow the instructions of the proper tribal authorities is affirmed in United States Code, Title 25, Section 48, which provides:

> Right of tribes to direct employment of persons engaged for them. Where any of the tribes are, in the opinion of the Secretary of the Interior, compe-

tent to direct the employment of their blacksmiths, mechanics, teachers, farmers, or other persons engaged for them, the direction of such persons may be given to the proper authority of the tribe. (R.S. Section 2072)

23. Legislative Power

To pass ordinance or resolutions necessary or incidental to the exercise of any of the foregoing powers.

At this point, any general qualifications upon the ordinance-making powers of the tribal council should be inserted. The following provision is found in the Rules and Regulations for Annette Islands Reserve:

> *Section 1.* The council shall have power to pass such ordinances for the local government of the Annette Island Reserve as shall not be conflict with the laws of the United States, the laws of the Territory of Alaska, or the rules and regulations prescribed by the Secretary of the Interior for the Annette Islands Reserve.
>
> A copy of each ordinance passed by the council and certified by the signature of the mayor or of the acting mayor shall, within three days after its passage, be handed by the secretary to the person in charge of the work of the Bureau of Education at Metlakahtla, who shall promptly forward the same to the Commissioner of Education, through the district superintendent of schools and the Chief of the Alaska Division. (Article III)

A constitution under consideration upon the Fort Belknap Reservation provides:

> The council may pass, repeal, or modify ordinances or resolutions by a majority vote, but except in case of emergency, general ordinances shall not take effect until 20 days after the date of passage. (Article II)

24. The Maintenance of Law and Order

To provide for the maintenance of law and order and the administration of justice.

In cases where the administration of justice is directly entrusted to the tribal council, some such provision as the following, taken from the Rules and Regulations for the Annette Islands Reserve, may prove acceptable:

Section 4. By the vote of a majority of its membership, the council shall have power to impose upon any violator of an ordinance passed by the council such a fine as may be deemed just, not exceeding ten dollars ($10) for each offense.

In each case, before the council proceeds to vote thereon, the person accused of such violation shall be given opportunity to appear before the council and make any statement that he or she may wish to make.

The secretary shall, within three days after such a fine has been imposed by the council, hand to the person upon whom the fine has been imposed written notification thereof, countersigned by the mayor or by the acting mayor, setting forth the amount of the fine and the reasons for which it has been imposed.

Fines thus imposed shall be collected by the secretary and by him deposited with the treasurer, to be expended at the direction of the council as other funds are expended.

Whenever a fine which has been thus imposed remains unpaid for a period of four weeks from and including the day upon which notification thereof was received by the delinquent, the council, by the vote of a majority of its membership, may, in lieu of the payment of the fine, require the delinquent to labor not more than ten (10) days on the streets or other public works of the reserve. The expense in connection with such sentence shall be paid from funds under the control of the council. (Article III)

Where it is expected that the tribal council will delegate judicial powers to a tribal court, some such provisions as the following, taken from the proposed constitution for Fort Yuma Reservation, may prove useful:

It shall have the right to set up, establish, and promulgate ordinances and regulations for the purpose of safeguarding and securing the peace and safety of residents of the Fort Yuma Indian Reservation and to establish and set up minor courts for the adjudication of minor claims or disputes arising amongst the members of the Quechan Tribe and for the trial and punishment of members of the Quechan Tribe charged with the commission of crimes or offenses set forth in such ordinances or regulations.

Similar to the foregoing provision is the following provision of the proposed constitution of the Pima Community of Arizona:

Section 14. The Community Council shall have power to make all laws which it shall deem necessary to the proper enforcement of law and order of the reservations—laws defining drunkenness, disorderly conduct, perjury, dishonesty, as well as laws prescribing a moral code, including definitions of marriage and divorce, adultery, fornication, and any other laws they may see fit to enact that offer no conflict with applicable federal statutes, and shall have power to fix penalties in the nature of fines or jail sentences.

Section 15. The Community Council shall prescribe no cruel or unusual penalties for violation of community ordinances and laws.

* * * * *

Section 17. The Council shall appoint all Community Judges and all Community Police whose duty it shall be to enforce, under the direction of the President, all applicable federal statutes and all laws and ordinances enacted by the Council. Judges and Police shall be appointed for terms of five years. (Article II.)

If it is intended to give the tribal council the power to pardon or reprieve persons convicted of tribal offenses, this should be specifically provided in the constitution.

25. Further Powers

To exercise such further powers as may be delegated to the _____ Tribe by the Secretary of the Interior or by any other official or agency of the government.

The inclusion of some such phrase looking toward the future is advisable so that the tribe may, without delay, take advantage of any further legislation supplementing the Wheeler-Howard Act and granting further powers of local home rule. In this connection, study should be given to the following provisions, taken from the proposed constitution for the Fort Yuma Reservation:

It shall have the right to conclude negotiations with the Commissioner of Indian Affairs, or with the Bureau of Indian Affairs, whereby the rights and duties herein provided for shall be gradually transferred from the Bureau of Indian Affairs or from the Commissioner of Indian Affairs to this Council over a period of time in order that the Council shall not be charged with responsibilities beyond its capacity due to inexperience, but such transfer of duties shall not be delayed longer than a period of five years from the date of the approval of this constitution by the Commissioner of Indian Affairs or by the Bureau of Indian Affairs. (Article 3)

26. Residual Powers

The foregoing enumeration of powers shall not be construed to limit the powers of the _____ Tribe, but all powers of local government not expressly entrusted to the tribal council by this constitution shall be reserved to the people of the _____ Tribe to be exercised by the adoption of bylaws or constitutional amendments as provided in Section 16 of the Wheeler-Howard Act.

The foregoing statement, or some equivalent statement, is advisable in order to protect the tribe against any oversights in the list of powers given above. Without some such statement it might be claimed that the tribe had yielded to the state or to the federal government power over matters not expressly referred to in the clause specifying the powers of the tribal council. In order to obviate any such claim, this "saving clause," or some similar provision, should be added.

SECTION 14

DECLARATION OF THE RIGHTS OF THE PEOPLE

In the Constitution of the United States and in the constitutions of the several states, there are contained "bills of rights," which set forth the rights of individuals which all officials of the government are supposed to respect. Various opinions may be held as to the efficacy of those provisions. Not only are they frequently violated, but they have often been misused to obstruct needed legislation desired by a majority of people.

Whether or not such a statement of the rights of the people is included in any tribal constitution, it is important to remember that the rights of the people cannot be guaranteed by any words of a constitution but must be defended by the enlightened understanding and resolute will of the people. "The price of liberty is eternal vigilance." Tyrannical government can be prevented more easily by provisions for adequate popular control of governmental actions (as, for instance, through the recall and referendum) than by written guarantee of civil liberties.

If it is thought desirable to include in the constitution a declaration of the rights of the people, the following provisions, taken from the constitution of the Choctaw Nation, adopted in 1890, may prove a helpful guide.

Article I. Declaration of Rights

That the general, great and essential principles of liberty and free government may be recognized and established, we declare:

Section 1. That all free men, when they form a social compact, are equal in rights, and that no man or set of men is entitled to exclusive, separate public emolument or privileges from the community, but in consideration of public services.

Section 2. That all political power is inherent in the people, and all free governments are founded on their authority and established for their benefits, and therefore they have at all times an inalienable and indefeasible right to alter, reform or abolish their form of government in such manner as they may think proper or expedient.

Section 3. That there shall be no establishment of religion by law. No preference shall ever be given by law to any religious sects, society, denomination, or mode of worship, and no religious test shall ever be allowed as a qualification to any public trust under this government.

Section 4. That no human authority ought in any case whatever control or interfere with rights of the conscience in matters of religion.

Section 5. That no person shall for the same offense be twice put in jeopardy of life or limb, nor shall any person's property be taken or applied to public use without the consent of the general council, and without just compensation being first made therefore.

Section 6. That no person shall ever be appointed or elected to any office in this nation for life or during good behavior, but the tenure of all offices shall be for some limited period of time, if the person appointed or elected thereto so long behave well.

Section 7. That the right of trial by jury shall remain inviolate.

Section 8. That every citizen has right to bear arms in defense of himself and his country.

Section 9. That the printing press shall be free to every person, and no law shall ever be made to restrain the rights thereof. The free communication of opinion is one of the inviolable rights of man, and every citizen may freely speak, write, and print on any subject, being responsible for abuse of that liberty.

Section 10. That the people shall be secure in their persons, houses, papers, and possessions from unreasonable seizures and searches, and that no warrant to search any place or to seize any person or thing shall issue, without describing the place to be searched and the person or thing to be seized as nearly as may be, nor without probable cause supported by oath or affirmation. But in all cases where suspicion rests on any person or persons of conveying or secreting whisky or other intoxicating liquors, the same shall be liable to search or seizure as may be hereafter provided by the law.

Section 11. That no free man shall be taken, or imprisoned, or disseized of his freehold liberties or privileges, or outlawed, or exiled, or in any manner destroyed or deprived of his life, liberty, and property, but by the judgment of his peers or the law of the land.

Section 12. That no person shall ever be imprisoned for debt.

Section 13. That excessive bail shall not be required, nor excessive fines imposed, nor cruel or unusual punishments inflicted.

Section 14. That all courts shall be open and every person for an injury done him in his lands, goods, person or reputation shall have remedy by due course of law, and right and justice administered without sale, denial, or delay.

Section 15. That the citizens have a right in a peaceable manner, to assemble together for their common good, to instruct their representatives, and apply to those invested with the powers of the government for redress of grievances, or other proper purposes, by petition, address, or remonstrance.

Section 16. That no power of suspending laws shall be exercised except by the general council or its authority.

Section 17. That in all criminal prosecutions, the accused has a right to be heard by himself or counsel, or both, to demand the nature and cause of the accusation, to be confronted by the witnesses against him, to have a compulsory process for obtaining witnesses in his favor; and in all prosecutions by indictment or information, a speedy and public trial by an impartial jury of the county or district where the offence was committed; that he cannot be compelled to give evidence against himself, nor can he be deprived of his life, liberty, or property but by due course of law.

Section 18. That all prisoners shall, before conviction, be bailable by sufficient securities, except for capital offenses, where the proof is evident or the presumption great, and the privilege of the writ of *habeas corpus* shall not be suspended, unless when in case of rebellion or invasion, the public safety may require it.

Section 19. That the general council shall have power to pass general laws in regard to the collection of fines, bonds, forfeitures, and court fees, and direct the manner of such collection.

Section 20. That no property qualification for eligibility to office, or for the right of suffrage, shall ever be required by law in this nation.

SECTION 15

BYLAWS: DUTIES OF OFFICERS

Under the Wheeler-Howard Act there is no difference in binding force between the provisions of a tribal constitution and the bylaws. Both the bylaws and the constitution must be approved by a majority of the adult Indians of the tribe or reservation and by the Secretary of the Interior. Both alike can be amended only in the same way.

It is, therefore, not a matter of much importance whether any provisions dealing with the tribal organization are placed in the constitution or in the bylaws of the tribe. In general it is expected that the more-general provisions will be made part of the constitution and that the more-specific and detailed provisions will appear as bylaws.

In this memorandum the following subjects are reserved for inclusion in the bylaws:

1. Duties of officers
2. Qualifications for office
3. Oaths of office, insignia, and ceremonials
4. Salaries of officials
5. Procedure of governing body
6. Judicial code
7. Criminal code
8. Law of domestic relations
9. Law of property
10. Law of taxation
11. Community welfare activities

It is, of course, entirely optional with each tribe whether or not to include in its constitution or bylaws a statement of the duties of the various officers of the tribe.

If brevity is a chief consideration, the following section, taken from the constitution and bylaws of the Business Committee of the Fort Peck Indian Reservation, may serve as a model:

> *Article III.* At its first meeting the business committee shall elect a president, vice-president, secretary, and treasurer from its own number. The duties of these officers shall be such as usually pertain to their offices.

However, such a provision, although easy to read and memorize, is not very helpful to an elected official who wants to learn exactly what he is supposed to do, or to some member of the tribe who wants to know what officer he should see with regard to some specific problem. For this reason various detailed statements of the duties of tribal officials are offered for consideration.

The duties of the highest officer of the reservation may vary considerably. As has been noted already in the discussion under Section 7, the principal officer may be entirely subordinate to the tribal council or he may have certain independent powers, such as the power to veto acts of the tribal council.

The duties of the principal chief are thus described in the constitution of the Osage Nation:

> *Section 8.* He may, on extraordinary occasions, convene the National Council at the seat of government.
>
> *Section 9.* He shall, from time to time, give to the Council information on the state of the government and recommend to their consideration such measures as he may deem expedient.
>
> *Section 10.* He shall take care that the laws be faithfully executed.
>
> *Section 11.* It shall be his duty to visit the different districts at least once in two years, to inform himself of the general condition of the country.
>
> * * * * *
>
> *Section 14.* Every bill, which shall pass the National Council, shall, before it becomes a law, be presented to the Principal Chief; if he approves, he shall sign it, but if not, he shall return it with his objections to the Council, who shall enter the objections at large on their journals, and proceed to reconsider it.
>
> If, after such reconsideration, two-thirds of the Council shall agree to pass the bill, it becomes a law; if any bill shall not be returned by the Principal Chief within five days (Sunday excepted) after the same has been presented to him, it shall become law, in like manner as if he had signed it. Unless the National Council, by their adjournment, prevent its return, in

which case it shall be a law, unless sent back within three days after their next meeting. (Article IV)

A constitution now under consideration by the Sioux of Standing Rock Reservation contains the following provision:

> *Section 3.* It shall be the duty of the Chief to preside over all meetings of the Tribal Council and to carry out all orders of the Tribal Council. All members of the Tribal Council and all sub-ordinate officers shall assist the Chief in all proper ways in carrying out the orders of the Tribal Council. The Chief shall be regarded by the Sioux of this Reservation in the same manner as were the Chiefs of the Tribe under our old Tribal life and government.

A constitution now under consideration on the Fort Belknap Reservation contains the following statement of a governor's duties:

> The governor shall be chairman of all meetings of the Council and shall be an ex officio member of all committees and commissions. He shall appoint all temporary committees unless the Council by a majority vote reserves the right to appoint such committee itself. The chairman shall vote in the Council only in case of a tie.

A constitution prepared by the Menominee Tribe in 1904, but never officially approved, contained the following statement of the powers of the chief official:

> *Article III.*
> *Section 1.* The chairman of the Business Committee shall hold office at a place to be designated by said Committee and shall see that the Menominee Tribe of Indians and each member thereof are protected in all their rights.
> *Section 2.* He shall make a full report of his official actions and proceedings to the Business Committee in writing at the beginning of each annual session thereof, and may also communicate his views and recommend to said Committee, at the commencement of every session, the adoption of such measure as he may deem to be for the best interests of the Menominee Tribe of Indians.
> *Section 3.* The chairman of the Business Committee shall see that all moneys and annuities due the Tribe from the United States or any other source are promptly paid over according to agreement.

Section 4. The chairman of the Business Committee shall have power to call special meetings of the Committee, and with the consent of the Business Committee to employ counsel to prosecute or defend any suit, claim, or demand in favor of, or against the Menominee Tribe of Indians; and such Committee shall make provision for the payment of such counsel or attorney who may be so employed.

The Rules and Regulations for Annette Islands Reserve contain the following statement of the powers of the chief officer of the reservation, designated as mayor:

Section 1. The mayor shall be the executive head of the Annette Islands Reserve. He shall preside at the meetings of the council, but he shall not vote except in case of a tie vote in that body, when he shall cast the deciding vote.

Section 2. The mayor shall call a special meeting of the council whenever he deems such procedure necessary, or when he is requested, in writing, to call such meeting by five or more members of the council. He shall notify each member of the council, the secretary, the treasurer, and the person in charge of the local work of the United States Bureau of Education, either by special messenger or through the United States mail, of the time and place of such meeting.

Section 3. The mayor shall sign all warrants drawn by order of the council on the treasurer.

Section 4. The mayor shall be chairman of the executive committee, hereinafter provided for, and he shall call a meeting of this committee at least once a month for the consideration of questions relative to the welfare of the community.

Section 5. The mayor shall have immediate control of the constables.

Where a constitution provides for the election of a vice-president or second chief, or similar officer, the bylaws may provide that "the vice-president (or second chief, etc.) shall act as president in the event of the death, resignation or absence from the reservation of the president (or principal chief, etc.)."

However, the existence of such an office is not necessary, especially when the chief officer of the reservation is elected by the council, which can easily meet to elect a successor.

Of great importance is the office of secretary or, where the duties of secretary and treasurer are combined, of secretary-treasurer. The following statement of the duties of a secretary is taken from a draft constitution for the Fort Belknap Indian Community now under consideration:

> The Secretary shall keep a faithful record of the meetings of the Council, shall conduct the official correspondence of the Fort Belknap Indian Community, shall maintain and distribute authorized copies of the Charter, Constitution, and Ordinances of the Fort Belknap Indian Community, and shall keep and preserve all official documents and records relating to the history and affairs of the Fort Belknap Indian Community.

The following statement of a secretary's duties is taken from the Rules and Regulations for Annette Islands Reserve:

> *Section 6.* The secretary shall keep the minutes of all of the proceedings of the council; he shall attend to the official correspondence of the council, and he shall be the custodian of all of the official documents of the Annette Islands Reserve.
>
> *Section 7.* The secretary shall collect, without commission, and give receipt for all taxes, fines, and fees levied by the council and shall deposit said payments with the treasurer, taking proper receipt therefor.
>
> *Section 8.* The secretary shall prepare for the signature of the mayor all warrants on the treasurer as ordered by the council.
>
> *Section 9.* The secretary shall be custodian of all public buildings and property on Annette Islands Reserve not under the direct supervision of the United States Bureau of Education.
>
> *Section 10.* The secretary shall keep a record of the births and deaths of the Annette Islands Reserve and shall report these vital statistics every month to the resident representative in charge of the work of the United States Bureau of Education.
>
> *Section 11.* The secretary shall be a member, ex officio, of the executive committee; he shall keep a record of its proceedings and shall present all recommendations of this committee to the council when it convenes.
>
> *Section 12.* The secretary shall post a copy of every ordinance passed by the council before it becomes operative in at least three public places on the reserve, and a fourth copy he shall, within three days after its passage, hand to the person in charge of the work of the United States Bureau of Education at Metlakahtla. (Article IV)

The same rules and regulations contain an excellent statement of the duties of a treasurer:

Section 15. The treasurer shall receive from the secretary all moneys collected by him, rendering proper receipts therefor.

Section 16. The treasurer shall pay out money only upon warrants drawn upon him by the secretary and countersigned by the mayor, or by the acting mayor. All warrants paid shall be preserved in his official files.

Section 17. The treasurer shall keep in a book which shall at all times be open to the inspection of the mayor, the secretary, the auditing committee, and the representatives of the United States Bureau of Education, a correct account of all moneys received and paid out by him.

Section 18. The treasurer shall be, ex officio, a member of the executive committee.

Section 19. The treasurer shall make an annual report to the council at the last meeting in December, giving a full account of all receipts and disbursements for the year.

The following statement of a treasurer's duties is found in a constitution under consideration on the Fort Belknap Reservation:

The treasurer shall receive all money or other property on behalf of the Fort Belknap Indian Community; shall make all payments authorized by the Council on behalf of the said community; and shall keep true, accurate and faithful accounts of all receipts and disbursements. Such accounts shall at all times be open to public inspection. The treasurer shall be personally responsible for any loss of money or property through his carelessness or dishonesty. In addition, the treasurer shall, before assuming office, file a bond of a reliable surety company.

The duties of a secretary-treasurer are thus set forth in a constitution recently prepared and submitted by the Seneca-Cayuga Tribe in Oklahoma:

The secretary-treasurer shall correctly record the proceedings of all meetings. He shall make out the order of the business for the chief, shall notify all committees of their appointments, shall have custody of the records and all papers of the council, which records and papers shall be open to inspection at any time, in his presence, by any member of the council desiring to read them. He shall keep a correct list of all members of the council, shall authenticate all accounts or orders of the council, and, in the absence of the chief and second chief, shall call the meeting to order until a chairman pro tem is selected. He shall render a written report at the annual meeting and at the expiration of his term of office the records and all papers in his possession shall be turned over to his successor. He shall issue notices of all meetings and conduct all general correspondence, as directed by the council. He shall receive all moneys of the council and keep an accurate account of receipts and disbursements. (Bylaws, Article I)

Where the constitution provides for the office of legal advisor or counselor the following statement of the duties of such an officer found in the constitution and bylaws of the Junior Yakima Indian Council may serve as a useful model:

It shall be the duty of the councellor to have charge of the legal department of the council.

It shall be the duty of the councellor to investigate all Indian problems which have been brought to the attention of the council and suggest and advise proper action on the same.

It shall be the duty of the councellor to secure information relating to laws or bills affecting Indian property rights and all other rights, and also all cases decided or pending in Federal or State Courts, or any other departments of the United States Government, affecting Indians or their rights, and supply said information to the President or the Board of Trustees of the council, and he shall have full charge of all legal actions on any and all matters pertaining to the property rights and all other rights of every kind of legal nature as may arise at any time. (Bylaws, Section 4)

An important official in the Pueblo of Laguna is the Mayordomo, a local officer in charge of public labor on the irrigation ditches, public property, and other community affairs. The duties of this office are thus set forth in the constitution of the Laguna Pueblo Indians adopted in 1908:

It shall be the duty of the Mayordomos to take charge, look after, and direct all work on ditches, dams, and roads. He shall have the power to appoint someone to take care of the general stock while any public work is being done under his supervision.

They shall make their reports to the officer in charge of their respective villages, which officer shall repeat such report to the court officers at the next regular meeting. In case the village officer deems it necessary for the Mayordomo to report in person at the convening of the court officers, he shall order him to do so *provided* he has a standing order from the Governor giving him the power to do so. In this case it shall be the duty of the

Mayordomo to obey the command, and if he should refuse it will be sufficient cause for further action by the Governor.

In all work in which the Mayordomos have charge, all who come under their jurisdiction are subject to their orders, and any willful disobedience of his orders shall be sufficient reason for the Mayordomo to fine the guilty party the usual fee for such disobedience. But if the person affected has reason to believe that he is being treated unjustly, he shall have the right to demand that the matter be brought before the court officers for adjustment. All fines in such cases shall go to the Mayordomo who made the charge.

It shall be his duty to take charge of all loose stock he may find on forbidden lands of the Pueblo, put them in a corral, or otherwise take care of them, and immediately notify the owner; also to take charge of any similar stock turned over to him by other members of the Pueblo. He shall collect the usual fee from the owner as a recompence for his services. In case the stock has been turned over to him by another party, he shall have one-half of the fee for his trouble, the other half going to the man who brought in the stock.

All damages to crops, etc., being determined according to the pueblo law hereto attached. (Section 13)

The duties of councilmen generally do not require a detailed statement since their duties are implied by the statement of the powers of the council. However, the following constitutional provisions on the duties of councilmen are worthy of note:

Regardless of personal opinion, it shall be the express and explicit duty of the business council to carry out the wishes of the majority of the tribe in all cases. (Constitution and Bylaws of the Hoopa Business Council, Article 2)

The Councilmen of either tribe shall not adopt any resolution or attempt to enter into any agreement to its own advantage that be detrimental to the interests of the other tribe, but shall at all time keep in mind the promotion of the common welfare and harmony of both tribes as a whole. (Fort Belknap Tribal Business Council, Constitution and Bylaws, Article 7)

Ordinarily the duties of special committees or boards will be established by the council at the time of the creation of the committee or board. It has been suggested, however, that a constitution may provide for certain important standing committees or boards or commissions. In such event, it would be proper to set forth in the bylaws the duties of such special committees. The following constitutional provisions deserve study:

> *Section 1.* The executive committee shall be composed of the mayor, who shall be ex officio, its chairman, the secretary, the treasurer, and the person in charge of the local work of the United States Bureau of Education. The executive committee shall meet at least once a month. Meetings may be called at any time either by the mayor or the local representative of the United States Bureau of Education.
>
> *Section 2.* It shall be the duty of the executive committee to make recommendations to the council regarding ways and means of bettering the conditions of the community. The secretary shall keep a record of the proceedings of the committee and shall report its recommendations to the council.
>
> *Section 3.* In the absence of a majority of the members of the council from the reserve, the executive committee shall carry on the work of the council and shall report its actions in full to the council at its next meeting: *provided* That the executive committee shall have no power to levy taxes or fines, or to repeal any ordinance passed by the council.
>
> *Section 4.* The Council may add to the duties of the executive committee from time to time.
>
> *Section 5.* It shall be the duty of the auditing committee, elected as provided in Article III, Section 7, of these rules and regulations, to audit all claims against funds controlled by the council and to report upon the same to the council at the next meeting of that body. This committee shall audit the accounts of the treasurer and make a report on the same to the council at the last meeting in December of each year, and at such other times as the council shall direct.
>
> *Section 6.* It shall be the duty of the public health committee, elected as provided in Article III, Section 7, of those rules and regulations, to assist the secretary in collecting and preserving the vital statistics, to assist the local representative of the United States Bureau of Education, who is a territorial health officer, in maintaining sanitary conditions throughout Annette Islands Reserve and enforcing quarantine regulations.

From a proposed constitution for the Fort Belknap Indian Community now under consideration:

Article XI. Duties of Commissioners of Lands
It shall be the duty of the Commissioners of Lands to distribute and revoke rights and interests in land, and to supervise the use, inheritance, and transfer thereof, in accordance with the Charter, Constitution, and Ordinances of the Fort Belknap Indian Community, and to maintain at all times accurate records of land ownership and tenure.

Article XII. Duties of Commissioners of Public Works
The Commissioners of Public Works shall maintain, supervise, and construct community buildings, roads, irrigation ditches, fences, and other improvements as may be determined upon by the Council. It shall be the duty of the Commissioners of Public Works to supervise all community labor which the members of the Fort Belknap Indian Community may be required to perform and to allot such labor in a fair and equitable manner.

Article XIII. Duties of Commissioners of Elections
The Commissioners of Elections shall be charged with the duty of promulgating and enforcing regulations concerning the time, place and manner of voting; of counting votes; and of announcing the election results and inducting new officers, provided, however, that such new officers shall be inducted as soon as possible after election and in no event more than one week after their election. The Commissioners of Elections shall supervise all popular elections and other votes. The Commissioners of Elections shall prescribe such oaths, ceremonials, and formalities as may seem just.

Article XIV. Duties of Commissioners of Public Welfare
The Commission of Public Welfare shall watch over the health and happiness of the members of the Fort Belknap Indian Community. It shall maintain adequate statistics of births, deaths, marriages, and divorces and prescribe rules for the registration thereof. It shall supervise and regulate all matters of health, charity, recreation, and education, cooperating with such Federal or State agencies in those fields as may be available. It shall from time to time with the approval of the Council make recommendations to the Federal Government or to the State Government concerning the needs and desires of the members of the Fort Belknap Indian Community.

From a statement prepared for the guidance of the Fort Peck Indians:

(6) Proper and necessary permanent or standing committees shall be provided for by the constitution and shall be elected or appointed at the first regular meeting of the general council, as follows:

1. Executive Committee, which shall consist of three members whose duty it shall be to transact all business for the tribe intervening regular meetings of the general council and as otherwise defined by the constitution and bylaws when approved.

2. Resolutions Committee, which shall consist of three members whose duty it shall be to study conditions among the Indians; to investigate complaints; to determine all matters necessary to be brought before the general council; and to prepare resolutions or other documents in accordance therewith to be submitted with proper recommendations for consideration. Action of the general council at any regular meeting to be limited as far as possible to the disposition of the resolutions and other matters so submitted. All matters of an individual nature desired to be submitted to the general council shall first be submitted with proper recommendations to the general council for consideration.

3. Credentials Committee, which shall consist of three members whose duty it shall be to pass upon the credentials and the seating of the delegates. Credentials to be furnished each delegate by the respective district councils and to be passed upon by the Credentials Committee before participation may be permitted in the regular sessions of the general council.

4. Legislative Committee, which shall consist of the president of the general council as ex officio member and three members to be elected in the regular manner by the general council, whose duty shall be to represent the Indians of the Fort Peck Reservation in tribal matters wherein it becomes necessary to deal direct with the governmental authorities in the City of Washington or elsewhere. At the direction of the general council and the approval of the proper authorities, one or more members of the Legislative Committee so created may be required or directed to travel wherever it may be deemed necessary and to officially represent the Indians of the Fort Peck Reservation in such a manner and to the extent that he or they be instructed.. Compensation and expenses to be paid in a manner to be determined and from funds as may be hereafter provided.

The subject of cooperation between officers of the tribe and employees of the Indian Service deserves careful study. The bylaws of an organized tribe should provide for the making of regular reports to the officers of the tribe by designated employees of the Indian Service and for the fullest possible discussion of all departmental plans and programs with the officers of the tribe or the people themselves. One method of securing proper cooperation is to make certain officers of the Indian Service ex officio officers of the tribe. Such officers would have no vote in tribal affairs but would be entitled to participate in all discussion and might be required to render official reports or committee reports from time to time.

The following statement of the relation of the superintendent to a tribal council is taken from the constitution and bylaws of the Hoopa Business Council, approved 1933:

> The superintendent shall assist the council in the promotion of a high standard of morals within the tribe.
>
> He shall submit to them a statement of all funds obtained from the sale of land, timber, right-of-ways, mining royalties, or any money that may have accrued from any other sources pertaining to the rights of the tribe.
>
> A copy of monthly disbursements shall be given to the council for reference and consideration.
>
> He shall see that all necessary literature for conducting of the business council's affairs are properly typed or mimeographed. (Article 17)

Under the legislative charter of the Eastern Band of Cherokee Indians the superintendent of the reservation is made ex officio secretary of the council:

> *Section 12.* That all acts of council, resolutions, etc., shall be signed by the chairman and the clerk, and countersigned by the chief, and certified to by the secretary, and that the agent appointed by the general government to supervise the schools or affairs of the Eastern Band of Cherokee Indians shall be, and is hereby made, ex officio, by virtue of his office, secretary of this corporation, with the custody of the books and papers appertaining to the same in all respects; *provided*, however, that if such agent fails to act the council may elect a secretary.

The rules and regulations for the government of the Fort Bidwell Indian Colony in California, adopted in 1933, provide that the agent in charge of the reservation shall act as treasurer.

It has already been noted that under the existing constitution of the Fort Belknap Tribal Business Council the superintendent of the reservation is an officio member of the tribal council.

Under an old constitution of the Neah Bay Village the heads of various local governmental services were made ex officio chairmen of appropriate committee of the Indian village council.

Special duties of judicial and legal officers are dealt with separately under Section 20.

SECTION 16

BYLAWS: QUALIFICATIONS FOR OFFICE

It is usual to include either in the constitution or in the bylaws a statement of the qualifications of tribal officers. Such qualifications restrict those eligible to hold tribal office by laying down specified requirements of age, degree of Indian blood, residence, sex, and/or character. While the Indian Office will interpose no objection to any reasonable qualifications, the value of constitutional provisions or bylaws laying down such qualifications is very questionable. Where those qualifications correspond to basic popular feelings and beliefs they will control the popular choice of candidates, even if they are not stated in the constitution or bylaws. On the other hand, if those qualifications do not represent the permanent feelings and beliefs of the tribe, their inclusion in a written constitution or written bylaws is of doubtful propriety. If it is thought best to adopt any such qualifications, the following provisions may be considered.

From the proposed constitution of the Pima Community of Arizona:

> *Section 3.* A person may be a member of the Community Council who shall have attained the age of twenty-five years and who shall have resided on the reservation for a continuous period of at least two years immediately preceding the date of said election, and who shall, when chosen, be an inhabitant of the District in which he shall be chosen and who is a full-blood Indian. And no person lacking these qualifications or any of them may qualify. (Article II)

From the constitution and bylaws of the Representative Council of the Cheyenne River Sioux Indians, adopted in 1925:

> *Article III. Qualifications for Office*
> A person to be eligible to election to any of the offices provided for in Article II hereof must be an allotted male member of the Cheyenne River

Sioux Indians not less than thirty (30) nor more than sixty (60) years of age, except in the case of the Secretary, to which position any allotted male member of the Cheyenne River Sioux Indians, over the age of twenty-one years, may be eligible.

From the constitution and bylaws of the Hoopa Business Council, adopted in 1933:

> *Article 3.* The business council shall be composed of seven enrolled members of the Hoopa Tribe, bona fide residents of Humboldt County, California, and twenty-one years of age or over.

From the constitution and bylaws of the Klamath Business Committee, adopted in 1929:

> *Article 16.* Any member of the tribe who is in the employ of the Indian Service shall be ineligible to membership in the business committee, but may have a voice in the discussion of questions before the committee, as provided in Article 6.

From a constitution adopted by the Menominee Indians in 1904, but never approved:

> *Section 16.* No member of the Business Committee shall, during the time for which he was elected, be appointed to any other office under the authority of the Menominee Tribe of Indians which shall have been created, or the emoluments whereof shall have been increased, during such time; and no person holding any office under the United States shall be a member of the Business Committee during his continuance in office, after the election in the year of 1906.

From the amended Constitution of the Eastern Band of Cherokee Indians, adopted in 1875:

> *Article III*
> *Section 1.* No person shall ever be eligible to any office or appointment of honor, profit, or trust who shall have aided or abetted, counseled or encouraged any person or persons guilty of defrauding the Eastern Band of the Cherokees, or who may hereafter aid or abet, counsel or encourage any pretended agents or attorneys in defrauding the Eastern Band of Cherokees.

The following provisions, concerning the qualifications for the position of secretary, are taken from the proposed constitution of the Quechan (Fort Yuma) Tribal Council:

(1) In order to insure the greatest measure of competency and efficiency it shall be the first duty of the Tribal Council, after having elected a President and a Vice-President, to give careful and impartial consideration to the selection and appointment of a Tribal Secretary who shall also serve as ex officio Secretary to the Quechan Tribal Council.

(2) Such selection and appointment shall be made upon the basis of the candidate's qualifications, firstly; as to character, past record, and reputation; secondly, as to the candidate's ability to properly keep the records and minutes of the Council; thirdly, as to the candidate's ability to properly understand the English language, and to properly and adequately interpret same into the Quechan language, in order that those members of the tribe who are unable to properly understand the English language shall, at all times, receive a true and accurate interpretation of the substance of all tribal records, contracts, or agreements and the proceedings of the Tribal Council. (Article 8)

SECTION 17

BYLAWS: OATHS OF OFFICE, INSIGNIA, AND CEREMONIALS

The induction or inauguration of tribal chiefs, headmen, or other officers was in early days a matter of greater importance. Public ceremonies made the occasion auspicious, impressed upon the minds of the people the picture of their own leaders, and impressed upon the minds of these leaders a vision of their new responsibilities. Speeches were made by the older men or women of the tribe to instruct the new leaders in their powers and duties. Insignia of office symbolized these new powers and duties.

It was natural under these circumstances for the officers of the tribe to take their work seriously. Many of the great Indian chiefs whose names have come down to us gave, without stint, of their time, their wealth, and, when necessary, their blood for the service of their people. Positions of leadership in the tribe were not regarded either as an opportunity for selfish exploitation of the tribe or as a regular job to be performed for wages. Tribal office was recognized as a difficult task and heavy responsibility which no honorable man could refuse to assume when requested to do so.

Many of the traditions and ceremonies which gave importance to positions of tribal leadership were wiped out in the attempt of the Indian Office to "civilize" the Indian. In many tribes today the election of tribal officers has ceased to be a matter of any importance. Few people attend a tribal election. Since no great honor is attached to the holding of office, many of the officers will attend council meetings only rarely, unless a large per diem salary is provided.

Of course, this situation is likely to change when the council is restored to a position of power, but power is dangerous unless it is accompanied by a sense of responsibility. It is important that the Indians who seek to reestablish local self-government shall not only select the best possible individuals for tribal office, but shall impress deeply upon the minds of these individuals the responsibilities. It is important that by the proper use of oaths and ceremonials

95

the obligations and the honor of public office should be made clear to the people and their chosen leaders. It is important when an election is completed that officers of the tribe shall recognize their responsibilities to the tribe as a whole, including those members of the tribe who have voted against them. It is important that the Indians give their best thought to devising ways of eliminating the spirit of selfishness and narrow partisanship which has disgraced some Indian tribal councils.

The following provisions from the Great Binding Law (Gayanashakgowah) of the Iroquois Confederacy point to a ceremony of induction which cannot be adopted in detail by other tribes but which embodies a spirit that may be invoked, perhaps in other ways:

28. When a candidate Lord is to be installed he shall furnish four strings of shells (or wampum) one span in length bound together at one end. Such will constitute the evidence of his pledge to the Confederate Lords that he will live according to the constitution of the Great Peace and exercise justice in all affairs.

When the pledge is furnished the Speaker of the Council must hold the shell strings in his hand and address the opposite side of the Council Fire, and he shall commence his address saying: "Now behold him. He has now become a Confederate Lord. See how splendid he looks." An address may then follow. At the end of it he shall send the bunch of shell strings to the opposite side and they shall be received as evidence of the pledge. Then shall the opposite side say:

"We now do crown you with the sacred emblem of the deer's antlers, the emblem of your Lordship. You shall now become a mentor of the people of the Five Nations. The thickness of your skin shall be seven spans— which is to say that you shall be proof against anger, offensive actions, and criticism. Your heart shall be filled with peace and goodwill and your mind filled with a yearning for the welfare of the people of the Confederacy. With endless patience you shall carry out your duty and your firmness shall be tempered with tenderness for your people. Neither anger nor fury shall find lodgement in your mind, and all your words and actions shall be marked with calm deliberation. In all of your deliberations in the Confederate Council, in your efforts at law making, in all your official acts, self-interest shall be cast into oblivion. Cast not over your shoulder behind you the warnings of the nephews and nieces should they chide you for any error or wrong you may do, but return to the way of the Great Law which is just and right. Look and listen for the welfare of the whole people and have always in view not only the present but also the coming generations, even those whose faces are yet beneath the surface of the ground—the unborn of the future Nation."

The proposed constitution of the Pima Community of Arizona prescribes the following oath for the president of the community:

> I do solemnly swear [or affirm] that I will faithfully execute the office of President of the PIMA COMMUNITY OF ARIZONA; and that I will, to the best of my ability, preserve, protect, and defend the Constitution of the United States and the Constitution of the PIMA COMMUNITY OF ARIZONA. (Article III, Section 2)

Oaths of office have been prescribed in many Indian tribal constitutions. The amended constitution of the Eastern Band of Cherokee Indians, adopted in 1875, contains the following provision for oaths of office:

> *Section 2.* Each member of the annual council, before he takes his seat to transact any business of the council, shall take the following oath (or affirmation):
> "I, A. B., do solemnly swear [or affirm] that I have not obtained my election or appointment as a member of this council by bribery or any undue or unlawful means or duress or fraud, used by myself or others, by my desire or approbation for that purpose; that I consider myself constitutionally qualified as a member of this council, and that on all questions and measures which may come before me I will give my vote and so conduct myself as in my judgment shall appear most conducive to the interest and prosperity of the Eastern Band of the Cherokee Indians, and that I will bear true faith and allegiance to the same, and to the utmost of my ability and power observe, conform to, support, and defend the constitution thereof."

The following oath is contained in the constitution and bylaws of the Klamath Business Committee, adopted in 1929:

> "I, _____, do solemnly swear [or affirm] that I will support and defend the Constitution of the United States against all enemies and faithfully and impartially carry out the duties of my office to the best of my ability, and will cooperate with the Superintendent in charge of the reservation in all proper efforts to promote and protect the best interests of the Indians of the Klamath Reservation and to assist them in every way toward better citizenship and progress."

The constitution of the Cherokee Nation, adopted in 1839, and the compiled laws adopted thereunder (addition of 1892), contain the following specific oaths for various tribal offices:

Oath of Principal Chief
"I do solemnly swear [or affirm] that I will faithfully execute the duties of Principal Chief of the Cherokee Nation and will, to the best of my ability, preserve, protect, and defend the Constitution of the Cherokee Nation." (Compiled Laws of 1892, Article IV, Section 7)

Oath of Council Members
"I, A. B., do solemnly swear [or affirm, as the case may be] that I have not obtained my election by bribery, threats, or any undue or unlawful means, used by myself or others, by my desire and approbation for that purpose; that I consider myself constitutionally qualified as a member of the _____ and that on all questions and measures which may come before me, I will so give my vote, and so conduct myself, as in my judgment shall appear most conducive to the interest and prosperity of the Nation, and that I will bear true faith and allegiance to the same, and to the utmost of my ability and power, observe, conform to, support and defend the Constitution thereof." (Article III, Section 12)

Oath of Treasurer
"I, _____, do solemnly swear [or affirm] that I will faithfully and to the best of my ability, perform the duties of Treasurer of the Cherokee Nation; that I will carefully preserve all books, records, papers, moneys, and other property coming into my custody by virtue of the office; that I will disburse the public moneys in conformity with the express provisions of the law, and without fear, favor, or partiality to anyone; that I will not lend, with or without interest, or otherwise use any of the public moneys or other property, for any use whatsoever not authorized by law; that I will be accountable to the Cherokee Nation for the acts of all subordinates appointed by me and serving in my office under me; that I will make true and correct reports of the condition of the Treasury whenever by law required so to do; and that I will turn over or account for to my successor in office or any person lawfully authorized to receive the same, all moneys, securities, records, papers, furniture, and other property of the Cherokee Nation that may be or may have come into my possession as Treasurer. So help me God." (Article II, Section 33)

Oath of Auditor

"I, _____, as Auditor, do solemnly swear [or affirm] that I will make and keep a correct registry of all certificates of national indebtedness, authorized by law to be registered; that I will faithfully and impartially register the same to the persons owning or presenting them, as required of me by law to do; and that I will, to the best of my skill and ability, perform all the duties required of me by law. So help me God." (Article III, Section 54)

Oath of Sheriff

"I, A.B., having been elected to the office of Sheriff of _____ district, do solemnly swear that I will well and truly execute the duties of my said office as defined and required of me by law, and my bond to execute, according to the best of my skill and understanding, without fear or partiality. So help me God." (Article IV, Section 61)

Oath of District Clerk

"I do solemnly swear [or affirm] that I will carefully file and preserve all books, papers, and documents that may come to my possession or be placed in my charge, by virtue of my office, and the same with the furniture and things belonging to the office, safely transmit unimpaired to my successor in office, upon notice from him of his readiness to receive them, that I will true record make of all matters and things required of me by law or the court to record, and that I will faithfully and truly execute all other duties which may devolve upon me to perform by virtue of my office, without favor, affection or partiality, and to the best of my ability. So help me God." (Article V, Section 75)

Oath of Solicitor

"You do solemnly swear, that as Solicitor or Prosecuting Attorney, for and in behalf of the Cherokee Nation, you will, to the best of your skill and ability, faithfully conduct all examinations of crimes committed, or person charged, and prosecute all persons indicted in pursuance of authority given you by law, without fear, favor, partiality, or malice, within the district of _____, during your continuance in office, and that you will not take or receive any remuneration of any person charged with any criminal offense within said district, or from any one else in behalf of such person, but be faithful to the Cherokee Nation in all prosecutions, and in the performance of all other duties required of a Solicitor to perform by law, to the best of your ability. So help you God." (Article VI, Section 91)

If it is thought that these oaths should not be set forth in detail in the constitution or bylaws, the constitution or bylaws might simply provide that commissioners of elections or other designated officials should prescribe such oaths, ceremonials and formalities of induction or inauguration as they might judge proper.

Insignia of office may be as important as oaths in creating the proper atmosphere of dignity and public responsibility in the performance of public acts. The bylaws of a tribe might well provide for a tribal seal and for seals of specific offices to be used in the execution of official documents. Badges or other symbols of office might likewise be provided for.

In the pueblos of New Mexico the canes given by the Spanish and Mexican governments and by President Lincoln are impressive insignia of the office of governor. It is possible that other tribes will wish to secure similar permanent insignia for their highest offices.

SECTION 18

BYLAWS: SALARIES OF OFFICIALS

The question of whether any salaries ought to be paid to tribal officials cannot receive a single answer for all reservations. In some tribes the tradition of service is so strong that payment of official salaries would be regarded as unnecessary and degrading. In other tribes it would be impossible to obtain the service of capable leaders without offering substantial payments. In each case the question must be considered of how much time the service in question will consume. The necessity and available means of travel on any reservation must be considered. Actual expenses of travel and losses through the interruption of paid work may be held to require compensation even if no regular salaries are paid. The constitution and bylaws of the Hoopa Business Council contain the following compromise provisions:

> *Article 15.* The office of business councilmen shall be strictly honorary and without compensation, except when valuable or meritorious services are registered by any member of the business council in the discharge of his duties, in which case claim may be made for compensation.

A similar provision is found in Article 15 of the constitution and bylaws of the Yankton Sioux Tribal Business and Claims Committee.

Where a schedule of salaries is to be fixed, the amount of such salaries should be based upon a consideration of the tribal funds available, upon the amount of labor that will be required by official duties, and upon the prevailing rate of wages in the locality for labor of equal difficulty. The schedule of official salaries now paid varies considerably from reservation to reservation. Salaries to tribal councilmen are usually paid upon a per diem basis. The following figures are reported from various reservations (these figures being in addition to compensation for traveling expenses):

101

$2.00 a day	Cheyenne River; Eastern Band of Cherokee
$2.50 a day	Menominee
$3.00 a day	Fort Peck; Fort Hall
$4.00 a day	Mescalero
$5.00 a day	Klamath; Sac and Fox
$7.00 a day	Navajo

Special annual salaries are usually paid to officers whose work continues day after day through the year. The following typical salaries are noted:

Annette Islands Reserve: Secretary, $10 per annum; Treasurer, $10 per annum

Laguna Pueblo: Governor, $50 per annum; other officials, $35 per annum.

Rosebud: Secretary, $100 per annum

Eastern Band of Cherokee: Principal Chief, $250 per annum; Assistant Chief, $125 per annum

Osage: Principal Chief, $900 per annum; Assistant Chief, $750 per annum; Councilmen, $500 per annum.

Choctaw: Chief, $2,000 per annum; Mining Trustee, $4,000 per annum; National Attorney, $5,000 per annum.

These salaries are paid out of tribal funds, either funds held by the United States or funds held directly by the tribe. In some cases special legislative authority for such payments has been obtained. The following sources of funds for salaries are noted as typical:

Fort Peck: Proceeds of labor of Fort Peck Indians of Montana (councils and delegations), Act of June 30, 1932

Sac and Fox: Proceeds of labor of Sac and Fox Indians of Oklahoma; rental and oil production from tribal lands.

Fort Totten: Superintendent reports, "At times compensation has been paid on day rate from 'Support of Indians and Administration of Indian Property' or from 'Indian Money Proceeds of Labor (Tribal)' or other appropriate funds such as Roads."

Cheyenne River: Cheyenne River Reservation three percent fund support

Mescalero: Indian moneys, proceeds of labor Mescalero Agency

Fort Hall: Fort Hall irrigation four percent fund

Laguna Pueblo: Funds derived from assessments upon members of pueblo by tribal council

SECTION 19

BYLAWS: PROCEDURE OF GOVERNING BODY

The governing body of an organized tribe, whether it is known as a tribal council or senate, or by any other name, will have work of great importance to do; and it is necessary that its procedure should be both efficient and democratic. In order to work efficiently, the council must meet regularly and promptly and proceed to the consideration of important problems without disorder or obstruction. In order to secure the loyalty of the council to the best interests of the people, it is necessary that the action of the council be deliberate, public, and based upon the widest knowledge of the wishes of the people and fullest understanding of their conditions.

The manner in which a tribal council is to work in order to secure these objectives offers a very important problem in the drafting of tribal bylaws.

Modern "parliamentary" rules of procedure will prove useful in certain tribes but entirely unworkable or undesirable in other tribes. Other modes of procedure may be suggested by the native political customs of the various tribes. Whatever system of procedure is thought best should be described briefly and clearly in the bylaws of the tribe.

In the first place, the bylaws of any tribe should fix a date and place for regular meetings of the tribal council and also for meetings of the entire tribe on those reservations where such meetings are possible. It is expected that each organized tribe will have a regular town hall or community house of its own for meetings and tribal business, or else will have the right to use agency or school buildings at regular times or whenever necessary.

The frequency of council meetings will depend upon the amount of work to be accomplished and upon the difficulties of travel at certain seasons. Existing tribal councils or business committees recognized by the Indian Office usually meet two, four, or six times a year, but then these organizations have, for the most part, little work to do and little power. Under a system of self-government, more frequent meetings will probably

103

be necessary. Thus, a number of actual and proposed constitutions include provision for regular monthly meetings.

The constitution of the Laguna Pueblo Indians, adopted in 1908, provides:

> *Section 5.* Unless otherwise ordered by the Governor, all meetings shall convene from 9 a.m. to 12 m. and from 1 p.m. to 4 or 5 p.m., as ordered by the Governor.
>
> Regular meetings of the court officers shall be held monthly on the last Saturday of each month.
>
> * * * * *
>
> *Section 8.* It shall be the duty of the Governor to see that all business on hand or coming up within any month be disposed of if possible before the beginning of the next month.

The Rules and Regulations for Annette Islands Reserve, Alaska, provide:

> *Section 7.* The council shall have regular monthly meetings, except during any period of the year when it would prove a hardship on the members of the council to leave their personal labors in order to attend such meetings. At such times the executive committee, provided for by Article V, Section 1, of these rules and regulations, shall carry on the work of the council and reports its action at the first regular meeting of the council thereafter. (Article II)

In addition to providing for regular meetings, the bylaws should specify the procedure for calling special meetings in emergencies. The following provision is found in a constitution recently submitted by the Indians of the San Carlos Reservation:

> *Section 3. Special Meetings*
>
> The chairman of the Council shall call a special meeting of the Council upon the request of two or more other Councilmen, upon request of a District, if at least one-third of its voting members request it, also upon request of the Superintendent; and the Superintendent shall in every case be served notice of such special meeting.
>
> A general meeting of the Tribe shall be called upon request of fifty-one (51) per cent of the qualified voters of a district, served upon the Superintendent, also upon request of the Superintendent. (Article IV)

Some provision should be made as to the number of persons required to attend council meetings in order to make the transaction of business lawful. Usually, it is provided that unless a majority of the members are present, no business may be transacted. Thus, the charter of the Eastern Band of Cherokee Indians, issued by the legislature of North Carolina in 1897, provides:

> *Section 10.* That there shall be an annual or grand council held on the first Monday in October of each and every year, and in cases of emergency the principal chief can call a special council, but no business can be transacted in either annual or special council unless a quorum of the members shall be present which shall consist of a majority of the members of council elected at the last preceding elections.

If it is deemed necessary to compel the attendance of council members at meetings through the levying of fines, the following provisions taken from the constitution of the Laguna Pueblo Indians might be adopted:

> *Section 9.* All court officers shall be required to be present at each regular monthly meeting, and each special meeting when called by the Governor, unless it should be absolutely impossible for him to be there; in which case he shall send a substitute and notify the Governor of his inability to attend, giving his reasons therefore. The Governor will then refer the matter to the court, and if in the opinion of the court, his reasons are justifiable he shall be excused; otherwise, he shall be subject to the usual fine of being absent without the proper reasons. (Constitution)
>
> *Section 10.* That in any case where a court officer is absent from a regular meeting, or a special meeting when properly notified, and his reasons therefore are not considered justifiable in the opinion of the court, he shall be fined the usual fee of 50 cents for each absence. (Bylaws)

The question may arise whether council meetings should be closed or open to the public and, if open at all, whether the public permitted to attend should be limited to members of the tribe and Indian Service employees.

The Rules and Regulations for Annette Islands Reserve permit the attendance of all outsiders, but make the right of outsiders to speak dependent upon the wishes of the council:

> *Section 8.* All regular meetings of the council shall be open to the public, but no one not having a seat on the council shall be permitted to

discuss matters before the council, except by permission or upon the invitation of the council. (Article II)

The proposed bylaws of the Quechan (Fort Yuma) Tribal Council provide that meetings of the council shall be open to all members of the tribe, but further provide for executive sessions, as follows:

> The Council may, upon motion duly passed, go into executive session. At such executive session all persons not directly concerned with the matter under discussion shall be excluded from the Council Chambers and any such person whose presence shall be required before the committee shall be designated by the President and no other person shall be allowed to be present other than the members of the Council and the Secretary.

A proposed constitution drafted by Indians of the San Carlos Reservation provides that all the meetings of the council "shall be public to the Indians and the government representative and may be attended by guests welcome to the Council." (Article IV, Section 2) The constitution of the Chickasaw Nation provides simply that "The business of both Houses shall be transacted with open doors." (Article IV, Section 13)

The bylaws of the Junior Chippewa Association of the White Earth Reservation contain the following provision permitting any member of the association to speak at council meetings:

> *VII.* Any enrolled member of the association is privileged to speak at regular and special meetings. This is especially urged upon all the members in order to draw out more deliberation and advance more ideas so as to come to better conclusions.

The question of attendance by nonmembers of the council at council meetings is only part of the much broader question: How may nonmembers of the governing council assist in the work of government?

Under the traditional forms of government in the United States, it is almost impossible for anyone to play an active responsible part in government unless he is a regularly elected or appointed official. Those on the outside can only criticize or "lobby."

The practice of many Indian tribes in the past was very different. Any member of the tribe was free to come before the council of chiefs or headmen to put forward some plan that he considered to be for the benefit of the tribe. If the members of the council thought the plan worth trying, they would generally authorize the one who suggested it to organize a group, either of members of the council or of other people, in order to carry out the proposed enterprise. While carrying out this enterprise, the person who organized it might be considered a temporary member of the council. If the matter finally turned out successfully, the person who had organized the enterprise might be given a permanent place on the council as a chief or headman.

Leadership, then, was not an exclusive monopoly of the elected or hereditary officers of the tribe. Anyone who wanted to assume leadership in some special project, whether in a hunting expedition, a building program, a war party, a social entertainment, or an irrigation project, might do so with the blessing of the council, provided only he could convince a sufficient number of his relatives and fellow tribesmen to cooperate with him in the venture. True, he received no salary for his tribal service, but he was paid by the respect of his fellow tribesmen. He was recognized as a leader of his people just as if he had obtained some title through a regular election or through inheritance.

In this way, anyone who was able to think out worthwhile projects for the benefit of the tribe could come before the recognized leaders of the people and receive their cooperation. Under these circumstances, the lot of the "agitator" was hard. If he had any constructive plans to suggest, people expected him to go before the council and expected the council to receive his suggestions sympathetically and help him to work out those suggestions. If, with the cooperation of the council, he could not make his plans work, then anybody could see that they were not worthwhile. If, on the other hand, a critic of existing policies made no attempt to work out his own new ideas, then people would realize that he was probably motivated by jealously rather than by the desire to render service to his tribe.

This form of procedure was, on the whole, very successful in securing a large measure of harmony within each Indian tribe. It required a great amount of tolerance and patience on the part of the tribal leaders, but it operated to reduce factionalism and to bring into the active service of the tribe many energetic individuals who, under modern forms of government, could only engage in destructive criticism.

Only recently, in the United States, the basic principles of this ancient Indian custom have been rediscovered and introduced into the structure of the federal government. In the last few years, many individuals who have criticized governmental policies have been appointed to special advisory committees, boards, code authorities, etc., and given the opportunity to try to put into practice the policies they advocated. This has resulted not only in introducing new ideas into governmental services, but also in diminishing the sources of purely negative criticism.

In order to establish or reestablish a procedure of this sort in tribal government, the bylaws of the tribe should provide that all who have matters to present that are not merely of a personal nature may appear before the council and receive a public hearing. The bylaws should further provide that *non-members of the council may be appointed to committees or given special offices by vote of the council*. As chairmen of special committees, individuals with constructive ideas for the benefit of the tribe could be authorized to work on their own initiative, but under the general supervision and authority of the tribal council.

A very important matter in the efficient conduct of the business of the tribal council is the maintenance of orderly procedure. Orderly procedure does not necessarily require an elaborate system of parliamentary rules of order. The constitution of the Laguna Pueblo Indians, for instance, deals with the matter of procedure very simply, in the following language:

> *Section 6.* The Governor being in full charge of all meetings, it shall be his duty to see that perfect order is preserved in every respect. In the discussion of all business but one person shall be allowed to speak at a time. When anyone wishes to speak he shall first ask permission of the Governor to do so before proceeding.

Where a detailed set of rules of order is desired, the bylaws of the Fort Belknap Tribal Business Council, adopted in 1921, may serve as a useful model:

> The following shall be the order of business which shall be subject to temporary change at any meeting by a majority vote:
>
> 1. Call to order
> 2. Roll call
> 3. Reading, correction, and adoption of the minutes of the previous meeting
> 4. Unfinished business
> 5. Report of committees
> 6. New business
> 7. Adjournment

The meeting shall be called to order as soon as it appears that a quorum is present.

If a Councilman, while speaking, be called to order he shall, at the request of the chair, take his seat until the question or order is decided.

Should two or more Councilmen rise to speak at the same time, the chair shall decide who is entitled to the floor.

No Councilman shall interrupt another in his remarks except to call to a point or order.

A Councilman shall not speak twice upon a question until all who wish to speak shall have had an opportunity to do so.

Speeches shall be limited to ten minutes, but this time may be extended by majority vote of the Council.

A motion shall be open for discussion only after it has been seconded and stated from the chair.

At the request of five members, the mover of a motion shall be required to reduce it to writing.

When a question is pending before the Council, no motion shall be in order except; to adjourn, to refer, for the previous question, to postpone indefinitely, to postpone for a certain time, to amend, which motions shall have precedence in the order mentioned.

Motions to lay on the table shall not be debatable except as limited by *Robert's Rules of Order.*

A motion to reconsider shall be entertained only when made by a Councilman who voted in the majority, and in order to carry shall receive a majority vote.

The reports of Committees shall be subject to amendments and substitutes from the floor of the Council as are other motions and resolutions.

No motion or resolution shall be voted upon until the mover or introducer has had a chance to speak if he so desires.

When a rollcall vote has been taken, and all the Councilmen present have had the opportunity to record their votes, the ballot shall be declared closed.

When a rollcall ballot has been ordered, no adjournment shall take place until the result has been announced.

Robert's Rules of Order shall be the guide on all matters not provided herein.

In choosing between such a set of rules as that given above and a simpler or more flexible form of procedure, two things should be borne in mind. In the first place, technical rules of order may offer an unfair advantage to those members of the tribal council who are learned in tricks of parliamentary procedure. The older Indians in certain tribal councils would be put at a serious disadvantage by the adoption of modern parliamentary rules of order. Where all the Indians likely to be elected to tribal office are equally familiar with the recognized parliamentary rules of order, this objection does not arise.

There is a second, and perhaps more serious, objection to the rules of order used in modern legislatures and other organizations. These rules of order are based fundamentally on the principle of "majority right." The individual who stands alone may not speak unless another person seconds his motion. His motion may be ruled out of order. Discussion on a motion may be closed before certain individuals have had an opportunity to speak. In those and other ways, a member of the council may find himself deprived of the right to *speak* on important questions, though, of course, he cannot be deprived of the right to *vote*.

Such a system of majority rule may be appropriate enough where people are accustomed to submitting to the decisions of majorities. But where there is no firmly established tradition of majority rule, it would seem much better to permit every man to have his say on every question, even though his fellow council members may consider his remarks boring or out of order, and to strive in all cases to reach unanimous agreement instead of ending discussion when a majority agreement is reached.

This is a much slower way of reaching decisions than the way of majority rule. In a large council or public assembly it may be quite impossible; but in a council of reasonable size, where there are no irreconcilable factions, the method of procedure by unanimous consent offers certain substantial advantages. For one thing, it tends to reduce personal animosities and jealousies within the council, which are likely to arise when any member feels that the majority is disregarding him. Also, it greatly simplifies the problem of law enforcement by avoiding a situation in which elected leaders of the people have declared their opposition to particular laws. Unanimity and harmony in the council offer a good example to the rest of the tribe. Finally, unanimous consent is likely to produce workable compromises in cases where majority decisions would be harsh and unworkable.

Experience with the jury system, where unanimous agreement is required for a verdict, shows that it is possible to reach unanimous agreement in a group of twelve men upon almost any question, even questions of great complexity; but this same experience shows that it will often take a long time to reach such agreement. The question for any tribe to decide is whether it is worthwhile to try to secure unanimous agreement in decisions of the tribal council in view of the increased time which will be required to convince minorities or to reach generally acceptable compromises.

One answer to this problem is suggested by the following provision in the Constitution of the Standing Rock Business Council, adopted in 1914, requiring that certain important decisions must be reached by unanimous agreement, while allowing majority rule on other less important questions:

> *Voting.* All decisions (minor) shall be by rising majority vote. All important decisions, Treaties, Adoptions and Resolutions to the Secretary of the Interior shall be by unanimous vote in writing.

If there is doubt as to whether unanimous agreement can be reached in all cases, and it is felt that at least a serious attempt should always be made to secure such unanimous consent, a provision like the following might be adopted:

> The members of the _____ Council shall attempt to reach a unanimous agreement on all questions involving the passage of resolutions or ordinances, the approval of contracts, or the making of recommendations to the United States Government. If unanimous agreement cannot be reached when the matter is first presented, the question shall be put over until the next day that the council shall be in session, at which time decision by majority vote shall control.

Another way of inducing unanimous agreement without making it an absolute requirement would be to provide that any member of the council (or else any *two* members of the council) should have the privilege to *postpone* any question for a period, say, of one month, or perhaps to require that any decision be put to a referendum of the tribe. In order to prevent undue use of this privilege for purposes of obstruction, the bylaws might provide that no member should call for more than one postponement or referendum (or possibly two or three) within a period, say, of one year. Under such a rule, the majority would always be anxious to win over the minority, or to reach a mutually satisfactory compromise, in order to avoid the trouble and delay involved in a postponement of voting or in the holding of a popular referendum.

Of course, these methods of encouraging unanimous agreement necessarily slow up the procedure of the council and may prove quite impracticable in a very large tribal council, or even in a small council that is torn by bitter factional disputes. Likewise, these methods may prove undesirable where individual members of the council are likely to oppose measures not because of honest beliefs, which may always be changed by argument, but because they have been bribed to do so. Finally, those methods may be quite unnecessary in communities which are accustomed to majority rule and minority obedience.

There are certain minor details of council procedure which should be specified in the bylaws of the tribe in order to ensure uniformity of practice.

Thus, the bylaws should determine whether or not members of the council may vote on matters in which they have a special personal interest or in which members of their household have such an interest.

Likewise, the bylaws should provide for the election by the council or the appointment by its presiding officer of a sergeant at arms to maintain order, if such an office is deemed necessary.

The bylaws should also specify the form of ordinances and resolutions. A suitable provision on this point would be

> All ordinances and resolutions adopted by the council shall contain the enacting clause, "Be it enacted by the Council of the _____ Tribe:" or "Be it resolved by the Council of the _____Tribe:" and shall bear the Seal of the Tribe.

Likewise, the bylaws should provide for the manner of published ordinances, for instance, by posting copies in designated places or by announcing such ordinances at public meetings. In this connection it will be noted that the procedure of reporting acts of the council at local district meetings is discussed under Section 6 of the memorandum.

Finally, the bylaws might contain a provision permitting public examination of all tribal records by members of the tribe or representatives of the United States Government and might specify the times and places at which such examination could be made. At the same time, provision should be made for transmitting copies of the minutes of council meetings to the Commissioner of Indian Affairs. These matters might be dealt with in a special section of the bylaws or else included in those sections dealing with the duties of the secretary and the treasurer. (See Section 15 of this memorandum.)

SECTION 20

BYLAWS: JUDICIAL CODE

The simplest method of administering justice is through the general representative body of the tribe. As was noted in the discussion under Section 7, the same body that passes laws may be given authority to enforce them and to punish offenders.

Such a provision is included in the constitution of the Laguna Pueblo Indians, Section 3, as quoted in Section 7 of this memorandum. A similar arrangement is established by the Rules and Regulations for Annette Islands Reserve, which provide:

> *Section 4.* By the vote of a majority of its membership, the council shall have power to impose upon any violator of an ordinance passed by the council such a fine as may be deemed just, not exceeding ten dollars ($10) for each offense.
>
> In each case, before the council proceeds to vote thereon, the person accused of such violation shall be given opportunity to appear before the council and make any statement that he or she may wish to make.
>
> The secretary shall, within three days after such a fine has been imposed by the council, hand to the person upon whom the fine has been imposed written notification thereof, countersigned by the mayor or by the acting mayor, setting forth the amount of the fine and the reasons for which it has been imposed.
>
> Fines thus imposed shall be collected by the secretary and by him deposited with the treasurer, to be expended at the direction of the council as other funds are expended.
>
> Whenever a fine which has been thus imposed remains unpaid for a period of four weeks, from and including the day upon which notification thereof was received by the delinquent, the council, by the vote of a majority of its membership, may, in lieu of the payment of the fine, require the delinquent to labor not more than ten (10) days on the streets or other

public works of the reserve. The expenses in connection with such sentence shall be paid from funds under the control of the council. (Article III)

Judicial administration through the general representative body or its executive committee is well-established practice with the Eastern Band of Cherokee Indians, with the Quinaielt Indians, and probably with other tribes as well. On none of the reservations where this simple method of administering justice has been in practice has any serious objection been offered against this procedure.

There are, of course, many reservations where such a system of judicial administration would be quite unworkable because the administration of justice would take up too much of the time of the council and leave insufficient time for the consideration of other problems. Where such is the case, or where for any other reason it is desired to have special officials designated as judges to handle judicial matters, it will be necessary to set forth in the constitution and bylaws how these judges are to be chosen and how they may be removed, what their powers are to be, and what forms of procedure they must follow.

On some reservations it may be thought desirable to have a judicial system corresponding as closely as possible to that of the state in which the reservation is located. Under such circumstances, those who are entrusted with the drafting of the tribal bylaws should make a careful study of the state laws governing the procedure of county or district courts and justices of the peace. If possible, they should attend sessions of these courts and make inquiries of the court officials in order to find out exactly what procedure is followed and the reasons therefore. The assistance of a local lawyer in this study might be very useful. On the basis of such a study, using the state laws as a model, those who are drafting the bylaws may attempt to draw up a judicial code which is similar to that of the surrounding white community and at the same time intelligible to the Indians concerned and applicable to their circumstances.

It will be noted that the Law and Order Regulations recently prepared by the Interior Department will not apply to any reservation which votes to adopt a constitution that provides for tribal courts. Any tribe that adopts a constitution which is approved by the Secretary of the Interior under the Wheeler-Howard Act is free to decide for itself whether it wants to adopt a judicial system patterned after that of the surrounding white communities, or to adopt the general Law and Order Regulations of the Interior Department without change, or to use these Law and Order Regulations as a model and make such changes as seem desirable, or to establish or perpetuate an entirely different judicial system.

A tribe that desires to adopt, without change, the departmental Law and Order Regulations may insert in its constitution or bylaws the following provisions:

> The administration of justice shall be vested in a Court of Indian Offenses, together with an Indian Police force, which shall function in the manner prescribed in Chapters 1, 4, and 5 of the Law and Order Regulations of the Interior Department, promulgated on _____.

Most tribes, however, would wish to make some changes in these regulations before adopting them as part of the tribal bylaws. Some of the changes which may be desired by various tribes are discussed below, in connection with the several sections of Chapters 1, 4, and 5 of the departmental Law and Order Regulations. Chapter 2, which treats of criminal offenses, and Chapter 3, which deals with domestic relations, will be taken up in later sections of this memorandum.

Chapter 1 [Courts of Indian Offenses], Section 1. Jurisdiction

For the sake of clarity it would be preferable to designate a tribal court, that is to say, a court establishment by a tribal constitution or bylaws, by some other name than Court of Indian Offenses, which is the title used for courts set up under departmental regulations. Various titles for such courts are available, including the following: Court of the _____ Tribe (or _____ Reservation, or _____ Band, or _____ Pueblo, or _____ Community); District Court and Supreme Court or Court of Appeals, where more than one court is set up by the constitution; Justice of the Peace; Peacemakers' Court; and Surrogate's Court, the latter term being used to designate a special court that deals with inheritance matters.

In specifying the limits of jurisdiction of such tribal courts, the following provisions taken from various tribal constitutions should be considered.

The proposed bylaws of the Quechan (Fort Yuma) Tribal Council define the jurisdiction of a tribal court as follows:

Tribal Court
(1) It shall be the duty of the Council to provide the necessary ordinance whereby there shall be established upon the reservation a Tribal Court.

Such Court shall be in the nature of a Court of Justice having jurisdiction over all minor crimes of a misdemeanor nature. It shall also function as a Small Claims Court and shall hear and try lawsuits involving any and all amounts up to and including Three Hundred Dollars ($300.00).

(2) This Court shall have jurisdiction over all such petty crimes or offenses against the peace and morals of the public and all such other offenses of a criminal nature as are listed as such in the Penal Code of the State of California. It shall also have jurisdiction over and shall try and determine such other crimes and/or offenses against the peace and dignity of the public as shall be designated by the Bureau of Indian Affairs and over all other crimes and offenses occurring on the reservation and which do not come within the jurisdiction of the Federal Courts.

Any decrees, judgments, rulings, or sentences emanating from this Court shall have full force and effect and shall be in accord with those decrees, judgments, rulings or sentences specified in the Civil Code and the Penal Code of the State of California for like offenses or conditions.

(3) Court shall have jurisdiction over all Indians upon the reservation and over such disputes or lawsuits as shall occur between Indians on the reservation and Whites who are also on the reservation, where such cases are brought before it by stipulation of both parties thereto.

(4) The duties and jurisdiction of this Court shall be more fully defined and established by the Federal Government acting through the Bureau of Indian Affairs or through such other bureau or department as will have proper authority to so act.

The laws of the Osage Nation contain the following simple statement:

The court established under the Government of this Nation shall have jurisdiction of all suits rising under the Constitution and laws of the Osage Nation. (Laws of the Osage Nation, Chapter 3, Article I, Section 2)

In the constitution of the Seneca Nation, as amended in 1893, the following provisions appear, governing the jurisdiction of the Peacemakers' and Surrogate's Courts, which are modeled after local state courts:

Section 4. The judiciary power shall be vested in courts to be known by the name of peacemakers' and surrogate's courts. The peacemakers' courts shall be composed of three members each, one court to be established upon the Cattaraugus and the other upon the Allegany Reservation, the members of each to be elected from residents of the respective reservations on the first Tuesday of May, A.D. 1893. The whole number of peacemakers shall be elected in the following manner: One for one year, one for two years, one for three years; one for each reservation for each and every year thereafter. Term of office, three years. The jurisdiction, forms of process, and proceedings under the law applicable to this court shall be the same as in courts of justices of the peace of the State of New York. The peacemakers on each reservation shall have the power to hold court and preserve order in the same manner as a justice of the peace and shall have the further jurisdiction to grant divorces as between Indians residing on the said reservations and to hear and determine all questions and action between individual Indians residing on said reservation involving the title or possession to real estate on said reservation. Any two of the peacemakers on either of said reservations shall have the power to hold courts and discharge all the duties of peacemakers' courts. . . .

The surrogate's court shall be composed of one person for each of the Allegany and Cattaraugus Reservations, and shall be elected from the residents of the respective reservations at the next annual election after the adoption of this constitution. [They shall] hold their office for the term of two years, and be elected every two years thereafter, and shall be known as surrogates, and shall have jurisdiction of all matters on each reservation for which they are respectively elected, the same as surrogates of the different counties of the Sate of New York, and the forms, process, and proceedings now adopted and in force among the surrogates of New York State shall be the forms, process, and proceedings in use and to be adopted in the courts hereby created, with the right of appeal from all decisions and determinations to the council of the Seneca Nation, the same as from peacemakers' court.

Chapter 1, Section 2. Personnel

The Indian tribe which assumes the responsibilities of self-government will probably want to provide that its judges shall be appointed by the tribal council or elected by the people of the tribe or district, instead of being appointed by the Commissioner of Indian Affairs as are the Indian judges of Courts of Indian Offenses.

The laws of the Muskogee (Creek) Nation contain the following provision on district courts:

> *Section 100.* There shall be established in each district, at such point as the citizens of the district shall decide, a District Court: to each Court there shall be attached one Judge, one Prosecuting Attorney, and a company of Light Horsemen, consisting of one Captain and four Privates.
>
> * * * * *
>
> *Section 115.* The Judge of each District shall be elected by the National Council at its regular session, for the period of two years, and shall be installed in the same manner as the national officers. (Compiled Laws, 1893, Chapter 3)

The proposed constitution of the Pima Community contains the following provision, which leaves to the council the determination of the number of judges and policemen:

> *Section 17.* The Council shall appoint all Community Judges and all Community Police whose duty it shall be to enforce, under the direction of the President, all applicable federal statutes and all laws and ordinances enacted by the Council. Judges and Police shall be appointed for terms of five years. (Article II)

The number of judges should be fixed with due regard to the amount of time required for the disposition of judicial matters, the area of the reservation and the available means of travel, and the funds available for judicial salaries. If these matters cannot be definitely determined at the time of drafting the bylaws, it would be well to leave the determination of the number and location of tribal courts to the future decision of the tribal council.

Chapter 1, Section 3. Meetings

The time, place and number of court sessions might be set forth in the bylaws or left to the tribal council to determine, by resolution or ordinance, or left to the court itself to determine by "rules of court."

Chapter 1, Section 4. Juries

The method of selecting jurymen, if jury trials are desired, might be fixed by the bylaws. The question of whether jury verdicts should be by unanimous vote or majority vote should receive consideration; so, too, should the question of whether the losing party in a civil case should be required to pay costs to meet the jurymen's fees. If so, it might be provided that either party demanding a jury trial in a civil action should file a bond for the payment of jury fees. The following provision on the oath of jurymen is found in the laws of the Muskogee Nation:

> *Section 110.* No person shall be competent to sit on any case as juryman until he has taken an oath, administered by the proper officer, to decide according to law and evidence, without favor or partiality. (Compiled Laws, 1893, Chapter 3)

Chapter 1, Section 5. Clerks

The tribe may wish to leave the selection of clerks with the tribal council or with the court itself, rather than with the superintendent. In this case the bylaws might provide for the designation by the tribal council of an appropriate government employee for the office of court clerk, or else might provide for the regular employment of such an official by the tribal council. In the latter case, of course, it would be necessary for the tribe to provide for any salary for such official.

Chapter 1, Section 6. Records

No changes suggested.

Chapter 1, Section 7. Professional Attorneys

Where laws and court procedure are too complicated and too difficult for some members of a community to understand, one of two things is necessary: either a system of pleading by lawyers must be introduced, or else the laws and court procedure must be simplified.

If the former alternative is adopted, the tribal council or the court might be authorized to determine who should be permitted to plead before the tribal courts and to control the conduct of such individuals. Of course, it is not necessary that persons should have a professional law training in order to practice before tribal courts. Knowledge of the applicable laws, ordinances, and regulations should be a sufficient qualification, if the applicant is of good character. The following provision on the admission of attorneys to practice before tribal courts is found in the laws of the Muskogee Nation:

> *Section 137 [Attorneys at Law].* Any person of good moral character, desiring to practice law before any District Court of this Nation, shall be privileged to do so by applying to one of the District Judges, who shall grant him a commission to practice law in that district, for which he shall pay the sum of ten ($10.00) dollars; and any person of good moral character desiring to practice in all the courts of this Nation, shall be permitted to do so by making application to one of the Supreme Judges, receiving a commission and paying twenty ($20.00) dollars for the same.
>
> *Section 138 [Unfaithfulness of Attorneys at Law].* Any attorney at law who shall be found guilty of unfaithfulness or deception in any way toward his client by accepting, receiving, or agreeing to receive any fee or present from any source by which the interests of his client shall be in any way endangered, shall be silenced from the bar of this Nation and prohibited from further practice before any of the Courts thereof, and shall be fined in the penal sum of one hundred ($100.00) dollars. (Compiled Laws, 1893, Chapter 3)

The following attorney's oath is prescribed by the laws of the Cherokee Nation:

> *Section 618.* Any person obtaining a license to practice law shall, before he is allowed to appear as an attorney in any court, take the following oath:
>
> "I do solemnly swear, that I will, to the best of my knowledge and ability, support and defend all causes that may be entrusted to my care and that in so doing, I will be true to the court and to the constitution and laws of the Cherokee Nation. So help me God." (Compiled Laws, 1892, Chapter 12, Article 9)

The laws of the Cherokee Nation likewise provide that judges and other tribal officials may not appear as lawyers before a tribal court:

> *Section 622.* No judge appointed under the authority of this Nation, shall be allowed to appear as counsel or attorney and practice law in the courts of this Nation.
>
> *Section 623.* Members of the executive council, and the executive secretary of the Cherokee Nation, are hereby prohibited from practicing

law, as attorneys, before any of the courts of the Cherokee Nation. (Compiled Laws, 1892, Chapter 12, Article 9)

Chapter 1, Section 8. Fines and Penalties

The bylaws might well provide for the supervision of work to be performed by way of judicial penalty. Likewise, the receipt and disposition of fine should be regulated by a specific provision.

Chapter 1, Section 9. Removal of Judges

As in the matter of appointments, an Indian tribe might wish to provide that judges shall be removed either by the tribal council or by the people at large, through a recall vote (see Section 11 of this memorandum), rather than by the Commissioner of Indian Affairs. The proposed constitution of the Pima Community provides:

> *Section 18.* Judges and police may be removed from office at any time by the action of four-fifths of the Council. (Article II)

Chapter 1, Section 10. Complaints

In some tribes it may be desirable to have oral rather than written complaints in civil cases. The laws of the Muskogee Nation contain the following provisions on the commencement of a civil action:

> *Section 103.* Any person wishing to enter suit before any of the District Courts of this Nation shall, in person or by attorney, appear before the District Judge and make known such wishes, stating the names of all persons whom he desires to have summoned as witnesses in his behalf, and the name or names of the person or persons against whom he wishes to institute suit; and it shall be the duty of the Captain of the Light Horse to summon such witness or witnesses to appear at the next session of the Court.
>
> *Section 104.* When the defendant is a citizen of a different district from that of the person suing, the person suing shall appear before the Judge of the district wherein the defendant resides and there enter suit.
>
> *Section 105.* In order that the parties against whom suit is instituted may prepare for trial, it shall be the duty of the Judge to give them due

notice, informing them of the nature of the suit and by whom instituted. Both the defendant or defendants and all witnesses shall be summoned at least ten days before the meeting of the Court.

Section 106. After all parties have been duly notified by the proper authority, and a decision has been reached, such decision shall be final, whether all parties were present or absent, unless the parties who have been absent during trial appear before the Judge within twenty days after the decision and render proper reasons for non-attendance, in which event another trial shall be allowed. (Compiled Laws, 1893, Chapter 3)

Chapter 1, Section 11. Witnesses

It may be questioned whether the superintendent should have power to issue subpoenas for attendance at a tribal court.

The matter of witness fees deserves consideration. The following provisions on this point are found in the laws of the Muskogee Nation:

> *Section 107.* Any person or persons, instituting a suit before any of the Courts of this Nation, when obtaining a summons for that purpose, shall file a bond, with sufficient security satisfactory to the presiding Judge, for the payment of such witnesses as he or she shall summon; and the defendant shall be required to file a bond or of the same nature for the payment of such witnesses as he or she shall cause to be summoned.
>
> *Section 108.* After the decision in a civil suit has been reached, should either party refuse to settle with the witnesses in accordance with the bond given, the Judge shall order his Light Horsemen to seize and sell any property belonging to such party until the amount of cost is collected.
>
> * * * * *
>
> *Section 111.* No person shall be allowed to testify in any of the Courts of this Nation without first taking an oath, administered by the proper authority, to testify according to the whole truth and nothing but the truth.
>
> *Section 112.* Each witness who attends Court in obedience to his summons by the proper authority shall be allowed one ($1.00) dollar per day while in service. (Compiled Laws, 1893, Chapter 3)

Chapter 1, Section 12. Warrants to Apprehend

Again, the question of whether a superintendent should have power to issue warrants, in matters properly within the jurisdiction of the tribal court, requires consideration.

Chapter 1, Section 13. Appeal

In most, but not all, American courts there is a right of appeal from the decision of a trial judge to some appellate body. It is generally thought that this right of appeal is a useful protection against the possibility of injustice.

On the other hand, many who have studied the question believe that the system of appeals is a serious obstacle to the proper administration of justice, because it causes long delays in situations where one of the two parties may not be able to bear any delay and because it constitutes an additional source of expense and tends to create disrespect for the position of trial judge.

Whether there should be a right of appeal from the decision of a tribal court and, if so, whether that right should be limited to cases of a serious nature are questions that each tribe must decide for itself.

Chapter 1, Section 14. Appeal Board

If appeals are to be permitted, the question arises: To what body shall this appeal be taken? The departmental Law and Order Regulations provide for appeals to an "Appeal Board." The following alternative methods of appeal should be considered:

1. Where there are more than two judges on a single reservation, appeals might be taken from the decision of a single judge to the entire body of judges, including the original judge, or to the judges other than the original judge.
2. An appellate court, with special judges, might be created on the reservation.
3. Appeals might be taken to the tribal council. A special vote of two-thirds or three-fourths, or even a unanimous vote, might be required for the reversal of a judicial decision.
4. Appeals might be taken by popular referendum. It would probably be advisable to limit the cases that could be put to referendum to matters of great importance affecting the entire tribe, such as decisions

holding some act of the tribal council or of a tribal officer to be
unconstitutional or invalid.

5. Finally, if the tribe so desires, a system of appeals from the tribal
   courts to the Secretary of the Interior, or to some other designated
   official of the Interior Department, could be arranged.

Through appropriate *legislation*, it might be provided that appeals from
tribal courts should be taken either to state or to federal courts.

Chapter 1, Section 15. Civil Actions

A schedule of costs might be included in the bylaws or placed within the
authority of the tribal council or the court itself to promulgate. The bylaws
of the Laguna Pueblo Indians contain the following provision:

> *Section 11.* That both the plaintiff and defendant shall each pay a
> fee of 50 cents for each and all cases which they may bring before the
> court for action.

Chapter 1, Section 16. Prisoners

Again, on reservations which have adopted constitutions, it may be questioned whether the *superintendent* ought to exercise any authority over
agreements for the care of Indian prisoners, such as Section 16 of the departmental Law and Order Regulations confers.

Chapter 1, Section 17. Commitments

In connection with the commitment of a person accused of tribal offenses, it
may be thought desirable to establish a regular system for preliminary hear-
ings as is provided in the following terms by the laws of the Muskogee
Nation:

> *Section 130 [Preliminary Examination].* Whenever the Prosecuting
> Attorney is seeking evidence upon which to base criminal prosecutions, he
> may have parties brought before the Judge of the District and there exam-
> ine them under oath.
> *Section 131.* If at such preliminary examinations any party shall have
> testified to certain facts, and shall at the regular trial so testify as to falsify

the preliminary testimony, and such falsification shall be willful, such party shall be guilty of perjury, and, upon conviction, shall suffer the penalty prescribed for perjury. (Compiled Laws, 1893, Chapter 3)

Chapter 1, Section 18. Search Warrants

No changes suggested.

Chapter 1, Section 19. Signatures

Provision might be made, at this point in the bylaws, for the design of judicial seals.

Chapter 1, Section 20. Power to Sign for Superintendent

This provision will be unnecessary if the power of the superintendent to sign subpoenas, warrants, etc., is terminated.

Chapter 1, Section 21. Substitute Judge

The matter of substitute judges is covered by the following sections of the laws of the Muskogee Nation:

Section 102. Should any District Judge, by sickness or other hindrance, be prevented from holding Court, at any time specified by law, he shall call a session at as near that time as he may deem best, but no District Court shall sit at one session for a longer time than twelve days.

* * * * *

Section 126. No Judge of any of the courts of this Nation shall engage in the trial of any case, nor shall any Prosecuting Attorney engage in the prosecution of any cause, where either of the interested parties are blood relations of said Judge or Prosecuting Attorney within the third degree.

Section 127. When the Judge or Prosecuting Attorney are related as above mentioned to the parties or either of the parties are interested, it shall be the duty of the Principal Chief to make *pro tem* appointments for said offices; said *pro tem* officers shall have administered to them by the regular officer the oath of office, and they shall only hold their *pro tem* appointments during the course of the trial for which they shall have been appointed. (Compiled Laws, 1893, Chapter 3)

Chapter 1, Section 22. Bail or Bond

The same laws of the Muskogee Nation provide, with respect to bail bonds:

> *Section 140 [Bond for Appearance in Court]*. Any citizen of this Nation who may be arraigned before the Court upon a charge of criminal offense, except murder, may be released from custody upon his giving bond for appearance and trial, in such sum as shall be determined by the Judge, with one or more sureties, who shall state, under oath, that he or they are possessed of property to the amount of the bond over and above his or their personal liabilities; and if any person after executing bond as herein required shall fail to appear at Court at the required time, and his sureties shall fail to cause his appearance within twenty days thereafter, then the bond shall be forfeited, and the amount collected by the Light Horsemen under the orders of the Court; and the officer collecting the bond shall receive 25 per cent thereof for his fee, and the remainder shall be turned into the National Treasury. (Compiled Laws, 1893, Chapter 3)

Chapter 1, Section 23. Restitution

No changes suggested.

Chapter 1, Section 24. Copies of Laws

No doubt an organized tribe will add authenticated copies of all tribal resolutions and ordinances to its court "library."

Chapter 1, Section 25. Parole

Consideration should be given to the question of whether the power to grant parole, reprieve, or absolute pardon should lie with the sentencing court, the tribal council, or some official of the tribe, such as the governor or the president of the council.

Chapter 1, Section 26. Interference with Court

No changes suggested.

Chapter 1, Section 27. Jurisdiction over Indian Employees

No changes suggested.

Arbitration

The matter of arbitration, not considered in the departmental Law and Order Regulations, may find a place in a tribal judicial code. The following provision, taken from the laws of the Choctaw Nation, may serve as a model:

Section XVI. Arbitration.

1. Be it enacted by the general council of the Choctaw nation assembled: When an arbitrator or arbitrators are chosen by two or more persons to decide and settle any matters in controversy, it will be necessary for each person in controversy to furnish their arbitrator or arbitrators all proofs, facts, and statements, or any evidence they may possess in finding the case, and upon impartial trial of the same by the arbitrators, as well as his or their opinion and judgment rendered on the matter in controversy, [the finding] shall be as final and binding on all the persons concerned in choosing an arbitration as if it were done in any court of justice. But in case the arbitrators cannot agree in forming a decision on any case before them, they shall have the right of choosing an umpire whose decision shall be final and conclusive. When a decision is rendered by an arbitrator or arbitrators on any matter in controversy, such decision shall be recorded in the nearest county court. (Compiled Laws, 1894, Laws governing Judicial Department)

Extradition

Another matter not specifically covered in the departmental Law and Order Regulations is the matter of extradition. The bylaws of a tribe may provide not only that the tribal authorities shall surrender persons to be tried in other jurisdictions (as provided in Chapter 1, Section 1, of the departmental Law and Order Regulations), but also that the proper authorities of the tribe may demand the return of persons arrested in other jurisdiction who have committed an offense against the tribe in question. Whether or not federal or state authorities would heed such requests for extradition is questionable and would depend upon the controlling state or federal statutes. Undoubtedly, however, such a request for extradition directed to *another Indian tribe* would be entitled to recognition. The following provision on the subject of extradition is taken from the laws of the Cherokee Nation:

> *Section 20.* Whenever it shall appear to the satisfaction of the Principal Chief that any person charged with a capital or other criminal offense has fled beyond the jurisdiction of the Cherokee Nation, and taken refuge in any other country, he shall make requisition upon the executive authority of such country for the arrest and rendition to the lawful authorities of the Cherokee Nation of the person so accused. (Compiled Laws, 1892, Chapter 1, Article 1)

Rules of Court

Since it may be necessary for a court to promulgate rules and regulations for the conduct of its business in matters not covered by the bylaws or ordinances of the tribe, some such provision as the following, taken from the laws of the Cherokee Nation, may prove useful:

Article XV. General Rules
> *Section 245.* Each court shall have the right to make and enforce such regulations for the orderly transaction of business and the preservation of order in and about the court, during its sessions, as may be deemed necessary and proper, and which shall not be in violation of law; and for every contempt or disrespect offered, or obstruction of business by the improper conduct of individuals, the court may impose a fine on any such person so offending of not less than one, nor more than fifty dollars at its discretion. (Compiled Laws, 1892, Chapter 3)

Chapter 4 [Civil Actions], Section 1. Law Applicable in Civil Actions

No changes suggested.

Chapter 4, Section 2. Judgments in Civil Actions

No changes suggested.

Enforcement of Judgments

Usually it will be found that a flexible provision on civil judgments, such as that prescribed by Chapter 4, Section 2, of the departmental Law and Order

Regulations, will make unnecessary any detailed provisions on the execution of such judgments. Under the provision cited, a tribal court will, when the defendant is unable to pay a given obligation in money, require such defendant either to turn over specific goods for the benefit of the injured party or else to perform specified labor for his benefit.

Where it is thought that these matters should be specifically provided in the tribal judicial code, instead of being left to the discretion of the judge, the following provisions on executions, taken from the laws of the Osage Nation, may prove suggestive:

> *Section 8.* That in all cases where a debt may be contracted, and it is agreed that property or trade shall be taken in payment of such debt, judgment shall be rendered accordingly; and the officer shall proceed to levy on the property of such debtor and to summon two disinterested citizens, who shall be sworn by him, to aid in the valuation of such property, fairly and impartially, and when such property is so valued by the sheriff and such other persons, the creditor shall receive the same at such valuation as may be fined by them.
>
> *Section 9.* The following description of property shall be exempt from sale to satisfy any debt or judgment and shall be reserved for the benefit of the owner thereof; viz: one horse or in lieu thereof, one yoke of oxen, one cow and calf, one sow and pigs, farming utensils, household and kitchen furniture, fifty bushels of corn, firearms, and one saddle and bridle, and it shall not be lawful for an officer to levy on any of the above-mentioned property.
>
> *Section 10.* When judgment is rendered, and the officer is whose hands an execution may be placed shall fail to find any property or effects in possession of the debtor to satisfy the same, and has cause to believe that some other person has in hands property or effects belonging to such debtor, the officer shall proceed to make inquiry of such person; and if such property or effects shall be pointed out, he shall proceed to make levy; but if such person shall refuse to give such information as may be satisfactory, the officer shall summon him before the clerk of the court, who shall require of him an oath to answer to the charges of holding in his possession the property or effects of such debtor.
>
> *Section 11.* It shall not be lawful for any officer to levy on the house, farm, or any other improvements, of any person or persons.

Chapter 5. The Indian Police

The departmental Law and Order Regulations on the subject of Indian police contemplate a police force entirely controlled by the superintendent of the reservation. Very likely, any tribe which sets up its own political organization will want to control its own police force, so that the departmental regulations on this subject will not be very helpful.

Normally, a police force is under the executive head of the government. Where the executive head is responsible directly to the council, the police force may be subject to the orders of the council. A simple provision on this point is that found in Rules and Regulations for Annette Islands Reserve, which provides:

> *Section 8.* The council shall have authority to employ such a number of competent persons as constables as it may deem necessary in order to enforce its ordinances, to define their duties and to fix their remuneration, if any. The constables shall be under the immediate control of the mayor or of the acting mayor, subject to the instructions of the council.

A flexible provision permitting the tribal council to establish and regulate a tribal police force, through tribal ordinances, is found in the proposed bylaws of the Quechan (Fort Yuma) Tribal Council:

> *Organization of Tribal Police Force*
> It shall be the duty of the Council to establish by ordinance a Tribal Police Force which shall have full jurisdiction upon the reservation. Such ordinances shall outline in detail the authority and duties of such Tribal Police Force and the manner in which such police force shall function. The Tribal Police Force shall be employees of the Council and shall be agents of the Tribal Court.

More-detailed provisions governing the appointment, tenure, and duties of Indian police are found in the laws of the Muskogee Nation, which contain the following provisions:

> *Section 122 [Light Horsemen].* The Light Horse Company shall be the police force of the district. They shall be elected on the third Tuesday in September, every two years, and installed by the District Judge. They shall serve all summons, make arrests, collect fines, and act as general bailiffs of the Court. The Captains of Light Horsemen shall receive the

sum of three hundred ($300.00) dollars per annum, and each of the Privates shall receive the sum of two hundred and seventy-five ($275.00) dollars per annum, and they shall be allowed to appropriate to their own use all fines collected from persons violating the law prohibiting the keeping or introduction of intoxicating liquors, and such other fines as may be provided by laws. But no citizen of this Nation shall be arrested at any election held in accordance with law, unless for breach of peace or violation of the law prohibiting the carrying of deadly weapons.

Section 123. The Light Horsemen shall collect all fines from any person who fails to obey a summons issued by the proper authority, and all fines thus collected shall be transmitted to the National Treasurer.

Section 124. Any Light Horsemen guilty of disobeying a legal order from the Judge, either by neglect or willfully, shall be removed from office. (Compiled Laws, 1893, Chapter 3)

In most American communities the office of prosecuting attorney is one distinct from the police force. Such an arrangement existed, for instance, in the Osage Nation, where the laws of the nation provided for the appointment of a prosecuting attorney by the national council upon the recommendation of the principal chief:

Article X. Duties of the Prosecuting Attorney

Section 32. The prosecuting attorney shall be elected at the same time and in the manner that executive councilors are elected, and his term of office shall be that of the National Council electing him, and such prosecuting attorney before he enters upon the duties of his office shall be commissioned by the principal chief, his compensation shall be two hundred dollars per annum.

Section 33. That it shall be the duty of the prosecuting attorney to prosecute in behalf of the Nation all persons charged with criminal offences that may be brought before the court of the Nation, and be required to take the following oath or affirmation: "You do solemnly swear that you as prosecuting attorney for and on behalf of the Nation will, to the best of your skills and ability, prosecute all persons charged with criminal offences that may be brought before the court, and that you will not take or receive any remuneration of any person charged with any criminal offence, but will be faithful to the Osage Nation in all prosecutions to the best of your ability, so help you God."

SECTION 21

BYLAWS: CODE OF MISDEMEANORS

The whole subject of penal law governing Indians is in a very complicated and chaotic state. This situation may be clarified and simplified where an Indian tribe undertakes to maintain and enforce its own penal laws, suited to its own conditions and circumstances. However, it is impossible for an Indian tribe to establish a code of laws of its own without taking into consideration the federal and state laws that are now applicable on Indian reservations. For this reason any discussion of possible provisions for an Indian tribal code of misdemeanors requires an analysis of the criminal laws which are now applicable on Indian reservations.

1. State laws are now applicable to any offenses committed by one non-Indian against another non-Indian, even though the offenses be committed on an Indian reservation. The Indian tribe is not concerned with such offenses.
2. Offenses committed by Indians outside of the reservation are subject to the same state laws that apply to other citizens. Again, the Indian tribe is not concerned with such offenses.
3. There are certain peculiar federal crimes, crimes against the United Sates, which are applicable to all citizens, both Indians and non-Indians. For purposes of jurisdiction, it makes no difference whether such crimes are committed within or outside of any Indian reservation. Such crimes, for instance, are counterfeiting, offenses against the postal service, and treason. A list of these crimes will be found in United States Code, Title 18, Part 1, Chapters 1–10. These crimes do not particularly affect the Indian tribe, even when committed by members of the tribe. Their suppression is peculiarly within the jurisdiction of the federal courts.
4. In addition to the foregoing federal criminal laws, which apply whether or not the culprit is an Indian and whether or not the offense has been committed on an Indian reservation, there are certain criminal laws

which apply peculiarly to territory under the control of the federal government. These laws cover matters which would ordinarily be subject to state laws and to state courts. But, because no state courts could exercise jurisdiction, the federal courts are authorized to enforce special federal criminal laws for such territories. These laws include laws for the punishment of murder, manslaughter, assault, attempted murder, rape, seduction, maiming, robbery, larceny, receiving stolen goods, piracy, circulating obscene literature, polygamy, unlawful cohabitation, incest, fornication, prize fighting, and certain other offenses, all of which are listed in United States Code, Title 18, Part 1, Chapter 11–13. These specific penal provisions are supplemented by a general provision, according to which any act that would be a crime under state laws, if committed in a place under state jurisdiction, is to be considered a federal crime when committed in a territory under federal jurisdiction. This is the effect of United States Code, Title 18, Section 468, which provides:

Section 468 (Criminal Code, Section 289). Offenses under State Laws
Whoever, within the territorial limits of any State, organized Territory, or District, but within or upon any of the places now existing or hereafter reserved or acquired, described in Section 272 of the Criminal Code (U.S.C., Title 18, Section 451), shall do or omit the doing of any act or thing which is not made penal by any laws of Congress, but which if committed or omitted within the jurisdiction of the State, Territory, or District in which such place is situated, by the laws thereof in force on June 1, 1933, and remaining in force at the time of the doing or omitting the doing of such act or thing, would be penal, shall be deemed guilty of a like offense and be subject to a like punishment. (As amended June 15, 1933, c. 83, 48 Stat.)

The federal laws, above discussed, have only a limited application to Indian reservations. United States Code, Title 25, Section 217, provides for the application of those laws in the following terms:

217. General Laws as to Punishment Extended to Indian Country. Except as to crimes the punishment of which is expressly provided for in this title, the general laws of the United States as to the punishment of crimes committed in any place within the sole and exclusive jurisdiction of the United States, except the District of Columbia, shall extend to the Indian country. (R.S. Sec. 2145.)

However, this provision is qualified by the succeeding provision, which contains the following language:

> *218. Exceptions as to Extension of General Laws.* The preceding sections shall not be construed to extend to crimes committed by one Indian against the person or property of another Indian, nor to any Indian committing any offense in the Indian country who has been punished by the local law of the tribe, or to any case where, by treaty stipulations, the exclusive jurisdiction over such offenses is or may be secured to the Indian tribes respectively. (R.S. Sec. 2146; February 18, 1875, c. 90, Section 1, 18 Stat. 318.)

It will be seen, then, that the federal penal laws, already discussed, applicable to territories under federal jurisdiction, will apply to offenses committed by whites against Indians and will also apply to offenses committed by Indians against whites (unless the Indian has been punished by his own tribe, in which case he cannot be published by a federal court), but do not apply at all to offenses committed by one Indian against another Indian.

The Indian tribe must leave to the federal courts the problem of punishing non-Indians who commit offenses against Indians. The Indian tribe can cooperate only to the extent of apprehending criminals and turning them over to the proper federal authorities. With respect to the punishment of Indians who commit offenses against non-Indians, the tribe may either turn such individuals over to the proper federal authorities for punishment or inflict punishment under its own authority.

5. We come finally to those federal penal laws which are applicable to crimes committed either by Indians or by non-Indians upon an Indian reservation. These laws cover the following offenses:

1. Murder	U.S. Code, Title 18, Sec. 548.
2. Manslaughter	" " " " "
3. Rape	" " " " "
4. Incest	" " " " "
5. Assault with intent to kill	" " " " "
6. Assault with a dangerous weapon	" " " " "
7. Arson	" " " " "
8. Burglary	" " " " "
9. Robbery	" " " " "
10. Larceny	" " " " "
11. Timber depredations on Indian lands	" " " " 104

12. Starting fires on Indian lands	"	"	"	" 107
13. Breaking fences or driving cattle on enclosed public lands	"	"	"	" 110
14. Inducing conveyances by Indians of trust interest in lands	"	"	"	" 115
15. Receipt of money under prohibited contracts	"	"	25	" 83
16. Purchases or grants of land from Indians "	"	"	"	" 177
17. Driving stock to feed on Indian lands	"	"	"	" 179
18. Settling on or surveying lands belonging to Indians by treaty	"	"	"	" 180
19. Sale of cattle purchased by government to nontribal members	"	"	"	" —
20. Arson (by non-Indians, or by Indian against non-Indian)	"	"	"	" 212
21. Assault with intent to kill (by non-Indian or by Indian against non-Indian)	"	"	"	" 213
22. Disposing or removing cattle from Indian country	"	"	"	" 214
23. Hunting on Indian lands	"	"	"	" 216
24. Selling intoxicating liquors: sale to Indians or introducing into liquor into Indian country	"	"	"	241, " 241a
25. Possession of intoxicating liquors in Indian country	"	"	"	" 244
26. Setting up distillery	"	"	"	" 251
27. Trading without license	"	"	"	" 264
28. Prohibited purchases and sales	"	"	"	" 265
29. Sale of arms	"	"	"	" 266

While this list of offenses may seem rather long considering the peaceable character of most Indians, it will be observed that dozens, and perhaps hundreds, of offenses punishable under the laws of most states are not made punishable by any federal laws when committed by one Indian against another Indian on an Indian reservation. Such offenses, for instance, as disorderly conduct, simple assault, adultery, embezzlement, forgery, and kidnapping are not covered by any applicable federal laws. An examination of any state criminal code will reveal many other crimes not covered by any applicable federal laws.

Each Indian tribe which undertakes the task of self-government will be expected to draw up a code of misdemeanors suitable to the conditions which obtain among the members of the tribe, and to enforce this code. Such a code will be, in effect, supplementary to the federal laws and will deal primarily with matters not covered by federal laws. No objection is seen, however, to the exercise of tribal jurisdiction over minor offenses, such as petty larceny, which are theoretically subject to federal prosecution, but which actually do not receive proper attention in the federal courts.

Heretofore, the suppression of offenses which are not covered by special federal statutes has been attempted by the Department of the Interior, acting through Courts of Indian Offenses or directly through superintendents, without the advice or consent of the Indians concerned. This arrangement has been, on the whole, very unsatisfactory. It is expected that when the Indians themselves assume responsibility for the maintenance of law and order in their own communities, the situation will be very much improved.

An Indian tribe that so desires may use the Code of Tribal Offenses included in Chapter 2 of the Law and Order Regulations recently promulgated by the Interior Department as a model for its own tribal code of misdemeanors. If this is done, it may be found desirable to eliminate some of the enumerated penal provisions, to add other provisions, to simplify or otherwise change the definitions of the various offenses, and to modify the attached penalties. In particular, the fines fixed in the departmental Law and Order Regulations may be entirely too high on certain reservations and at the same time entirely too low on other reservations. In any attempt to set fines for specified offenses, more definite than the flexible departmental provisions which contain a maximum but no minimum, it should be remembered that a fixed fine will fall *unequally* upon the well-to-do Indian and the needy Indian. Equality of punishment demands inequality of money fines in accordance with inequality of wealth.

Any tribe may, of course, instead of using the departmental Law and Order Regulations as a model, use the penal code of the state in which it is situated, or the municipal codes of ordinances of neighboring towns, as models. In general, these codes will be found very much more comprehensive and more detailed than the Code of Tribal Offenses drawn up by the Interior Department.

SECTION 22

BYLAWS: LAW OF DOMESTIC RELATIONS

An organized Indian tribe must decide for itself whether it will assume jurisdiction over marriages and divorces or will leave such matters wholly to state authorities.

If the tribe itself wishes to have its own laws of marriage and divorce, it might be advisable to include those laws in the written bylaws of the tribe so as to eliminate any question as to their binding force.

Whether any particular civil or religious ceremony is to be required in order to validate a marriage, whether marriages by tribal custom are to be recognized, and, if so, what formalities tribal custom requires are questions which each tribe must decide for itself. In reaching a reasonable decision on these controversial matters, a tribe should consider the ease or difficulty with which members of the tribe may secure state marriage licenses or divorce decrees, the need for maintaining accurate records of marriage for the purpose of determining heirs and for other administrative purposes, and the respect and dignity due to the marriage relationship.

The following laws on marriage and divorce, taken from the laws of the Cherokee Nation, may serve as a useful guide in a discussion of tribal laws on this subject:

Article XX. Marriage and Divorce

Section 92. Marriage, so far as its validity in law is concerned, is a civil contract, to which the consent of the parties, capable in law of contracting, is essential.

Section 93. Every male person who shall have attained the age of eighteen years, and every female person who shall have attained the age of fifteen years, shall be capable in law of contracting marriage, if otherwise competent. But in all cases where the male is less than eighteen years of age, and the female less than fifteen years of age, the consent of the mother, father, or guardian of such minor shall be given; otherwise such marriage shall be null and void, unless it shall appear that the parties have no parent or guardian then living and at the time of marriage are self-dependent.

Section 94. No marriage shall be contracted whilst either of the parties has a husband or wife living; nor between parties who are nearer of kin than first cousins, whether of the half or of the whole blood; nor between parties who are insane or idiotic.

Section 95. Marriages may be solemnized by any of the judges of the courts of this Nation, or by the clerks of the several districts, or by any ordained minister of the Gospel in regular communion with any religious society. And any marriage contracted in writing in the presence of two or more attending witnesses, who shall sign the marriage contract as such, shall be lawful.

Section 96. No particular form of marriage shall be required in the solemnization of marriages, except that the parties shall solemnly declare in the presence of the judge, clerk, or minister officiating, or the attending witnesses, that they take each other as husband and wife, *provided* that citizens of the United Sates, or those of other than Indian nationalities, inter-marrying among the Cherokees, shall first comply with the law governing such cases.

Section 97. It shall be the duty of all persons contracting marriage in the presence of witnesses, or who shall, within the Nation, join two citizens thereof in wedlock, or who shall so join a citizen thereof with a citizen of any other government, to report the same to the clerk of the district in which such marriage was solemnized, for registration, giving the names of the contracting parties, their ages and previous places of residence, and the clerk shall at once make record of the same, in a book to be kept for that purpose.

Section 98. Every person, a citizen of this Nation, who shall, within the Nation, violate the provisions of this act, by joining minors in the bonds of matrimony without the consent of the father, mother, or guardian, except as hereinbefore expressly provided, shall be liable to a fine in any sum not exceeding one hundred dollars, or to imprisonment not exceeding six months, as the discretion of the court having jurisdiction.

Section 99. All marriages which are herein prohibited on account of consanguinity between the parties, or on account of either of them having a former husband or wife then living, shall be absolutely void in this Nation, without any judgment of divorce or other legal proceeding, *provided* that the issue from such unlawful marriage shall nevertheless be legitimate; *provided,* also, that when the man, having by a woman one or more children, shall afterwards intermarry with such woman, such child or children, if recognized by him, or proven to be his, shall thereby be legitimate.

Section 100. A divorce from the bonds of matrimony may be adjudged by the circuit courts of this Nation, on action brought in the district where the parties or one of them reside, on application by petition or complaint of the aggrieved party.

Section 101. Actions for divorce shall be conducted in the same manner as any other actions in courts, and the court shall have power to enforce its judgments as to other cases; and when a judgment of divorce from the bonds of matrimony is granted in this Nation by a court of competent authority, such judgment shall fully and completely dissolve the marriage contract as to both parties.

Section 102. A divorce from the bonds of matrimony may be adjudged for any of the following causes: viz., for adultery; for imprisonment for three years or more; for willful desertion and neglect for the term of one year next preceding the filing of the complaint or petition; for extreme cruelty, whether by violence or other means; and for habitual drunkenness for one year immediately preceding the filing of the complaint or petition.

Section 103. The court in granting a divorce shall, in all cases where there are minor children of the parties divorced, make such order concerning the care, custody, and maintenance of such children as it shall deem proper and just, having due regard to the age and sex of the same.

Section 104. When a judgment of divorce has been granted, and the parties shall afterwards intermarry, the court, upon their joint application, and upon satisfactory proof of such marriage, may revoke all judgments or orders of divorce, alimony, and subsistence, which will not affect the rights of third persons. (Complied Laws, 1881, Chapter 12)

The following provision, recognizing existing marriage, is taken from the laws of the Muskogee Nation, compiled 1892, Chapter 23:

Section 308. From and after the passage of this act, all marriages between citizens, who are now living together as man and wife, are hereby legalized.

A particularly critical problem exists on some reservations where white men may be tempted to marry women of the tribe in order to share in tribal property. An attempt to bar such intermarriages takes form in Sections 4 to 7 of the proposed constitution of the Pima Community, cited in Section 4 of this memorandum.

The following laws on this subject were established by the Cherokee Nation in an effort to protect the property and the womanhood of the nation against unscrupulous whites:

Article XV. Intermarriage with White Men and Foreigners
    Section 66. Whereas the peace and prosperity of the Cherokee people require, that, in the enforcement of the laws, jurisdiction should be exercised over all persons whatever, who may from time to time be privileged to reside within the territorial limits of this Nation, therefore every white man, or citizen of the United States, or of any foreign state or government desiring money, a Cherokee, Delaware, or Shawnee (December 10, 1880) woman citizen of the Nation shall be and is hereby required to obtain a license for the same from any of the district clerks of the several districts, and make the oath or satisfactory showing to such clerk that he has not a surviving wife from whom he has not been lawfully divorced. And unless such information be freely furnished to the satisfaction of the clerk, no license shall issue.
    Section 67. Every white man or person applying for license, as provided in the preceding section of this act, shall, before obtaining the same, be required to present to the said clerk a certificate of good moral character, signed by at least ten (10) respectable citizens of the Cherokee Nation who are Cherokees, Delawares, or Shawnees by blood and who shall have been acquainted with him at least six months immediately preceding the signing of such certificate, together with a "certificate of good moral character, signed by the county clerk, and sealed with the seal of the county of which he was last a voter." (December 10, 1880)
    Section 68. Before any license as herein provided shall be issued, the person applying shall be, and is hereby, required to pay to the clerk to whom application is made the sum of five dollars, for the benefit of said clerk, and additional sum of five dollars for the benefit of the Cherokee Nation; and all sums, so received for the benefit of the Nation, shall be turned over by the clerk to the national treasurer on the first Monday in November of each year, beginning with 1881 (December 10, 1880) and be also required to take the following oath:
    "I do solemnly swear, that I will honor, defend, and submit to the constitution and laws of the Cherokee Nation, and will neither claim, nor seek, from the United Sates, or any other government, or from the judicial tribunals thereof, any protection, privilege, or redress incompatible with the

same, as guaranteed to the Cherokee Nation by the United States in treaty stipulations entered into between them. So help me God."

Section 69. Marriages contracted under the provisions of this act shall be solemnized as provided by the laws of this Nation, or otherwise shall be null and void.

Section 70. No marriage between a citizen of the United States or of any foreign nation and a female citizen of this Nation, entered into within the limits of this Nation except as hereinbefore authorized and provided, shall be legal; and every person who shall engage or assist in solemnizing any such marriage shall, upon conviction before any district court of this Nation, be fined one hundred dollars; and it shall be the duty of the solicitor of the district in which such person may reside to collect the same, for his services, to twenty-five per cent of the amount collected and shall place the remainder into the hands of the treasurer to be by him credited to the general fund.

Section 71. Every person performing the marriage ceremony, under the authority of a license provided for herein, shall be required to attach a certificate of marriage to the back of the license and return it to the person in whose behalf it was issued, who shall within thirty days therefrom place the same in the hands of the district clerk, whose duty it shall be to record the same and return it to the owner.

Section 72. Every adopted citizen of the Cherokee Nation, by marriage or otherwise, who shall use the intercourse law or laws (as they are termed) in the prosecution of a Cherokee Indian, for any criminal offense committed within the limits of the Cherokee Nation, shall forfeit his rights of citizenship to the same, and be subject to be dealt with as other intruders in the country, and shall be removed out of this Nation.

Section 73. Should any man or woman, a citizen of the United States or of any foreign country, become a citizen of the Cherokee Nation by intermarriage and be left a widow or widower by the decease of the Cherokee wife or husband, such surviving widow or widower shall continue to enjoy the rights of citizenship, unless he or she shall marry a white man or woman, or person (as the case may be) having no rights of Cherokee citizenship by blood; in that case, all of his or her rights acquired under the provisions of this act shall cease.

Section 74. Every person who shall lawfully marry under the provisions of this act, and afterwards abandon his wife, shall thereby forfeit every right and privilege or citizenship of this Nation.

Section 75. Property of every description, possessed within the limits of the Cherokee Nation by an adopted citizen, shall, in case such adopted citizen abandon his wife without lawful cause, be the absolute property of such wife, or wife and her children. But whenever such abandonment shall be planned or effected by the wife for the purpose of ridding herself of her husband, then and in that case such wife shall be entitled to only such property as shall be awarded—upon application of either party for divorce—by the court having jurisdiction.

Where a tribe does not desire to assume jurisdiction in divorce cases, it may adopt some such provision as the following, found in the bylaws of the Laguna Pueblo Indians:

> *Section 3.* That no divorces shall be granted by the officers of the Pueblo of Laguna. They shall have the right, however, to examine the case and try to mutually adjust the matter, if possible, by giving wholesome advice to the parties concerned. Should they find a probable reason for divorce, they shall advise the complaining party to take his or her case before the proper State Authorities for further action in the case.

SECTION 23

BYLAWS: PROPERTY

Perhaps the most important part of the body of laws of any community is that part which deals with the property of the community and its members. The most basic human right is the right to security against privation and want. Without the food, shelter, and other materials needed for healthy and happy living, one cannot enjoy any other human rights. These things must be enjoyed by all the members of any society if that society is to be successful and stable.

In most Indian tribes the chief source of livelihood is the land. The most important problem to which such a tribe can give its thought in laying the foundations of its future social existence is the problem of land tenure.

Of course, it must depend, in part at least, upon a man's own efforts whether he is able to enjoy the material things that a good life requires. A community of lazy and inefficient individuals can be prosperous only if it preys upon some other community. But work alone does not guarantee security. If a man does not own the tools and materials of production and can secure the use of such tools or materials only by hiring out his labor to another, he must work for what another man is willing to pay, must work for another's profit rather than for his own livelihood. The system of property ownership under which a man works will, therefore, determine whether he is to enjoy the product of his own labor. Under a system which permits some men to receive an income without working, others will have to share part of what they produce with those who do not work.

If any Indian tribe wishes to perpetuate a system of individual ownership of land which allows sales or leases of allotments to outsiders, or simply to members of the tribe, it is inevitable that a time will come (as it has already come to many Indian and white societies) when many men will find themselves landless, homeless, and without means of support, while others will be prosperous.

If any Indian tribe desires, upon mature consideration of the problem, to live under such an individualistic system, the Indian Office will not object. The Indian Office will continue the attempt to relieve the distress of the unfortunate and to assist the more fortunate members of such a community to keep the land they have thus far held.

On the other hand, a tribe in which the wealthy Indians will make no sacrifices of any sort for the benefit of their own relatives and tribesmen cannot reasonably ask the non-Indian taxpayers of the United States to be more generous. When lands are to be bought and credit made available for Indians, those communities will receive special consideration which have attempted to set up a system of land ownership that promises security to the present and future members of the tribe.

In the rich experience of the Indian race, certain eminently satisfactory arrangements for the ownership and management of land have been evolved. In general, those Indian tribes which have been permitted to control their own affairs in matters of land ownership have insisted on the principle that land shall not be owned by an individual unless it can be used by an individual, and that those lands which can most profitably and most efficiently be used by the entire community shall be owned by the entire community. This means, concretely, that such lands as are to be used by individuals for homes, gardens, etc., shall be possessed by individuals, and that grazing lands and other resources, such as oil, coal, timber, and water power, which cannot be effectively developed and utilized by single individuals, shall be owned by the tribe as a whole.

This general principle will find different application on different reservations. The amount of land that an individual may properly use for himself and his family will vary with the fertility of the land and with the available methods of agriculture. The nature of the lands and resources that require community development will vary from reservation to reservation.

The following applications of this general principle are worthy of consideration.

In the Pueblo of Laguna, unimproved lands are owned by the pueblo itself. This is provided for in Section 5 of the Bylaws of the Laguna Pueblo Indians:

> That all the members of the Pueblo are declared co-owners of all lands of the Pueblo that are *unimproved*. Unimproved land shall mean all lands belonging to the Pueblo of Laguna, except that which has been granted to the various members of the Pueblo, by the officers thereof, for cultivating or other purposes as may be designated by the officers.

Such lands may be used by any members of the pueblo, but those whose flocks or herds exceed a certain number must pay a regular grazing fee for the use of the land.

In addition to grazing land, the pueblo is the sole owner of all natural resources on the reservation so that, in case of the discovery of any minerals, all members of the pueblo would benefit. The pueblo is likewise the owner of property used for public purposes, such as community buildings and plazas.

Individual possession is granted to members of the pueblo in accordance with the following provision of the Laguna constitution:

> When any member of the Pueblo desires a piece of unimproved Pueblo land, he shall select his land and then make his application for same to the officers then in charge of the Pueblo. If the officers decide to grant him the land, or any part thereof, they shall mark out the boundaries of same. The Grantee shall thereafter have full possession of said land, unless the officers have cause to dispossess him for the violation of the Pueblo Laws regarding same, hereto attached. (Section 16)

This provision is supplemented by the following recently proposed amendments to the Laguna bylaws:

> *Section 6.* Time limit for making improvements upon land allotted to individual members by the Officers shall be 3 years and following clauses to be incorporated:
>
> *Clause 1.* The safeguarding of minor children whose parents are deceased, as to ownership to such allotments previously made to such minors' deceased parents.
>
> *Clause 2.* In case of sickness or disabilities from other causes to any allottee, which would be the means of preventing such allottee from carrying out good and honest intentions toward making desired improvements within the 3-year-limit period, said allottee shall not be subject to forfeiture at a period of such disability.
>
> *Clause 3.* Unmarried sons and daughters of families, when still under parental roof, are not eligible for allotments; only at a time when such sons and daughters shall have become married, then such allotments of land shall be made.

The amounts of land assigned are now fixed by the following schedule:

Allotments of Unimproved Community Land

Allotments of unimproved land for farming, under irrigation ditches: Size as follows: 5 chs. long by 4 chs. wide

Dry-land farming land, not under irrigation ditches, but solely dependent on rain: Size as follows: 6 chs. long by 5 chs. wide

Land allotments for homes and corrals: For residences or homes, to be as follows: ½ chs. all around

Allotments for corrals, as follows: ½ chs. all round

Additional allotments for home-yard space to be allotted only after the building or buildings are erected.

It will be noted that no fee need be paid by the individual who desires a plot of land to cultivate and improve. By performing the necessary work the individual secures complete possession of the land, although title remains in the pueblo. The retention of title by the pueblo is important because it makes it impossible for the individual to lose his land to any outsider and thus safeguards Indians ownership. But for all practical purposes, the individual is the owner of the land on which he lives. Thus Section 6 of the Laguna bylaws provides:

> That the right of full possession shall be guaranteed to any member of the Pueblo holding lands granted to them by the officers of the Pueblo for cultivation or other purposes: *Provided* that no member holding said lands shall rent same to an alien, or if it is land secured for cultivating purposes, he shall cultivate same within *two years* from the date he was given possession. Any violation of the above provision shall be sufficient cause for the officers to dispossess him of said land. He shall have the right, however, to rent or sell said lands to any other member of the Pueblo after he has secured permanent possession of same.

Under the laws of the pueblo, this individual ownership does not carry with it an unlimited right to dispose of the land. Thus, it is provided that leases to outsiders may be made only by the officers of the pueblo. The purpose of this provision is to safeguard the entire community against the danger of unwise arrangements with outsiders which an individual might make and which might bring undesirable aliens into the community, or open the way to undesirable trades or practices, or allow outsiders to take up lands needed by members of the Indian community.

These purposes are secured by the following provisions:

That no lease of land shall be given to any person not a member of this Pueblo for any purpose whatever, except by decision of the officers of the Pueblo of Laguna assembled for that purpose. The officers of the Pueblo will then have the power to execute such lease in the name of the Pueblo; and all such leases must be signed by all of the court officers of the Pueblo, otherwise it shall be null and void.

A somewhat similar arrangement to that found at the Pueblo of Laguna is established by the constitutional charter of the Eastern Band of Cherokee Indians. This charter provides:

Section 22. That the council of the Eastern Band of Cherokee Indians shall direct the management and control of all property, either real or personal, belonging to the band as a corporation; but no person shall be entitled to the enjoyment of any lands belonging to the Eastern Band of Cherokee Indians as a corporation or a tribe, or any profits accruing therefrom, or any money which may belong to said band as a corporation or as a tribe, unless such person be of at least one-sixteenth of Eastern Cherokee blood, and in case that any money derived from any source whatever, belonging to the Eastern Band of Cherokee Indians, shall be distributed among the members thereof, the same shall be divided per capita among the members entitled thereto.

Under this authority the band has adopted the following resolution on the distribution of tribal lands:

Whereas the land belonging to the Eastern Band of Cherokee Indians is limited in extent, and whereas it is necessary that it be utilized to the fullest extent possible for the benefits of the Indians who are members of the tribe: be it RESOLVED by the Eastern Band of Cherokee Indians in council assembled,

(1) That in assigning holdings from the tribal lands to individual Indians it shall be understood and agreed by all concerned that the one to whom the holding is assigned must make bona fide entry on said lands within a period of 12 months from the date of said assignment; that during each year for the first 5 years after the holding is assigned the individual must clear and put into cultivation 1 acre of land (1 acre per year making a total of 5 acres in 5 years); that the Indian assigned the holding must within 2 years construct a suitable home on said holding; and that all laws and

regulations regarding the cutting or disposition of timber on said holding must be complied with in spirit and in letter;

(2) That any Indian to whom a holding of land has been assigned who abandons same and fails to utilize it during a period of 5 years shall forfeit all right, interest, and title to same which shall revert to the band;

(3) That the provisions of Sections 1 and 2 above shall apply equally to all members of the band, including those who have hitherto received holdings, provided the date from which the conditions run shall be that on which this resolution is ratified;

(4) That this resolution shall not be interpreted to mean that one who holds land cannot lease his holding or sell his possessory right to another Indian according to custom and subject to the approval of the business committee;

(5) That the acceptance of a holding of land by any Indian shall be prima facie evidence of acceptance of these conditions, and failure to comply with any of these conditions shall subject the holder to forfeiture of his claim;

(6) That all acts and resolutions previously passed, which may be in conflict with this resolution, are hereby repealed.

Passed and ratified in open council by four members voting for the act and none voting against it.

The following written form is used by the authorities of the Eastern Cherokee Band in making assignments of lands:

Whereas _____, who is an enrolled member of the Eastern Band of Cherokee Indians, has applied for a holding of land subject to the provisions of the law under which this band of Indians is incorporated and the rules and regulations prescribed by the Indian council thereunder;

And whereas the said _____ has not exhausted _____ right to such a holding:

Be it RESOLVED by the Eastern Band of Cherokee Indians in council assembled that the said _____ be and _____ hereby is assigned a holding of land located as follows: [to be more specifically and definitely located and marked under the direction of the business committee of this band].

It is understood and agreed that this assignment of a holding conveys only a possessory interest in the said holdings, and that the title to the said land remains in the Eastern Band of Cherokee Indians.

It is further understood and agreed that the said _____ must make bona fide entry on said holding within a period of 12 months from the date of this assignment; that during each year for the first 5 years from the date of this resolution this assignee must clear and put into cultivation 1 acre of land (1 acre each year making a total of at least 5 acres in 5 years); that the person assigned this holding must within 2 years construct a suitable home on said holding; and that all the laws and regulations regarding the cutting of timber on said holding must be complied with in spirit and in letter.

It is further understood and agreed that should the assignee fail to utilize said holding during the period of 5 years, _____ shall forfeit all right, interest, and title to said holding which shall revert to the Eastern Band of Cherokee Indians.

It is further understood and agreed that the assignee can lease said holding or sell _____ possessory right to another Indian according to established custom and subject to the approval of the business committee.

The acceptance of this holding shall be prima facie evidence of the acceptance of these conditions and failure to comply with any of these conditions shall subject the holder to forfeiture of _____ claim.

The complete description of this holding as finally selected and marked under the direction of the business committee is recorded on the back of this page.

A somewhat similar arrangement is approved by the Rules and Regulations for Annette Islands. These Rules and Regulations contain the following provisions on land tenure:

Section 1. The council, at any of its regular monthly meetings, shall be authorized to issue to any member of the Annette Islands Reserve unprovided with a parcel of land in the town of Metlakahtla the following permit:

Permit No._____   Metlakahtla, Alaska
                                     (Date)_____, 19____

This certifies that _____, of Metlakahtla, is authorized to enter upon and occupy that tract or parcel of land in Metlakahtla, on Annette Island, in the Territory of Alaska, more particularly described as follows: viz., Lot No. _____ of the town of Metlakahtla, according to the adopted plat thereof, and measuring _____ feet by _____ feet.

This permit shall be the evidence thereof, except it be before by us canceled upon our register by a two-thirds vote of the membership of the council for abandonment or for other reason deemed by the council to be good and sufficient, or except it be before by us canceled upon the request of the person to whom it has been issued.

Done by our order, under our seal, the day and year first above written.

THE TOWN AND ASSOCIATED COMMUNITY OF METLAKAHTLA

By _____, Mayor

_____, Secretary of the Council

Section 2. The council is authorized to issue similar permits for the occupancy and use of such tracts of land, other than mineral land, on Annette Islands as are cultivable to any member of the community who may be willing to clear and cultivate the same; not more than 10 acres of such land shall be assigned to any one person.

A description of each parcel of land thus assigned shall be made by the person in charge of the work of the Bureau of Education on Annette Islands, and the description of each tract of land assigned shall in each case be written out in full in the permit covering its assignment.

Section 3. A fee of five dollars ($5) shall be paid by each member of the Annette Islands reserve hereafter receiving, under these rules and regulations, a permit to occupy land, other than mineral, within the reserve. Such fees shall be collected by the secretary and by him deposited with the treasurer, to be expended for public purposes, as the council may direct.

Section 4. Every permit to occupy a lot within the town of Metlakahtla or to occupy a tract of land within Annette islands Reserve issued under these rules and regulations shall be made in triplicate. The original permit shall be held by the person to whom it has been issued; the duplicate copy shall be preserved by the secretary in the official records of the Annette Islands Reserve; the triplicate copy shall be sent by the secretary to the Commissioner of Education.

Section 5. All permits to occupy land within the Annette Islands Reserve in force at the date of the approval of these rules and regulations are recognized as of equal validity with those issued hereafter under Section 1 of this article. An official record of such permits shall be made and preserved by the secretary, and a list certified by the mayor, stating the names of the persons holding such permits, the dates of the permits, and the number of the lot in the town of Metlakahtla covered by each permit shall be sent by the secretary to the Commissioner of Education, together with a copy of the adopted plat of the town of Metlakahtla showing the numbers and dimensions of such lots.

Section 6. Should any permit to occupy land within or without the town of Metlakahtla be canceled for abandonment or misdemeanor, as provided in Section 1 of this article, the person whose permit is canceled shall receive for improvements upon said allotment such compensation, payable from the funds under the control of the council, as may be fixed by a two-thirds vote of the entire membership of the council. Such improvements for which compensation has thus been made shall be the property of Annette Islands Reserve. The council shall have power by its permit to transfer to another person said allotment with the improvements thereon upon such terms as the council may prescribe. A full and complete record of all such proceedings, certified by the mayor, shall in each and every case be sent by the secretary of the council to the Commissioner of Education. (Article VI)

It will be noted that the chief industry on the Annette Islands Reserve, the canning of fish, is operated on tribal property, for the benefit of the entire tribe. Individual possession attaches only to lands used for domestic purposes.

The principle applied in each of the foregoing provisions is thus stated in the first article of the constitution of the Cherokee Nation, adopted in 1839:

Section 2. The lands of the Cherokee Nation shall remain common property; but the improvements made thereon, and in the possession of thecitizens of the Nation, are the exclusive and indefeasible property of the citizens respectively who made them, or may rightfully be in possession of them; *provided* that the citizens of the Nation possessing exclusive and indefeasible right to their improvements, as expressed in this article, shall possess no right or power to dispose of their improvements, in any manner whatever, to the United Sates, individual states, or to individual citizens thereof; and that, whenever any citizen shall remove with his effects out of the limits of this Nation and become a citizen of any other government, all his rights and privileges as a citizen of this Nation shall cease; *provided, nevertheless,* that the National Council shall have power to readmit, by law, to all the rights of citizenship, any such person or persons who may, at any time, desire to return to the Nation, on memorializing the National Council for such re-admission.

Moreover, the National Council shall have power to adopt such laws and regulations, as its wisdom may deem expedient and proper, to prevent citizens from monopolizing improvements, with the view of speculation.

The productive management of the land and resources (water, minerals, timber, etc.) of the Indian community is a matter of the greatest importance.

Unfortunately, little can be said on this subject that would be of general application, since the problems of production vary so considerably from reservation to reservation. Some suggestions of value, however, may be found in the setup worked out at the Fort Bidwell Indian Colony in California. Section 12 of the rules and regulations for the government of the Fort Bidwell Indian Colony, adopted and promulgated in 1938, provides:

> *Section 12.* The specific regulations for the government of this Colony shall be in part as hereinafter set out and shall be subject to amendment, extension, or retraction through a majority vote of the Executive Council at any time, when coupled with the assent of the Agent in charge and that of the Chief of the Colony.

A. No Indian or Indian family shall be permitted to have permanent residence on this reservation, except those to whom new houses have been assigned.

B. Visits from relatives or friends of those having residence on the reservation shall be permitted but shall be limited to 14 days at any one time and shall not exceed 30 days in any one calendar year.

C. Any unusual conditions developing under the restrictions of Subarticle B shall be considered on their own individual merits in each case and, if it appears advisable to do so, further time may be extended visitors through an affirmative vote of the entire Executive Council if concurred in by the Agent in charge and the Chief of the Colony.

D. Whatever profits may accrue to the membership of the Colony, whether derived from the farm, dairy, or other sources, shall be prorated among the several members of the Colony according to the actual number of days of labor performed by each member.

E. The Colony project stands hereafter on a self-sustaining basis and there shall be set aside 25% of its net income from all sources to be used as a fund for repairs and replacement of farm tools, machinery, or other necessary equipment which may from time to time be needed for the profitable operation of the farm or dairy.

F. Monies that are received from the project and due the members of the Colony shall be paid to them immediately upon their receipt, after the 25% deductions above referred to shall have been made.

G. The Agent in charge shall act as Treasurer, receiving and paying in accordance with these regulations.

H. The 25% deductions from net income, referred to above, shall be placed on deposit to the credit of the Colony as a whole to be checked against by the Treasurer as needs require.

I. The judgment of the Treasurer as to what constitutes a legitimate need shall be sufficient for the contracting and payment of any obligation not to exceed $25.00. When an obligation in excess of $25.00 is necessary, the judgment of the Treasurer must be concurred in by a majority of the Executive Council.

J. The Treasurer shall keep an accurate and satisfactory account of all money received and disbursed. Such accounts to be open and subject to inspection of the Executive Council at any time.

K. At the close of each month the Treasurer shall prepare a statement showing expenditures for the current month with proper receipts attached, which statement shall be audited and signed by the Executive Council after which it shall be sent to the Superintendent of the Sacramento Indian Agency at Sacramento, California, to be preserved as a permanent record.

L. All wages now paid or hereafter to be paid to residents of this Colony for fence and road work shall be held by the Agent in charge for the exclusive purpose of purchasing dairy cattle in order that a dairy may be established on this reservation as an integral part of our farm policy.

M. From the 25% of the net profits derived from the dairy, when established, a definite part shall be set aside for the purchase of a sufficient number of hogs and chickens to eventually supply the needs of the members of the Colony. The exact amount to be used for this purpose shall later be determined by vote of the Executive Council.

N. All Indians resident on this reservation are hereby pledged to assist in the construction of dams in the two waterways leading down from the mountains on this reservation in order to provide a sufficient supply of irrigation water to extend the crop season some two months longer.

O. The number of horses permitted on this reservation is hereby limited to include one work team and one riding horse per family and shall for no reason be extended to allow more.

P. No other horses than those permitted in the paragraph first above shall be allowed to winter or be fed on the reservation.

Q. Horses allowed to remain on the reservation under the provisions of Sub-Article O shall be retained for work upon the farm as occasion demands, this being the sole reason for allowing them on the reservation under any circumstances.

R. Agency-owned horses are to be used for farm work only when the number of individually owned horses is insufficient to take care of the farming demands, and then their use shall be restricted so as to reserve them for those Indians owning no horses.

S. Under the general supervisory direction of the Executive Council, the following more or less distinct duties are to be carried out by the party placed in immediate charge and assigned to that particular work, as follows:

Billie Burns, Water Boss: Responsible for the proper irrigation of all field crops and gardens, including the community garden. To see that all irrigation ditches are clean of weeds, head gates repaired, and levees in shape to make satisfactory irrigation possible.

Connan Dick, Gardener: Responsible for the proper preparation of the ground, planting, cultivation, and care of all individual gardens and the community garden.

Nom DeGarmo, Blacksmith: Responsible for the proper repair of all tools and farm machinery, including the sharpening of plowshares, babbitting of boxings, welding of broken parts, and other general blacksmithing work.

Johnnie Paddy, Implements & Machinery: Responsible for the proper housing of all farm implements and machinery and for their proper use afield. To keep a proper check on all hand implements and to see that they are returned to the shop after use.

Wylopia Jack, Painter: Responsible for the painting and proper repair of all buildings on the entire reservation.

Ray Archie, Dairyman: Responsible for the proper handling and care of the dairy, including the feeding and care of the dairy herd, milking operations, handling of the milk, weight records of individuals, disposal of the product, time of the men under his direction, care of the barn and silo and milk utensils.

A. W. Johnson, Fire Chief: Responsible for, in addition to his present duties as Chief of Police, the organization of a hose company, its drill and the proper working condition of all fire extinguishers, fire hoses, fire-hose carts, and other fire-fighting equipment.

Johnnie Paddy, Boss, Labor Crew #1: Responsible for the proper assignment of duties to all men in his crew, their satisfactory work, and the keeping of their time.

Henry Barr, Boss, Labor Crew #2: Responsible for the proper assignment of duties to all men in his crew, their satisfactory work, and the keeping of their time.

Executive Council, Park and Road Committee—Willie Burns, Nom DeGarmo, Simon Hawley, Johnnie Paddy, and Luther Clemente: Responsible for the proper care and attractiveness of the public square and lawns, trimming of trees, grading and gravel work on roads of the reservation, removal of trash and debris, and all similar duties tending to beautify the grounds.

T. In addition to the foregoing and to what may be added through subsequent amendments, this Executive Council reserves to itself broad powers to determine questions of policy as they may affect either the residents of the reservation or have bearing on the community project. It recognizes, at the same time, the restrictions of governmental authority as it steps down through duly authorized representatives and yields to all such proper restrictions. Furthermore, it pledges all of whatever authority it now possesses to a constructive use for the betterment of the Colony undertaking at large, for the benefit of the individuals resident thereon, and, indirectly, to the advancement of the best interests of the Indian in this state.

The productive use of community property always involves labor. This labor may be paid for, if funds are available, or required as a contribution from all the members of the community. The logging operations conducted by the Menominee Tribe are carried through on a basis of regular wages for all labor performed, the proceeds of the operations becoming part of the tribal fund. At some other reservations no direct payment is made for community labor, but all members of the community are required to contribute equally to projects which all members of the community may enjoy equally. Thus, the Rules and Regulations for Annette Islands Reserve provide:

Section 3. The council shall have authority to direct, by its ordinance, that every able-bodied male resident of Annette Islands Reserve shall perform, without remuneration, in each calendar year not more than two days, labor, of eight hours each, on the streets, roads, wharves, public buildings, or other public improvements within the Annette Islands Reserve undertaken by order of the council.

The secretary shall keep a record of the labor thus performed, showing the dates, the number of hours, and the character of the service rendered by each person.

A more limited labor requirement is that set forth in the laws of the Muskogee Nation requiring work on public roads:

> *Section 274 [Work on Roads].* All male citizens over the age of eighteen years shall, at the call of the District Judge, without good reason for neglect, work on the public roads or pay for the benefit of those working, the sum of one ($1.00) dollar per day during the time in which such work is being done in the District. The District Judge shall have collected all sums due in accordance with this law. (Compiled Laws 1893, Chapter XVII)

A more-detailed set of rules for work on irrigation ditches, and other public works of benefit to the community, is found in the constitution and bylaws of the Laguna Pueblo Indians. The duties of the Mayordomo in this regard are set forth in Section 15 of the Laguna constitution, cited in Section 15 of this memorandum. The following regulations appear in a body of recently proposed amendments to the bylaws:

> *Regulations Governing the Duties of Mayordomos*
> *Community Work:* Before the commencement of any community work, of whatever nature, and at conclusion of such work, it shall be the duty of the Head Mayordomo or any Staff Officer, if present, to give a short address in nature of encouragement, cooperation, praise, etc., to his men.
>
> This regulation in the future prohibits any member on such Public Work from leaving such after conclusion of such day's work, prior to the command to be given by such Mayordomo or Staff Officer for ceasing such day's labors on any community or public labor. Violation of this regulation by any member or members absenting him or themselves, without the proper permission, shall be subject to a fine in amount of 25 cents for each offense in violation of this regulation.
>
> * * * * *
>
> *Granting Temporary Leave, Other Than Sick Leave from Any and All Public Work:* Mayordomos under this clause are authorized to grant temporary non-sick leaves of absence to members from any Public Work, where necessity will warrant such leave, at a time when such Public Work might be contemplated or already under way . . . , provided, however, that all requests for such excuses or leaves, are made by such members any time prior to commencement of such Public Work, and such requests to be made in person by members who seek such excuses or leaves.
>
> * * * * *

Emergency Leaves in Cases Where Most Urgent, from Causes beyond Human Control: Mayordomos shall grant leaves of absence to members so requesting such leave while on actual duty on any Public Work, of whatever nature, in cases of urgent emergencies, of whatever nature, beyond human control, such as sudden sickness while in line of duty, accidents, etc.

* * * * *

Granting of Sick Leaves by Mayordomos: Mayordomos shall have the authority to grant sick leaves to men and young men who are subject to any Public Work who might become suddenly ill prior to or when such work might be commenced and already in operation. In this clause is included also leaves for such men or young men whose immediate member or members of their families might become suddenly ill. Such members subject to Public Work, who are granted such sick leave, are to remain home until full recovery of such illness is in evidence and are not to devote themselves to any kind of work whatever.

Instead of prescribing any definite regulations in the tribal bylaws governing community labor, a tribe may leave to its tribal council the power to deal with this subject, from time to time, by ordinance. The following provision is found in the proposed bylaws of the Quechan (Fort Yuma) Tribal Council:

(2) It shall be the duty of the Council, to pass all necessary rules and regulations consistent with the Constitution, which shall have for their purpose the equalization of community labor in community projects such as building of necessary roads, fences, ditches, buildings, or other similar projects upon the reservation, and which are entirely and essentially of and for the benefit of all the residents of the reservation.

The distribution of the products of community labor should be particularly provided for in the constitution or bylaws of any tribe. Where the labor is entirely on public works such as roads, dams, community buildings, etc., no problem of distribution is presented. All the members of the community enjoy these things. But when the community labor is devoted to the production of goods that may be consumed or sold, the questions arises: How shall distribution of the goods or of the proceeds of their sale be made?

Where regular wages are paid to those who work on the community projects, the product belongs to the community as a whole. Provision should be made for the distribution of such product, or of the money returns derived from its sale, by the tribal council, in furtherance of public purposes. Where the returns are sufficient to permit of per capita distributions, bylaws should be drawn governing the dates and amounts of such distributions.

The foregoing arrangements with respect to community property offer no difficulties of application on a reservation which has not been allotted, or has been allotted only in part. The problem of establishing a similar system upon a reservation which has been completely allotted is very much more difficult.

The following program for effecting a change from the allotment system to a system of tribal ownership, with individual possession of improved lands, is laid down in a proposed constitution for the Pima Community, submitted by Indians of the Gila River and Salt River Reservations:

Article VIII. Tenure of Land

Section 1. All lands within the confines of the Salt River and of the Gila River Reservations shall ultimately become Communal property.

Section 2. All Trust Patents heretofore issued by the United States Government, covering lands on either of the above named reservations, shall be respected during the lifetime of the allottee, provided the allottee expresses to the Council a desire for such respect and provided the said allottee occupies said allotment and handles it in such a manner as to insure the economic use of said land and of all water appurtenant thereto. However, two consecutive years of disuse of land and appurtenant water shall be considered ample evidence of abandonment and in such event the allotment shall at once revert to the community and become communal property. On the death of an allottee, each tract of land so held under Trust Patent, shall revert to the PIMA COMMUNITY OF ARIZONA and shall, from the date of the death of the allottee, become communal property.

Section 3. The title to all so-called inherited or heirship allotments, which shall be in the class designated as inherited or heirship on the date of the adoption of this Constitution, shall as of that date revert to the Pima Community of Arizona and become communal property.

Section 4. It shall be the duty of the Community Council to administer Communal property in such a manner as to insure the economic use of the land and of all water appurtenant to it, and in such a manner as to procure the greatest benefits for the Community.

Section 5. The title to all allotments which have no water appurtenant thereto, whether inherited or otherwise, shall revert to the Pima Community of Arizona, as of the date of the adoption of this Constitution, and become Communal property.

Section 6. It shall be the duty of the Community Council to administer the Communal property described in Section 3 above in a manner that will prove of greatest benefit to the community.

Section 7. The title to all allotted lands which have heretofore been leased to whites, which leases shall be in effect on the date of the adoption of this Constitution, shall on the date revert to the Pima Community of Arizona and become Communal property, and all rentals accruing on such lands from that date shall likewise become Communal property, subject to disposition by the Community Council for the benefit of said Pima Community.

Section 8. On the death of an allottee, the allotment of such allottee shall immediately revert to the Pima Community of Arizona and become Communal property. However, there shall be no ouster of the heirs, neither of the first nor of succeeding generations, so long as such heirs shall be able to occupy and handle the property without traction among themselves, and in such a manner as to insure the economic use of the land and of the water appurtenant thereto.

Other programs may be devised for modifying the allotment system and establishing a larger domain of tribal land by encouraging voluntary sale allotments or heirship lands to the community in exchange for cash or corporate certificates, or by limiting the amount of land that a single individual may own and prohibiting the devising of restricted lands to persons who already have more than a fixed amount of land.

Some of the advantages of tribal ownership of grazing land and other natural resources that cannot be effectively developed and utilized by individuals may be obtained by securing leases of such land or resources to the tribe from the individual owners of the land.

The problem of developing a program for the modification of the allotment system is too complex and varies too much from reservation to reservation to warrant the statement in this memorandum of any general solution. Any serious attempt by the Indians concerned to settle this problem in a satisfactory manner will meet with the sympathetic cooperation of the Interior Department, and if necessary the Interior Department will support special legislation which such a program may require.

Despite the distinction we have drawn between community property and property possessed by individuals, it must be remembered that the individual in possession of land, whether the land be allotted or assigned, is always subject to regulations imposed by his local government for the protection of the interests of the community. Thus it is to the common interest

of the Indians of the community to prevent alienation of Indian lands to outsiders. A provision to this effect is contained in Article 1, Section 2, of the
constitution of the Cherokee Nation, cited earlier in this section of this memorandum. The importance that was attached to such restrictions upon alienation by the Cherokee Indians is evidenced by the Cherokee statute of
December 2, 1842, which made the attempt by any Indian to dispose of
Indian lands to the United States or any official of the United States a crime
punishable by death.

To a certain extent the Wheeler-Howard Act and the terms of restriction
contained in deeds and trust patents safeguard the Indian ownership of
Indian lands. It may be well, however, to supplement and strengthen those
restrictions, particularly in the matter of leases. It might, for instance, be
provided in the bylaws that the Indian tribe or Indian cooperative associations or Indian individuals should have a preference on all leases of
restricted Indian lands, as against outsiders.

Closely related to the problem of disposition of individual lands during
life is the question of the disposition of heirship lands. Any plan for the set-
tlement of the heirship problem must consider four objectives: (1) It must
prevent the division of holdings into unusable units; (2) it must avoid the
sale of Indian heirship lands to outsiders; (3) it must cut down the tremendous expense entailed by the present system of distributing small rentals
among dozens or hundreds of heirs; and (4) it must prevent the monopoliza-
tion of land by individuals who had the misfortune to be born in unhealthy
families.

The simplest solution of the heirship problem is through the establishment of community ownership of land. Where such a solution is not feasi-
ble, the following program, contained in the proposed bylaws of the Fort
Belknap Indian Tribal Association, may prove suggestive:

5. The Tribal Council hereby prohibits the sale or alienation of Indian
lands, either individual or tribal, to persons other than members of the
tribe, except on specific authorization by the United States Congress.

6. The Tribal Council hereby provides that all inherited lands must be kept
intact as originally allotted, and must pass to the oldest direct descendent
who is without land holdings, provided such heir is a qualified member of
this Association. No title shall pass into the possession of nonqualified
members of this Association, though such heirs may be permitted to reside
upon the reservation and make use of selections of lands during their lifetime, provided they secure the consent of the Tribal Council to such action.

7. All lands belonging to deceased Indians, who do not have heirs that can qualify under the preceding provisions, shall revert to the tribe and be available for reallotment to orphans or landless members of the Association, provided, however, that direct heirs of the deceased relative may arrange exchanges of allotments with the approval of the Council whereby improved lands may be held in the family and unimproved lands in their stead revert to the tribe for reallotment as herein provided. The order of succession and right to exchange privileges will be determined by the Council for each individual case, though the customary practice will be for the older heir to receive preference, should such be requested.

8. In the event that any aged and destitute Indian member of this Association desires to transfer his original or inherited allotment to the tribe before his death, the same may be accepted, provided the Council will authorize a payment of a monthly pension, of not less that $10.00 and not more than $25.00, to such individual from tribal or gratuitous funds under their control or specifically appropriated for this purpose.

9. Allotments cannot be transferred by will to other than landless Indian members of this Association. Aged and destitute Indian members of this Association may transfer by will to landless Indians, who are eligible under this section, their original allotments or inherited lands in return for their support and maintenance during their declining years by such beneficiary, provided that such agreement has the approval of the Tribal Council.

10. When a duly qualified and enrolled member of this Association shall reach the age of five years and still remain landless, his legal guardian shall be permitted to purchase from tribal holdings, an allotment suitable to the future needs of the child but not in excess of the present allotment unit, payment for which may be made in twenty annual payments either from combined income of the family or from lease rentals upon this tract or both.

11. The Tribal Council shall seek either gratuitous or tribal grants to purchase all reservational lands now alienated through direct gift to the state for school purposes, or through the past issuance of patent in fee, or disposal through inheritance under state laws, or allotment to Indians who can not qualify for membership in this association.

12. Present holdings of inherited lands must be transferred, in original units, to the next-oldest landless heir of the present heir who owns the larger interest in the holding. When the estate is held in equal parts by two or more heirs, the oldest then living heir may have the right to choose to whom the land may be transferred.

If the heirship problem cannot be settled at the time of drafting the tribal constitution and bylaws, some such provision as the following, taken from the proposed constitution of the Quechan (Fort Yuma) Tribal Council may be valuable as a reminder of unfinished business.

(5) The Council shall, through study, investigation, research, and analysis, seek to determine a just and equitable solution to the problems arising from allotment and heirship conditions as they apply to lands on this reservation. It shall publish its findings and recommendations and shall make the necessary reports and recommendations to the several departments of the Federal Government involved, in conformity to those articles and sections of the Constitution having to do with such questions.

(6) It shall endeavor to arrive at a just and equitable policy and program, whereby the rights of posterity shall be safeguarded and concurred and shall prosecute this study and investigation with diligence and dispatch to the end that such evils as now exist shall be removed and done away with at the earliest possible date.

In dealing with the mechanics of administering heirship estates, the following provisions, taken from the laws of the Muskogee Nation, may prove useful:

Chapter XIV. Wills and Administration: Wills
    Section 257. The last will and testament of any deceased person shall be valid; and if any person shall die without having made a will, not having had the opportunity to do so, and it can be established by two respectable witnesses that the deceased did, prior to his death, express verbally the manner in which he desired his property to be disposed of, such nuncupative will be valid. No will shall be valid unless the testator shall have been in his or her proper mind and such fact testified to by two respectable witnesses; *provided* that no will shall be valid when it is proven that it was made to avoid the payment of just debts.

Section 258. If any person claim to be the child of a deceased male person, and it should be proven that such person did not, during life, recognize the claimant as his offspring, then such claimant shall not be entitled to any share in the estate of the deceased.

Section 259. No person shall bring any claim against a deceased person without two respectable witnesses who shall have been present at the time the debt was created, or unless such claimant shall hold a written obligation. In either case where the deceased has property, it shall be collected, otherwise the debt shall not be good.

[Administration]

Section 260. If any male citizen die without having made a will, the Judge of the District wherein such deceased person resided shall grant letters of administration to any citizen of this Nation who may request it, and such person shall be required to give bond in double the value of such estate, with at least two good sureties, each of whom shall also own property equal to twice the value of such estate.

Section 261. All estates of deceased persons shall be valued by the Judge and two disinterested persons.

Section 262. The administrator shall at all times be required to make and provide liberal means for the support and education of all heirs of the deceased, to make any trade that may be of advantage to such estate, and to advise and direct the affairs of such heirs until they shall have become of age, according to law, or until such heir shall marry, in which event the administrator shall turn over to such heirs of his or her inheritance everything connected with the estate that may have been placed in his care, or its equivalent in money or other property.

Section 263. If an administrator, when required to do so, fails to turn over everything connected with an estate of which he shall have charge, or its equivalent in money or other property, the proper authority shall seize the goods or property of his sureties and appropriate therefrom a sufficient amount to make up any deficiency that may occur in the value of the estate; and if any person shall sign a bond as surety, and afterwards dies, the estate of such surety shall in all cases be held responsible.

Section 264. If no person shall ask letters of administration, the Judge shall appoint a suitable person who, upon giving sufficient bond and security, shall act as administrator.

Section 265. In case of the death of a female, if there be a husband and children living, he shall have the preference of administratorship, and in the event of there being no children living the nearest relative shall have the preference.

Section 266. The administrator or administratrix of an estate shall be entitled to 25% of every dollar's worth of such estate that may be rendered at the expiration of such administration.

Section 267. The lawful or acknowledged wife of a deceased husband shall be entitled to one-half of the estate, if there are no children, and a child's part, if there should be children, in all cases where there is *no will.* The husband surviving shall inherit of deceased wife in like manner.

Section 268. The homestead and kitchen furniture, one work horse, one cow and calf, and one breeding sow shall be exempt.

Section 269. Provided that an estate is solvent, the administrator shall settle up and cancel all debts and accounts against the estate out of the estate's effects. (Compiled Laws, 1893)

The problem of regulating the *use* of individual property, so as to prevent soil erosion, wasteful destruction of natural resources, and other improper uses of land, should engage serious consideration. The problem is perhaps too variable to warrant any definite regulations in the bylaws of any tribe, but power should be clearly vested in the proper tribal authorities to place reasonable restrictions upon the use of land within the reservation.

The foregoing considerations, advanced with respect to *land*, apply equally to various other forms of property, both tribal and individual.

Considerations with respect to the use of tribal lands apply equally to tribal herds, sawmills, agricultural machinery, minerals, water power, and as well to tribal funds.

The regulation of the use of personal property is a matter closely related to the regulation of land use. It would be possible to include in the bylaws of an Indian tribe detailed provisions on the fencing in or fencing out of livestock; the disposition of strays; the registration of brands; the definition of civil trespass and the measure of damages therefore; and limitation on the export of hay, firewood, or other products which may be needed on the reservation. In general, however, these are matters which should be dealt with by tribal ordinances rather than in the bylaws.

SECTION 24

BYLAWS: TAXATION

For certain tribes which enjoy large tribal funds or prosperous tribal industries, self-government will not involve the necessity of taxation. Other tribes
must face this necessity and supplement other sources of income by taxes in
order to carry out the functions of local self-government. This does not
mean that such a tribe will be expected to raise taxes from its members to
pay for the work that has hitherto been performed by the Indian Service out
of federal appropriations. The Interior Department will favor the indefinite
continuance of federal appropriations for those functions that have hitherto
been carried out by the Indian Service. If the tribal authorities take over
these various functions, such as law enforcement, the maintenance of land
records, the care of buildings, and the construction and maintenance of public improvements, then it is planned to make the proper appropriations available to the tribe and its employees instead of using such appropriations for
the salaries of Indian Service employees. But there will be certain things that
a tribe may undertake to do outside of the line of ordinary Indian Service
activities, and for these things it may be impossible to obtain federal appropriations. In such cases the tribe will have to resort to taxes.

It is likely that the salaries of members of the tribal council will have to
be paid from taxes where no tribal funds are now available for that purpose.
Other incidental expenses of government may have to be paid out of taxes.
Finally, expense involved in economic enterprises that a tribe may undertake for the mutual profits of its members may be paid for out of taxes.

The question of what kinds of taxes should be levied deserves careful
consideration. The simplest of all taxes is a poll tax levied alike upon all the
adult members or sometimes upon all the adult male members of the community. Such a tax, however, falls harshly upon the needy members of the
community, unless provision is made for exemptions where circumstances
warrant.

A much fairer tax, which is just as easy to collect, is an inheritance tax. Models for such taxes may be found in the legislation of almost every state. The following provision is taken from the proposed constitution and bylaws of the San Carlos Reservation:

Section 3. Special Support of Tribe Members
It is the resolution of the voting community of this Reservation that a system of levying an income tax, and possibly other auxiliary methods, be established for the creation and maintenance of a fund wherewith to prepare for the support by the Tribe of those of its members that may elsewise be destitute in old age, or that, in earlier life, may not be able to earn their livelihood by their own work. Funds gained for such purpose shall be used only for such purpose and shall be placed in the hands of a bonded U.S. officer, under regulations approved by the Indian Department. How this provision is best to be set in operation shall be considered by the Council, in conjunction with competent advisors, and shall be laid down as a bylaw, subject to approval by the Tribal vote.

Perhaps the most popular of all Indian taxes is a tax on non-Indians residents within the reservation. The following provisions, taken from the laws of the Cherokee Nation, offer an example of such a tax:

Article XXX. Trade and Intercourse
    Section 12. Every person transacting, or proposing to transact, a mercantile business in the Cherokee Nation shall make application, and receive license, for that purpose from the National Council. Such applicant shall make affidavit setting forth the name and style of the party or firms, and of every member or partner thereof, the place where he or they design to trade, and the nature of the business or merchandise; and he shall pay into the general fund of the national treasury, on the receipt of such license, the sum of one-fourth of one per cent on all bills of purchase and shall continue to pay at the same rates, and at the beginning of each quarter thereafter, for all new or additional bills of goods received and offered for sale.
    Section 13. Every person, who shall attempt to trade or otherwise dispose of merchandise, goods, or wares, without previously obtaining a permit or license, shall be fined, on conviction thereof, before a court of competent jurisdiction, in any sum not less than one hundred dollars, nor exceeding twenty thousand dollars, for each and every offense, at the discretion of the court, *provided* that the treasurer may issue license to a citizen or citizens of the Nation, only when the National Council is not in

session, on the payment of the proper tax, and upon compliance with the requirements of this act, which license shall be good until the adjournment of the sessions of the National Council next ensuing.

Section 14. Should it appear that any false affidavit has been made, either by omitting to name or misnaming any principal or partner to a mercantile firm, or by rendering any false invoice of goods, or by suppression of, or by failure to render, an invoice, then, and in that case, the person so falsely representing such firm shall be deemed guilty of perjury. And be proceeded against accordingly.

Section 15. The executive clerk shall, at the close of each annual session of the National Council, furnish to trade, granted under this act, with all the names of each firm; and the treasurer shall keep a correct record of all such licenses, together with such as he may grant between the annual sessions of council, showing to whom issued, the nature of the business, and the place or places where such parties may trade.

Section 16. Every peddler or trader, entering the Nation on foot, horseback, or in wagons or otherwise, with trinkets, jewelry, books, pictures or other prints, or with merchandise of whatever description, shall, before offering such effects for sale, obtain from the treasurer, or from the district clerk of the district in which he proposes to begin to sell, a written license or permit for that purpose. Such peddler or trader shall produce, for the information of the treasurer or district clerk, a full invoice or list, verified on oath, of his stock on hand and pay a tax thereon at the rate of five per cent; *provided* that sacred or moral literature, introduced for sale or gratuitous distribution by colporteurs, preachers of the Gospel, or by other agents of Christian societies, shall be exempt from taxation, *provided also* that improved stock and poultry, breadstuffs, meats, uncanned fruits and vegetables, grain for food, and seeds of every kind for planting shall also be exempt from taxation.

Section 17. It shall be, and is hereby made, the duty of the sheriff of any district in which any person shall have violated the intent of this act to seize such person with his merchandise, vehicles, team, storehouse, or place of business, and them safely keep until the case can be reported and acted upon by the lawful authority, in conformity with the treaties and laws of this nation, or with the intercourse laws of the United States. (Compiled Laws 1881, Chapter 12, Article 3)

Other provisions on taxation are cited in Section 13 of this memorandum.

SECTION 25

BYLAWS: PUBLIC WELFARE

It is the chief business of government to make people happy and to eliminate suffering. This task involves all sorts of disagreeable restrictions on the conduct of members of the community. But a government which becomes completely identified with these disagreeable tasks cannot win the respect and loyalty of its citizens.

In addition to those aspects of government which involve coercion, which minister to human happiness by repressing types of conduct that cause unnecessary misery, there are other activities in which a government may engage that minister more directly to human happiness, activities that do not involve any regulation of conduct. Such activities, for instance, the guidance of cooperative economic enterprise, have been discussed incidentally in many of the foregoing sections. Other activities of a similar sort which have escaped any considerable comment are social recreation, education, charity, the grant of credits, and the rendering of assistance to those members of the tribe who have been unjustly dealt with by government officials or other outsiders or who are in need of counsel in trying circumstances.

These grounds of activity do not need to be set forth in detail in the constitution or bylaws of the tribe. The provisions of such constitution and bylaws are primarily designed to preserve peace and to prevent disputes. But where there is no coercion, peace is natural and disputes are rare. All that is essential, in the way of formal organization, is that responsibility for these "public welfare activities" should be properly allocated, so that they may be efficiently carried out.

The following provisions taken from various tribal constitutions indicate something of the nature of these activities.

The proposed bylaws of the Quechan (Fort Yuma) Tribal Council contain the following provisions on charity, education, and other welfare activities:

Charity.

In conformity to certain clauses in the Constitution it shall be the duty of the Council to pass all necessary regulatory rules and regulations covering charity work on the reservation, and it shall interest itself in such work and the proper regulation thereof to the extent of making a study of the causes and corrective measures necessary to remove, insofar as is possible, the need for charity amongst the members of the tribe.

It shall further administer or control the administration of charity upon the reservation in order that solicitation and expenditure of charitable funds shall be conducted in an orderly and systematic manner and that the rights to do same shall not be abused. It shall seek the assistance of such charitable organizations as are consistent with its purposes, and it shall cooperate in every manner with those agencies which truly seek to render assistance or aid to the poor and needy.

* * * * *

Education.

(1) The Council shall pass the necessary rules and regulations and shall take such action as will seek to promote and increase learning and education amongst the members of the tribe. It shall make a study and analysis of the problems arising from illiteracy and shall seek to eliminate this condition at the very earliest date. The Council shall make a study of the present school system upon the reservation and shall make the necessary recommendations thereon to the proper bureau or departments, together with a plan for improving the same.

(2) The Council shall at all times encourage and support all activities seeking to increase learning and education amongst the residents of the reservation and shall make a sustained effort to procure for the members of the Tribe the highest type of educational facilities. It shall, if necessary to gain these ends, enter into negotiations with nonreservation schools, particularly those of higher learning, to the end that the younger members of the tribe shall have every possible advantage in procuring that degree of learning and education that will best fit them to meet the problems incident to modern civilization and advancement.

(3) The Council shall pass the necessary rules and regulations and shall enforce same whereby compulsory education of minors shall be exacted. It shall prevent child labor on the reservation during school period and shall pass necessary rules and regulations to this end. It shall, if it deems proper, employ a tribal truant officer who shall have the duty of enforcing the provisions of this section.

Social Welfare.

The Council shall foster and encourage a high type of social welfare work amongst the residents of the reservation, and it shall encourage and promote by every practical means a proper system of social and home education in home economics, social hygiene, home demonstrations, agronomy, and farm demonstration, and it shall lend full support and cooperation to the several state, county and federal departments and agencies which seek to promote such social welfare and agricultural development work.

The Council shall, if it so deems proper, initiate and promote a system of agricultural contacts and shall award prizes and ribbons for superior achievement in agricultural and livestock development and shall adopt any other means which it deems wise to foster and encourage such development.

The constitution and bylaws of the Winnebago Indian Tribal Council contain this provision for the handling of personal complaints:

Article VIII. It shall be the duty of said Council to receive and to forward to the Department of the Interior, through the Superintendent for said tribe, all complaints of any member of said Council or tribe, or any matter or subject pertaining to the rights of said individual complainant or to the welfare or best interest of the tribe, providing such complaint be in writing and is signed by the complainant. The Council may, if it wishes, make and forward with such complaint its recommendation as to what, if any, action should be taken by the Department of the Interior.

The following provision in the proposed constitution of the San Carlos Reservation points to an attempt by the tribal council to maintain sympathetic and efficient personnel in the Indian Service.

Section 6. Approbation and Complaints

(a) The Council shall request the Superintendent to furnish them with the names of all Civil Service probationers or temporary employees under Civil Service regulations on the San Carlos Reservation that are nearing the end of their probation periods, and shall advise with the Superintendent in the matter of their probation periods, and shall advise with the Superintendent in the matter of their being given permanent position as Civil Service employees on the Reservation.

(b) In case of complaint or charges against any Civil Service officers or employees, the Council, when deeming action necessary, shall in discretion observe the requirements of right, equity, and law, so the accused have ample opportunity to hear and answer complaints or charges. Specific and incriminating charges must be sustained by written statements sworn to before a justice of the peace or other person authorized to take affidavits.

The laws of the Cherokee Nation (compiled 1895, Chapter 12, Article 11) provided for the publication of a regular Indian newspaper.

Indian ingenuity should discover many other worthy tribal enterprises that may serve the welfare of the tribe and strengthen the loyalty of the people to the ideal of self-government.

APPENDIX A

MODEL CONSTITUTION

CONSTITUTION AND BYLAWS FOR THE _____ TRIBE OF
INDIANS OF THE _____ RESERVATION

We, the people of _____ tribe, in order to establish this
constitution and bylaws.

Article I: Territory

The jurisdiction of the _____ tribe of Indians shall extend to the
territory within the confines of the _____ reservation as
defined in [the Treaty of _____, date, or Executive Order of
_____, or Act of Congress of _____] and to such
other lands as may be hereafter added thereto under any law of the United
States, except as otherwise provided by law.

Article II: Membership

Section 1. The membership of the _____ Tribe of Indians shall
consist of
    (a) All persons of Indian blood whose names appear on the official
        census rolls of the tribe as of April 1, 1935;
    (b) All children born to any member of the _____ Tribe who
        is a resident of the reservation at the time of the birth of said
        children.

Section 2. The General Tribal Council shall have the power to promulgate
ordinances subject to review by the Secretary of the Interior covering future
membership and the adoption of new members.

Article III: Governing Body

Section 1. The governing body of the _____ Tribe of Indians shall be the General Tribal Council, which shall be composed of all the qualified voters of the _____ reservation.

Section 2. All enrolled members of the _____ Tribe who are 21 years of age or over shall be qualified voters at each election.

Section 3. The General Tribal Council shall elect from its own members by secret ballot (a) a chairman, (b) a vice chairman, (c) a secretary, (d) a treasurer, and (e) such other officers and committees as may be deemed necessary.

Section 4. The General Tribal Council shall meet on the first Mondays of January and July. Within thirty days after the ratification and approval of this constitution and bylaws, a General Tribal Council shall be called by the present tribal council (or by the Secretary of the Interior) for the purpose of electing the officers named herein, and it shall transact such other business as may be necessary. The officers elected at this meeting shall serve until the July meeting, at which time their successors shall be chosen. Thereafter, officials shall be chosen at the July meeting. The chairman, or 25 percent of the qualified voters, may, by written notice, call special meetings of the General Tribal Council.

One-third of the qualified voters of the tribe shall constitute a quorum at any special or regular meeting.

Section 5. There shall be an executive committee, consisting of the president, secretary, and treasurer of the General Tribal Council, which shall perform such duties as may be authorized by that Council.

Article IV: Powers of the General Tribal Council

Section 1. Enumerated Powers
The General Tribal Council of the _____ Reservation shall exercise the following powers, subject to any limitations imposed by the statutes or the Constitution of the United States:
   (a) To negotiate with the Federal, State and local governments;
   (b) To employ legal counsel, the choice of counsel and fixing of fees to
        be subject to the approval of the Secretary of the Interior;

(c) To veto any sale, disposition, lease, or encumbrance of tribal lands, interests in lands, or other tribal assets of the tribe;

(d) To advise the Secretary of the Interior with regard to all appropriation estimates for Federal projects for the benefit of the _____ Reservation prior to the submission of such estimates to the Bureau of the Budget and to Congress;

(e) To manage all economic affairs and enterprises of the _____ Tribe in accordance with the terms of a charter that may be issued to the tribe by the Secretary of the Interior;

(f) To promulgate and enforce ordinances, which shall be subject to review by the Secretary of the Interior, governing the conduct of members of the _____ Tribe providing for the manner of making, holding, and revoking assignments of tribal land or interests therein and providing for the levying of taxes and the appropriation of available tribal funds for public purposes; providing for the licensing of nonmembers coming upon the reservation for purposes of hunting, fishing, trading, or other business, and for the exclusion from the territory of the tribe of persons not so licensed; and establishing proper agencies for law enforcement upon the _____ Reservation;

(g) To charter subordinate organizations for economic purposes and to delegate to such organizations, or to an subordinate boards or officials of the tribe, any of the foregoing powers, reserving the right to review any action taken by virtue of such delegate power;

(h) adopt resolutions not inconsistent with this constitution and the attached bylaws, regulating the procedure of the Council itself and of other tribal agencies, tribal officials, or tribal organizations of the _____ Reservation.

Section 2. Future Powers. The General Tribal Council may exercise such further powers as may in the future be delegated to the Council by members of the tribe or by the Secretary of the Interior or any other duly authorized official or agency of the State or Federal Government.

Section 3. Reserved Powers. Any rights and powers heretofore vested in the _____ Tribe but not expressly referred to in this constitution shall not be abridged by this Article, but may be exercised by the people of the _____ Tribe through the adoption of appropriate bylaws and constitutional amendments.

Section 4. Manner of Review. Any resolution or ordinance which, by the terms of this constitution, is subject to review by the Secretary of the Interior, shall be presented to the superintendent of the reservation, who shall, within ten days thereafter, approve or disapprove the same.

If the superintendent shall approve any ordinance or resolution, it shall thereupon become effective, but the superintendent shall transmit a copy of the same, bearing his endorsement, to the Secretary of the Interior, who may, within ninety days from the date of enactment, rescind the said ordinance or resolution for any cause by notifying the tribal Council of such decision.

If the superintendent shall refuse to approve any ordinance or resolution submitted to him, within ten days after its enactment, he shall advise the Council of his reasons therefor. If these reasons appear to the Council insufficient, it may, by a majority vote, refer the ordinance or resolution to the Secretary of the Interior, who may, within ninety days from the date of its enactment, approve the same in writing, whereupon the said ordinance or resolution shall become effective.

Article V: Amendments

This constitution and bylaws may be amended by a majority vote of the qualified voters of the tribe voting at an election called for that purpose by the Secretary of the Interior, provided that at least 30 percent of those entitled to vote shall vote in such election; but no amendment shall become effective until it shall have been approved by the Secretary of the Interior.

It shall be the duty of the Secretary of the Interior to call an election on any proposed amendment upon receipt of a petition signed by one-third of the qualified voters, members of the tribe.

BYLAWS OF THE _____ TRIBE

Article I: Duties of Officers

Section 1. Chairman of Council. The Chairman of the Council shall preside over all meetings of the Council, shall perform the usual duties of a Chairman, and exercise any authority delegated to him by the Council. He shall vote only in the case of a tie.

Section 2. Vice Chairman of the Council. The Vice Chairman shall assist the Chairman when called upon to do so, and in the absence of the Chairman he shall preside. When so presiding, he shall have all the rights, privileges, and duties as well as the responsibilities of the Chairman.

Section 3. Secretary of the Council. The Secretary of the Tribal Council shall conduct all tribal correspondence and shall keep an accurate record of all matters transacted at Council meetings. It shall be his duty to submit promptly to the superintendent of the jurisdiction, and Commissioner of Indian Affairs, copies of all minutes of regular and special meetings of the Tribal Council.

Section 4. Treasurer of Council. The Treasurer of the Tribal Council shall accept, receive, receipt for, preserve, and safeguard all funds in the custody of the Council, whether they be tribal funds or special funds for which the Council is acting as trustee or custodian. He shall deposit all funds in such depositary as the Council shall direct and shall make and preserve a faithful record of such funds and shall report on all receipts and expenditures and the amount and nature of all funds in his possession and custody at such regular meetings of the General Tribal Council and at such other times as requested by the Council or the executive committee.

He shall not pay out or otherwise disburse any funds in his possession or custody, except in accordance with a resolution duly passed by the Council.

The Treasurer shall be required to give a bond satisfactory to the Council and to the Commissioner of Indian Affairs.

Section 5. Appointive Officers. The duties of all appointive boards or officers of the community shall be clearly defined by resolution of the Council at the time of their creation or appointment. Such boards and officers shall report, from time to time as required, to the Council, and their activities and decisions shall be subject to review by the Council upon the petition of any person aggrieved.

Article II: Ratification of Constitution and Bylaws

This constitution and these bylaws, when adopted by a majority vote of the voters of the _____ Tribe voting at a special election called by the Secretary of the Interior, in which at least 30 percent of those entitled to vote shall vote, shall be submitted to the Secretary of the Interior for his approval and shall be enforced from the date of such approval.

Source: Felix S. Cohen Papers, Box 8, Folder 106, August 19, 1935.

APPENDIX B

OUTLINE OF TRIBAL CONSTITUTION
AND BYLAWS

CONSTITUTION

1. Name of tribe or community.
2. Statement of purpose.
3. Territory. What territory shall be covered by the Constitution? Consider the present boundaries of the reservation, possible future additions, and possible exclusion of certain reservation lands from tribal jurisdiction (e.g., lands in white ownership).
4. Membership.
   (a) Present membership. Shall this be determined by census or allotment rolls or otherwise?
   (b) Right to membership of descendants. Should descendants having less than a minimum degree of Indian blood be required to submit the matter of their adoption to the council, or should all future descendants be recognized as members, regardless of the degree of Indian blood?
   (c) Loss of membership. Should continuous absence from the reservation for a period of years or for life operate to end a person's membership? Should membership be terminated for other reasons?
   (d) Procedure for adoption of new members.
5. Organization of governing body.
   (a) Number and titles of elected officers.
   (b) Basis of representation. Should officers represent the entire reservation or several districts or other groups?
   (c) First election. Who should call and supervise the first election?
   (d) Tenure of office.
   (e) Time of elections.
   (f) Appointment of nonelective officers. Consideration should be given to the appointment of special boards for the various tasks the tribe

may wish to undertake, for instance, a land board, a credit board, a board of elections, a board of public works.
6. District organization. Should there be local district organizations? If so, consider:
   (a) District boundaries.
   (b) Special officers for district government.
   (c) Jurisdiction of district councils or other district officers. Should these officers or councils have power to pass ordinances of their own or should they administer the general tribal ordinances?
7. Powers of self-government.
   (a) Grant of specific powers. The following powers, subject to certain qualifications, may be enjoyed by a tribe organized under the Indian Reorganization Act. What powers a given tribe shall exercise and what these qualifications shall be will depend upon the experience, desires, and circumstances of each tribe. Certain of these powers may be exercised only subject to review by the Secretary of the Interior. The recommendations of the tribe on this matter will be given due consideration.
     (1) Negotiation with government agencies.
     (2) Employment of legal counsel.
     (3) Veto power over disposition of tribal assets.
     (4) Advice on appropriation estimates.
     (5) Control over tribal territory: assignments of lands, exchange of allotments for assignments, control of tribal enterprises.
     (6) Appointment of officers, boards, and commissions.
     (7) Appropriation of available funds for public purposes. Under existing law the only funds available to a tribe are those which it may raise from taxes or contributions or those tribal funds which Congress specifically appropriates for the use of the tribal council.
     (8) Requisition of labor for public purposes.
     (9) Taxation.
     (10) Exclusion of trespassers from reservation.
     (11) Law and order: promulgation of ordinances, establishment of courts, appointment of judges and policemen.
     (12) Eminent domain. Should the tribe have the power to condemn the property of members needed for public purposes? For what purposes? How should fair compensation be fixed?
     (13) Regulation of commerce and use of property. Under this heading should be considered the types of ordinances that

may be necessary to protect the members of the tribe against nuisances, against exploitation, against destruction of natural resources, etc.

(14) Control of inheritance. It should be noted that under existing law, the tribe may not interfere with existing state law governing heirship with respect to allotted lands.

(15) Regulation of domestic relations.

(16) Appointment of guardians.

(17) Control of elections.

(18) Regulation of procedure of tribal government.

(b) Qualification of certain powers by requirement of tribal referendum, manner of referendum.

(c) Acceptance of future grants of power.

(d) Reservation of any additional powers not enumerated above to the tribe, to be exercised through bylaws or constitutional amendments.

8. Conduct of elections and nominations.

(a) Right to vote. Who shall have the right to vote? What shall the age requirement be? Shall there be any residence requirement?

(b) Time and place of voting.

(c) Manner of voting.

(d) Procedure for nominating candidates.

9. Removal from office.

(a) Forfeiture of office (by reason of continuous absence, conviction of crime, etc.)

(b) Removal from office by council or other body.

(c) Popular recall of officials.

(d) Procedure for filling vacancies caused by death or removal.

10. Popular participation in government.

(a) Means of informing tribe of official acts. How shall the members of the tribe be kept informed of the acts and plans of their representative? What provisions should be made for general tribal meetings or district meetings?

(b) Popular initiative. Shall the members of the tribe have the right, by petition or otherwise, to require a popular vote on certain measures?

(c) Popular participation in committees. Should members of the tribe (or Indian Service employees) be encouraged to serve on regular and special council committees or boards, to deal with matters in which they are particularly competent?

11. Land.
    (a) Maintenance of tribal title to tribal land; prohibitions against allotment or sale of tribal land.
    (b) Procedure for making assignments of tribal land.
        (1) Tenure of assignment.
        (2) Reversion for nonuse. Upon what conditions shall assigned lands be considered abandoned and available for reassignment?
        (3) Reassignment at death of assignee. What preferences shall be given to the assignee's dependents?
        (4) Persons entitled to receive assignments.
        (5) Amount of land included in assignment.
        (6) Voluntary exchange of allotments for assignments.
        (7) Assignments of shares in large community tracts.
    (c) Use of unassigned tribal lands.
    (d) Use of proceeds from leasing or other disposition of unassigned lands for charity and other public purposes.
    (e) Guarantee of existing rights of private ownership.
    (f) Procedure for carrying out land policies. What body or official shall make assignments? Shall there be an appeal from these decisions to a court or to some other tribal body or to the Secretary of the Interior?
12. Amendments. Procedure for proposing and voting upon amendments to constitution and bylaws (partly specified in Wheeler-Howard Act).

Bylaws

1. Duties of officers.
    (a) Duties of individual officers and of regular boards, commissions, or standing committees.
    (b) Review of acts of officers by council.
2. Qualifications for office.
3. Certification, installation, and oaths of office.
4. Salaries. Shall any salaries be paid to tribal officials, and if so, in what sums and from what source of revenue?
5. Meetings and procedure.
    (a) Date and place of regular meetings.
    (b) Quorum.
    (c) Calling of special meetings.
    (d) Rules of order. Shall all meetings be public to the tribe?

6. Judicial code. Jurisdiction, powers, and duties of judges and other legal officers. The proposed Law and Order Regulations of the Indian Office may serve as a model for this topic and the succeeding topic.
7. Code of misdemeanors.
8. Domestic relations.
   (a) Marriage
   (b) Divorce.
   (c) Care of dependents.
9. Law of property.
   (a) Inheritance.
   (b) Control over issuance of fee patents and sale of lands. Shall the tribe make recommendations to the Secretary of the Interior, for or against the issuance of fee patents to allottees or the sale of restricted lands?
   (c) Leases. What control shall the tribe have over the leasing of tribal lands, allotments and heirship lands?
   (d) Regulations of grazing, control of erosion, and abatement of nuisances.
   (e) Control of prospecting and mining.
   (f) Control of hunting and fishing.
   (g) Regulation of industry and commerce.
10. Tribal taxation. How shall the tribe raise the necessary funds for tribal government?
11. Public welfare.
    (a) Charity.
    (b) Education.
    (c) Recreation.
    (d) Social work.
    (e) Public health.
12. Indian Service personnel.
    (a) Cooperation of Indian Service employees with tribal government through reports, service on committees, etc.
    (b) Handling of tribal council of complaints and charges against employees.
    (c) Recommendations for federal appointments by petition, by tribal council, or otherwise.
13. Procedure for adoption of constitution and bylaws (specified in Wheeler-Howard Act).

Source: Felix S. Cohen Papers, Box 8, Folder 106, no date.

APPENDIX C

MODEL CORPORATE CHARTER

1. The _____ Tribe is hereby created a body corporate and politic of the United States of America.
2. The name of the corporation shall be the Incorporated _____ Tribe.
3. The said Incorporated _____ Tribe shall have perpetual succession with power to sue and be sued in courts of law and equity within the jurisdiction of the United States; but the grant or exercise of such power to sue and to be sued shall not be deemed a consent to the levy of any judgment, lien, or attachment upon the restricted property of the _____ Tribe.
4. The said Incorporated _____ Tribe shall be a membership corporation. Its membership shall consist of those persons entitled to membership in the _____ Tribe, now or hereafter, as provided by the constitution of the said tribe adopted on _____ and approved by the Secretary of the Interior on _____.
5. The management and governance of the affairs of the Incorporated _____ Tribe shall be in the manner set forth in the constitution of the said tribe. The council or the tribe shall, in addition to all other duties, perform the duties customarily entrusted to the board of directors of a membership corporation.
6. No property rights of the _____ Tribe shall be impaired by the incorporation of the tribe, but the tribe, as incorporated, shall continue to have and control all property, real and personal, and all legal and equitable interests in such property, heretofore vested in the _____ Tribe, and shall likewise be subject to all existing debts and liabilities of the said tribe, except where such debts or liabilities are cancelled pursuant to law.
7. The Incorporated _____ Tribe shall issue to each of its members a nontransferable certificate of membership evidencing the

equal share of each member in the assets of the incorporated tribe. The officers of the Incorporated Tribe shall distribute equally, among the members of the tribe, all profits of tribal enterprise, over and above sums necessary to defray tribal obligations to members of the tribe or other persons and over and above all sums which may be devoted to the construction of public works, the costs of public enterprises, the expenses of government, the needs of charity, or other tribal purposes. Such dividends shall be declared during the month of January, in each year, and shall be paid during the ensuing year in monthly installments.

8. The Incorporated _____ Tribe shall have the following corporate powers:

(a) The power to adopt and alter at its pleasure a corporate seal.

(b) The power to purchase, take by gift, bequest, or otherwise, own, hold, manage, operate, and dispose of property of every description, real and personal; but such power shall not extend to the sale or mortgage by the tribe of any land included in the limits of the _____ Reservation, or to the issuance of leases or permits covering such lands for a period in excess of ten years; and all losses and permits issued prior to January 1, 1940, must be approved by the Secretary of the Interior.

(c) The power to borrow money from the Indian Tribal Credit Fund established by Section 10 of the Act of June 18, 1934 (Public Law No. 383, 73d Congress), or any other governmental credit agency, and to use such funds directly for the purchase of lands for tribal use and for the economic development of tribal resources, properties, and industries, or to advance moneys thus borrowed to individual members of the Incorporated _____ Tribe, or to associations entirely consisting of such members, in furtherance of the purposes specified by the relevant statutes of Congress and regulations of the Interior Department.

(d) The power to purchase restricted Indian lands and to issue in exchange therefor interests in corporate property under the following conditions:

(1) *Kinds of land to be acquired.* It shall be the duty of the Incorporated _____ Tribe, so far as its resources permit, to purchase all heirship lands which cannot be conveniently partitioned among the heirs, all lands of old or incapacitated Indians who desire to exchange their lands for a life pension, all excess lands of members of the tribe owning more than the maximum unit of land ownership fixed by the tribal council,

and all lands needed for public purpose, as defined by the constitution and bylaws of the _____ Tribe. The _____ Tribe may in addition acquire by voluntary surrender, in exchange for corporate interests, any lands which may be incorporated into tribal grazing units, or other areas under tribal ownership.

(2) *Forms of Compensation.* Compensation for lands thus acquired shall be made either by payments on installment equally distributed over a ten- year period, or by the issuance of corporate securities in any of the following forms:

a. *Grazing permit.* In consideration of the grant to the Incorporated _____ Tribe by _____ of the following property _____, the Incorporated _____ Tribe hereby grants to _____ permission to graze _____ head of _____ for a period of _____ years upon tribal lands of the Incorporated _____ Tribe, without charge.

b. *Old age pension.* In consideration of the grant to the Incorporated _____ Tribe by _____ of the following property _____, the Incorporated _____ Tribe hereby agrees to pay to _____ the sum of _____ dollars upon the first day of each month so long as _____ shall live.

c. *Assignment of land.* In consideration of the grant to the Incorporated _____ Tribe by _____ of the following property _____, the Incorporated _____ Tribe hereby assigns to _____, for his exclusive use and occupancy _____. Unless _____ shall make substantial improvements of the said land within a period of two years, it shall revert to the Incorporated _____ Tribe; upon the further condition that such land shall not be encumbered or alienated in any manner nor leased except to a member of the _____ Tribe and upon terms approved by the tribal council; and upon the further condition that _____ may designate the person or persons to whom the land above described shall be assigned upon his death, provided any such designee must be a member of the _____ Tribe and otherwise entitled to receive an assignment of tribal land under the constitution and bylaws of the said tribe.

d. *Proportionate interest in tribal lands.* In consideration of the grant to the Incorporated _____ Tribe by _____ of the following property, _____, the Incorporated _____ Tribe hereby assigns to _____ and to his heirs and assigns forever, a proportionate interest in tribal _____ land and in the income therefrom, based upon the ratio which shall obtain in any year between the area of land above described and the total area of tribal _____ land. This interest shall not be transferable except with the consent of the tribal council, but may be devised and inherited.

(3) *Amount of compensation.* The amount of compensation to be paid by the Incorporated _____ Tribe in any of the foregoing transactions shall be determined by the council of the tribe, or fixed by designated officers thereof and ratified by the said council. In all transactions consummated prior to January 1, 1940, the determination of the tribal council with respect to the amount of compensation may be revised by the Secretary of the Interior upon petition of any person aggrieved or upon petition of any member of the tribal council, and the transaction may be voided within six months of its consummation, if the Secretary shall find that such compensation is unreasonably low or clearly excessive or has been fixed by fraudulent or improper means.

9. The foregoing enumeration of powers shall not be construed to impair the authority of the _____ Tribe in matters of government not comprised within this corporate charter.

10. The Incorporated _____ Tribe is recognized to be an instrumentality of the Federal Government for the administration of Indian Affairs, and none of the property of the said Incorporated _____ Tribe shall be subject to state or local taxation, but any dividends distributed by the said tribe in excess of $200 per capita shall be subject to any state taxes upon income or profits which would be applied to a cooperative marketing association of citizens of the state.

11. This charter shall not be revoked or surrendered except by act of Congress, but may be amended by resolution of the council of the

_____ Tribe, ratified by a two-thirds vote at a proper referendum, and approved by the Secretary of the Interior.

12. This charter shall be effective from and after the date of its ratification by a majority vote of the adult Indians living on the _____ Reservation.

Approved by the Secretary of the Interior
on the _____ day of _____, by virtue
of the authority conferred by Section 17
of the Act of June 18, 1934, (Public Law No.
383, 73d Congress), after receipt of a
petition by at least one-third of the adult
Indians residing on the _____
Reservation for the issuance of a charter of
incorporation.

Approval recommended:
John Collier   Harold L. Ickes
Commissioner of Indian Affairs   Secretary of the Interior
Washington, D. C.
Date _____

                                        CORPORATE SEAL
                        I hereby certify that the foregoing
                        charter was ratified at a special election
                        by a majority vote of the adult Indians
                        on the _____ Reservation.

_____ Reservation
State of _____
_____ day of _____, 1935
                        _____, President
                        _____, Superintendent
                        _____ Reservation

Source: Felix S. Cohen Papers, Box 7, Folder 104, September 25, 1935.

SELECTED BIBLIOGRAPHY

"Biographical Sketch." *Rutgers Law Review* 9 (Winter 1954): 345–53.

Clarkin, Thomas. "Felix Solomon Cohen." In *American National Biography*, vol. 5, John A. Garraty and Mark C. Carnes, eds. New York: Oxford University Press, 1999, 160–62.

Cohen, Felix S. "How Long Will Indian Constitutions Last?" In *The Legal Conscience: Selected Papers of Felix S. Cohen*, Lucy Kramer Cohen, ed. New Haven: Yale University Press, 1960, 222–29.

Cornwell, Joel R. "From Hedonism to Human Rights: Felix Cohen's Alternative to Nihilism." *Temple Law Review* 68 (Spring 1995): 197–221.

Deloria, Vine, Jr. "Laws Founded in Justice and Humanity: Reflections on the Content and Character of Federal Indian Law." *Arizona Law Review* 31 (1989): 203–23.

————. "Reserving to Themselves: Treaties and the Powers of Indian Tribes." *Arizona Law Review* 38 (Fall 1996): 963–80.

Feldman, Stephen M. "Felix S. Cohen and His Jurisprudence: Reflections on Federal Indian Law." *Buffalo Law Review* 35 (Spring 1986): 479–525.

Grinde, Donald A., Jr. "A Symposium on *Native Pragmatism: Rethinking the Roots of American Philosophy*." *Transactions of the Charles S. Peirce Society*, vol. xxxix, no. 4 (Fall 2003): 557–60.

Haas, Theodore, ed. *Felix S. Cohen, a Fighter for Justice*. Washington, D.C.: Chapter of the Alumni of the City College of New York, 1956.

Haycox, Stephen. "Felix Cohen and the Legacy of the Indian New Deal." *Yale University Library Gazette* 64 (April 1994): 135–56.

"Legal Realism and the Race Question: Some Realism about Realism on Race Relations." Note. *Harvard Law Review Association* 108 (May 1995): 1607–24.

Levi, Edward H. "The Legal Conscience: Selected Papers of Felix S. Cohen." Book Reviews. *Harvard Law Review* (June 1962): 1686–91.

Martin, Jill E. "A Year and a Spring of My Existence: Felix Cohen and the *Handbook of Federal Indian Law*." *Western Legal History* 8 (Winter-Spring 1995): 35–60.

————. "The Miner's Canary: Felix S. Cohen's Philosophy of Indian Rights." *American Indian Law Review* 23 (1998): 165–79.

Newton, Nell Jessup, ed. *Cohen's Handbook of Federal Indian Law.* Newark, N.J.: LexisNexis, 2005.

Obituary. *New York Times,* October 20, 1953.

Philp, Kenneth R., ed. *Indian Self-Rule: First-Hand Accounts of Indian-White Relations from Roosevelt to Reagan.* Salt Lake City: Howe Brothers, 1986.

Rostow, Eugene. "Felix Cohen." *Yale Law Journal* 63, no. 2 (December 1953): 141–43.

Soifer, Aviam. "Descent." *Florida State University Law Review* 29 (Fall 2001): 269–76.

Tsuk, Dalia. *Architect of Justice: Felix S. Cohen and the Founding of American Legal Pluralism.* Ithaca, N.Y.: Cornell University Press, 2007.

————. "The New Deal Origins of American Legal Pluralism." *Florida State University Law Review* 29 (Fall 2001): 189–268.

————. "Pluralisms: The Indian New Deal as a Model." *Margins Law Journal* (2001). Lexis/Nexis, 1–52.

Waldron, Jeremy. "'Transcendental Nonsense' and System in the Law." *Columbia Law Review* 100 (January 2000): 16–53.

INDEX

Tribal council *(continued)*
parole and, 126; personnel and, 117; police force and, 130; popular initiative/referendum and, 52, 53, 54; powers of, 56, 75, 174–76; public welfare and, 168–71; removal of judges and, 121; salaries for, 165; secretary of the, 21; sergeant at arms of the, 21; supervision of Indian Service employees and, 71; treasurer of the, 21; tribal government and, 33, 34, 35; tribal property and, 57; as tribal title, 20. *See also names of specific tribal councils*
Tribal courts: chiefs and, 38, 39; condemnation of property and, 68; governing body and, 29; judicial code and (*see* Judicial code); offices/ titles and, 20; self-government and, 73; territory and, 13
Tribal court systems, xxix
Tribal customs. *See* Customs
Tribal funds, 57, 58, 67, 101, 102, 155, 165
Tribal governance/government, xvii, xix, xxii, xxv, xxix; abolishing old forms of, 8–9; chiefs and, 37–39; older forms of, 19–20; relation of the Indian Service to, 33–36; self-government and, 62; tenure of office and, 47; in white communities versus older forms, 19–20. *See also* Government
Tribal legislature, as tribal title, 20
Tribal members. *See* Members
Tribal membership. *See* Membership
Tribal offenses, 74, 124, 127
Tribal Organization Committee (TOC), xxiii, xxiv, xxv, xxvii, xxix
Tribal organizations. *See* Organizations
Tribal powers, 36, 56
Tribal property. *See* Property
Tribal self-government. *See* Self-government
Tribal senate, as tribal title, 20
Tribal solicitor, as tribal title, 21
Tribal sovereignty, xi, xvi, xviii, xix
Tribes: appropriate names for, 5; bylaws for (*see* Bylaws); chiefs and, 37, 38, 39; Cohen's legal work for, xvi, xvii; constitutions for (*see* Tribal constitutions); defrauding, xxxi; district organization for, 22; elections for, 40, 45; governing body for, 28, 32, 33; government of (*see* Tribal governance/government); IRA and, xxii; judicial code for (*see* Judicial code); name of organization for, 5; offices of, 20–21; popular initiative/referendum and, 50, 54; preserving ancient traditions in, 19–20; problems in, 19; self-government in (*see* Self-government); sovereignty and, xviii; tenure of office for, 47; termination and, xvi; territory for, 13; titles in, 20, 21. *See also names of specific tribes*
Trustees: board of, 20; mining, 21
Tsosie, Rebecca, xxxii
Tsuk, Dalia, xix
Two-chambered legislature, 32

Uintah and Ouray Reservation, district organization on, 22
Unanimous consent/agreement, 110–12

Unanimous vote, 118–19
Undemocratic organizations, 70
Unified government, xxix, 28, 29–30
Uniformity of practice, 112
United States: administration of tribal property and, 67; American Indians and, xviii; Cherokee Nation and, 160; condemnation of property and, 68, 69; Constitution of the, 76; crimes against, 132; definition of territory of tribes of, 13; funds from, 102; governing body in, 31, 106, 107; tenure of office and, 47; treatment of Indians, xvii
United States Constitution, 32
United States government, 112
University of Connecticut School of Law, xi
Upper court, 21
Utes of the Consolidated Ute Agency, tenure of office for, 47

Vacancies, tenure of office and, 48
Veto power, 32, 32n, 33, 34, 52, 56, 57, 80
Vice-president, 82
Violations, xvi
Virgin Islands, xiv
Voting, xv, 121; chiefs and, 37; district organization and, 22; elections and, 40, 41; governing body and, 108, 110, 111, 112; majority, 119; popular initiative/referendum and, 50, 53; qualifications for, 63; self-government and, 62, 63; unanimous, 118–19

Warrants, xii; to apprehend, 123; search, 125
Washington, Lummi of, 47
Welfare, social, 60. *See also* Public welfare
Welpley, Mrs., xxvi
Wheeler-Howard Act: adopting constitutions under, 3; bylaws in, 79; Cohen and, xxiv, xxv, xxvi; condemnation of property and, 69; counsel and, 59; judicial code and, 114; lands and, 60; name of organization and, 5; negotiations and, 60; popular initiative/referendum and, 54; powers by, 56, 74, 75; property and, 58, 160; voting qualifications and, 63
Wheeler-Howard bill, xv, 58
White communities: forms of government in, xxix, 19; judicial code and, 114
White Earth Reservation, governing body for, 106
Whites: intermarriage with, 17, 18, 139–42; misdemeanors and, 134
Wills, 60
Winnebago Indian Tribal Council: public welfare of, 170; self-government and, 59
Wisconsin: Menominee Tribe of, 8
Witnesses, 122
Woehlke, Walter V., xxi, xxiii, xxvi
Women, voting and, 63

Yakima Tribe, 10–12
Yankton Sioux Constitution: popular initiative/referendum and, 51–52; tenure of office for, 49
Yankton Sioux Tribal Business and Claims Committee, 101

www.ingramcontent.com/pod-product-compliance
Lightning Source LLC
Chambersburg PA
CBHW022355280326
41935CB00007B/190